Nothing Left To Lose

Nothing Left To Lose
or
How <u>Not</u> to Start a Commune

a memoir

JEFF RICHARDS

CIRCUIT BREAKER BOOKS

Published by
Circuit Breaker Books LLC
Portland, OR
www.circuitbreakerbooks.com

NOTHING LEFT TO LOSE, OR, HOW NOT TO START A COMMUNE
© 2024 by Jeff Richards

This is a work of creative nonfiction. The events are portrayed to the best of the author's memory. While all the stories in this book are true, some names and identifying details have been changed to protect the privacy of the people involved.

Cover image courtesy Anne Sager.
Book design by Vinnie Kinsella.

ISBN (paperback): 978-1-953639-20-2
ISBN (ebook): 978-1-953639-19-6

To Connie, Ben, Hannah, and Baird
With love and affection

Freedom's just another word for nothin' left to lose.
—Janis Joplin and Kris Kristofferson

Chapter One

THE APARTMENT RICK SAGER AND I SHARED FOR SEVENTY-TWO BUCKS a month was behind the Opera House on the first floor of a red-brick bungalow downhill from the Denison University campus. The house sagged in the middle. I could walk downhill from my bed at the Elm Street end of the house and uphill to the kitchen table on the Opera House end. The bathroom was so small that we had to slide sideways to squeeze past the tub in order to fiddle with the radiator bleed valve. We painted the bathroom black and hung a black light. We painted the kitchen dark green and the final room, purple. On the wall next to the front door, I hung a western blanket, a Day-Glo cow skull, and a print of a fierce looking Iroquois brandishing a tomahawk. The rest of the pictures were psychedelic—Jim Morrison bent over his microphone, Jimi Hendrix bent over his guitar, a field of marijuana with the caption "This Bud's for You."

We had all the accessories of the psychedelic life except for the drugs. Once we smoked banana peels thinking it would get us high. That was Rick's idea. He got the idea off a Donovan song, something about an "electrical banana," but we found out later that the banana referred to a vibrator. But that was the closest we came to getting high until October 19, 1967, when Nat Koenig knocked on the door. I was alone.

Nat was a theater major, a muscular guy with soft eyes and an elastic face, a natural actor. I admired this quality in him, as I did his talent in attracting the opposite sex. His latest chick was Margie Walker, a short-haired blond with a husky voice and tomboy personality. She could drink us under the table, which was important to us in those days. I was half in love with her because she was such a free spirit. I could say anything to her. Just like a guy—a beautiful one. She reminded me of Kim Novak. I could understand how Nat felt. He had followed her to Mexico during the summer, and that was why he was here now. He wanted to share with us the dope he had purchased down there.

"I hid it in coffee cans. Then I put the coffee on top and resealed the cans. You know, like Juan Valdez."

"Sure, sure. You snuck it across the border in your suitcase," I said.

"Sure, man, but only two cans. The very best. Acapulco Gold."

He unsealed one of the cans and poured the coffee on the side table next to the bed. At the bottom of the can was a baggie full of the golden flakes—or at least they looked gold to me.

"The sun and the salty wind off the Pacific combine to create the color and the potency." He waved his hands over the can as if he were performing a magic trick.

He flopped down in the easy chair and whipped out a pack of Zig-Zag papers. I watched him carefully lick two sheets together then crease one end. He sifted through the baggie, separating the sticks and seeds from the pure stuff that he sprinkled over the paper. He rolled the joint on his knee.

"Where's Rick?" he asked.

"He's uphill working at the cafeteria."

Rick was a scholarship student, and they had called him at the last minute to fill in for someone else.

"Don't worry. Don't worry," said Nat. "We can handle it. We'll smoke alone. Then when Rick and Margie turn up, we'll smoke again. You and I will get twice as high."

Nat rolled a couple more joints and stashed them in his breast pocket. "We'll save this for later."

He laughed greedily and lit the bone, took a deep draw, and held it in while speaking in a squeaky voice. "You got to pull it deep in your lungs and hold it there. When you breathe out, there should be no smoke left."

I tried this several times and coughed up smoke. The third try, I succeeded. My throat was raw. I was not a smoker. I shrugged. "Nothing's happening."

"Don't worry," he said again. He pulled a tweezer-like item out of his breast pocket. "A roach clip. You clip it to the roach, the end of the weed that's black and gunky where all the good stuff collects."

I wasn't sure what he meant, but I followed his example, holding the roach by the clip close to my mouth and sucking in. I didn't want to burn my lips. Finally, all I could do was sniff in the smoke by covering one nostril with a finger and sniffing in with the other, as Nat did.

I lay back in my chair, ready to take off like a rocket, but all I could feel was a bit sleepy.

"I'll spin one of your records," said Nat as he moved across the room in slow motion. I followed him with my eyes. I felt like a heavy wind had picked up and was pushing me back in my chair. But that wasn't unusual, I thought. I was looking at Nat, and he was looking at me. He put on "Mellow Yellow" by Donovan.

"How are you feeling?" he asked from where he was sitting on the edge of my bed.

"Fine. But when am I going to turn on?" I asked, gripping the arms of my chair tightly. The wind had picked up.

"You're already on," he said, grinning. "Lit up like a lighthouse."

Rick trudged in an hour later, after his shift was over at the cafeteria. "This place smells like, I don't know, a field of skunk cabbage," he said as he sniffed the draperies.

Margie showed up not long after with a bottle of Wild Turkey. "You've been smoking without me," she carped.

Nat pulled the joints he had rolled from his breast pocket with a flourish. We sat in a circle passing the joints and the bottle of bourbon until we were whacked out, our eyes glazed over like zombies, our brains collapsed on the floor, each of us lost in disconnected thoughts and images until the munchies took over. We gravitated to the kitchen. Rick poured a bag of potato chips into a bowl. I grabbed the sour cream and the dried Lipton onion soup. I mixed the two together to make a very tasty and crunchy onion dip. Nat heated the pigs in blankets. And Margie found a two-day-old tub of fried chicken wings in a corner of the fridge. She heated the wings, sliced carrots and celery. She concocted a mixture of honey and mustard. We seemed to take an hour to go through the whole process. But it was ten minutes. We rushed back into the next room. I grabbed the card table in the corner and unfolded it. Rick grabbed the folding chairs. We gobbled down our plunder. We traded jokes about the mustard. It looked like poop, but it wasn't gray. It was the texture of bird poop. Maybe that was where they got the name poop deck. Maybe sea gulls hung around in the lanyards above the poop deck and pooped.

Margie said she didn't like poop talk and launched into talk about Earl Harris, a tall, skinny senior with a thick mustache and sideburns we all knew and didn't like. He was too serious, studying to be a Baptist minister. Margie said he was in one of her advanced Spanish classes where they studied the classics, Cervantes and García Lorca. "He told me once he gets his divinity degree, he wants to work in Central America as a missionary."

"That must be a difficult task, converting all those Catholics," said Rick as he suppressed a burp and gazed into Margie's icy-blue eyes.

"Yes, that's true in a way." She smiled at Rick and turned to Nat. He was leaning back in his chair and yawning, as if the subject bored him. "What do you think? Isn't it amazing that Earl already knows what he wants to do when he graduates?"

"I suppose it is, but then considering that, he's like the rest of us. Maybe he'll have to put off his plans until Uncle Sam is finished with him."

We switched to a chat about the draft because for Nat and me—Rick was a junior—our student deferments would be up in

June when we graduated. Nat thought he might try for conscientious objector.

"You'll never pull that one off," I said, "unless you're a Quaker."

"I'll convert tomorrow, and if that doesn't work, I'll flee to Canada. Maybe I'll refuse to serve. They'll put me in jail."

Margie drifted to the kitchen. I followed her. She cut four orange slices, muddled them in short glasses with bitters, and poured in bourbon, ice, sugar water, and cherries. She stirred the drinks. "Old-fashioneds," she said. "I'm a Southern girl, and I love anything with bourbon in it."

"My parents drink old-fashioneds, but they use rye," I said, smiling. "They're from Ohio."

"Wise guy," said Margie.

"Yeah, once when I was a kid, I took a sip of one of their drinks when they weren't looking. It was nasty."

"Here, try this." She handed me one of the glasses.

I took a sip. "Hey, that's pretty good," I said.

"I can make a mean mint julep, a Sazerac, a Manhattan, you name it. My dad taught me how."

"That's a weird thing for your father to do."

"Well, he's a weird guy. He thinks the South won the Civil War," she said, leaning toward me. She looked like she was about to topple over, so I held on to her arm.

"You know, I invited Nat to Atlanta last summer to meet my family. That was a big mistake. My father didn't like him." She wiped away a tear. "I think it's because Nat's Jewish."

"What's wrong with being Jewish?" I asked, though I knew perfectly well what was wrong with it as far as some people were concerned. I suggested that she should tell her father to fuck off, though that was not going to happen either. Margie, I think, was enough of a Southern belle to know her place. It was sad because I knew they were in love, and now this talk about Earl Harris was only a way to make Nat jealous.

She admitted as much. "Okay, maybe I'm using Earl to get at Nat, but I'll tell you what," she said, slamming her old-fashioned down on the table and spilling a few drops on her hand. "Last weekend I caught him at Eleventh Street Market with Erin McAllister. You know, the pretty red-headed actress? They were sitting in a booth drinking beers and laughing. His arm was around her shoulder."

"Did he see you?"

"Yeah, he saw me, but he pretended he didn't."

"Because you were with Earl?"

"Oh, man, you're a smart-mouth." She reached over and pinched my cheek. Sometimes she made me feel like a baby. I didn't like that.

She poured more bourbon in her glass and strolled into the living room, where Nat was still leaning back in his chair, holding his draft card in one hand and a Zippo lighter in the other. "Do you think I ought to burn it?"

"No way," said Rick. Nat snapped open the lid and ran his finger along the flint wheel, producing sparks but no flame. "You burn your card, you can't go to Tony's, Midway's, Eleventh Street Market. No booze."

"I'll burn it in June." Nat snapped the Zippo closed and placed it back in his pocket along with the card.

Margie kicked the chair out from under Nat and ran off laughing. She hid behind me. He chased after her. He reached his big mitts around my body. She jumped aside. He feigned left. She feigned right. I couldn't tell if he was mad or if this was an alcohol-infused romp. Nat pushed me backward into Margie. We piled on top of each other on the bed. Margie was on the bottom. She started screaming and kicking us away, but she was still laughing between gasps. At one point she tweaked my nipple. I jumped a mile in the air. I tried to pay her back in kind, but Nat knocked my hand away.

"No fair," he said. Then he grabbed her breast, and they fell into an embrace that ruined the fun until Rick started a pillow fight. We had six pillows, two of them feather. We whacked them against each other until they broke and feathers were flying over the room. Rick grabbed one of the hard foam pillows as Margie was coming at him with another. He stepped aside and whacked her in the face—too hard, as it turned out, because it produced a nosebleed. My roomie was horrified. He ran into the bathroom and grabbed some toilet paper. He handed it to her. She wadded it up and stuck it in her nostrils and grimaced. She stuck out her tongue at him while he pleaded for forgiveness.

"Don't worry," she said. "These things happen."

We sat there a long moment catching our breath until Nat got the bright idea that we needed to get more stoned. "This alcohol is no good for us. Negative vibes."

We slogged out to the front porch and collapsed in the lawn chairs we kept there. Nat rolled a joint that we smoked as we passed around Margie's bourbon to soothe our itchy throats. It was a warm fall day, the air so still I could almost hear the leaves falling from the oak tree across the street ping against the pavement.

"What do we do now?" asked Rick, yawning and stretching his arms. We were not the typical-looking denizens of our college. Not frat boys in chinos and closely cropped hair. Nor a sorority girl in a pleated skirt and flip bob haircut like Jackie Kennedy. We were the hip generation. Denim was our uniform. Rick in his bib overalls and flowered shirt, his tight curls exploding from his head like an atom bomb. Nat in his bell-bottoms and tight T-shirt showing off his muscles like an updated Stanley Kowalski. He actually played the Brando role in his junior year. That was how he hooked up with Margie. She had played Blanche DuBois. But she didn't look sultry now. She was more like a motorcycle chick, blond hair tied up in a ponytail, dressed in black denim, gold skull-and-crossbones earrings dangling from her ears. I had also seen her in granny dresses, but this was not her now. Me, I followed my father's advice: "Never call attention to yourself." I wore jeans, a black, lightweight sweater, and loafers duct-taped to keep the soles from flapping.

Preppy style. My hair was unkempt, my sideburns scraggly—my only concessions.

So, this was us. We were out of our minds and bored to death until a red-and-silver colored Trailways bus pulled up at the curb in front our abode full of what looked like college students dressed like us. Revolutionaries. On their way to the Pentagon march, if I could judge from a hand-painted sign taped to one of the windows:

Bring our GIs
Home *NOW!*

The bus door creaked open, and a skinny, stooped-over driver in a blue service cap and a badge stepped out.

"You know how to find Slayter Hall?" he asked in a resigned voice. He seemed tired, bags under his eyes like he hadn't slept in days.

Before we could answer, Nat sprinted down the porch stairs, past the driver, and onto the bus.

"Holy cow, protesters," he yelled, raised his hands like a choir-master, and launched into Country Joe and the Fish's "1-Feel-Like-I'm-Fixin'-to-Die Rag."

The students on the bus stomped their feet and sang along with Nat until the tired bus driver threw down his cap. "Hey, hey, stop all that," he yelled, waving his hands. "You want to go to your goddamn prep rally, you got to act civilized."

The one and only town cop car pulled up behind the bus. A short, fat cop struggled out of one side, a tall, skinny one out of the other. They must've been out on patrol. Normally they hung out in the police station, which was next door to us in a basement room of the Opera House.

They came around the side of the bus.

"Qui-et-t," yelled the short cop. He had his hand on his holster as if he were going to draw, only there wasn't any pistol. "This is a peaceful town. We got us a noise ordinance here."

The tall cop pushed the short one aside. "You looking for the college?" he asked the bus driver.

"Yes, sir, we need to pick up passengers behind Slayter Hall. You know how to get there?"

While the two cops directed the bus driver, Nat scurried back into the apartment, managed to find my Country Joe LP, placed the speakers by the door where it could be easily heard, and turned up the sound full blast. He ran down the porch steps again, yelling at the top of his lungs, "One, two, three, four, we don't want your fuckin' war."

The students on the bus stomped their feet and took up Nat's chant. The bus seemed to rock from side to side with their racket. The cops covered their ears. They stumbled up the stairs to my apartment but not before Nat. He blocked the door.

"Let us in," growled the shorter one, trying to yank Nat aside.

"You got a search warrant?" asked Nat, crossing his arms.

"'Course I don't. Need a judge to sign a warrant before it's legal."

The other cop pushed his buddy aside and threatened Nat with a billy club. "Turn off that record player before I smash it to smithereens."

"Well, you put it that way." Nat went back into the apartment to the record player, lifted the needle, and sauntered back to the porch, smiling at the law.

There was a slight tension in the air, but it wasn't that bad, seeing as these were small-town police. They couldn't call for backup. All the backup was here. We sat down in our chairs. Relaxed. The driver slogged up the steps of his bus and slid behind the wheel. He was about to close the door when Nat and Rick jumped aboard.

"We'll show you how to get up there," said Nat.

"Only paying passengers allowed," said the tired driver, his cap askew on his head.

The students protested. The driver shrugged and closed the door before Margie and I could climb aboard. The bus bounced down the road toward campus, leaving a trail of smoke behind.

"Oh, well, I didn't want to go anyway," said Margie.

We sat on the porch swing next to the lawn chairs and listened to the rusty chains that hung from the ceiling creak as we rocked back and forth. I inched my arm around her shoulder. The two cops parked their car and sat on the bench outside the door to their office. They watched us like hawks as if we were constructing a pipe bomb or something. Then they went inside. I tried to kiss Margie. She pushed me away.

"Please, you don't want to do that. Nat's your friend."

"You're right. You're absolutely right." I felt ashamed. I hung my head. "But if Nat wasn't your boyfriend, I swear I'd do my damnedest to, you know...you know..."

"Make love to me."

"That's it. That's it exactly," I said.

She laughed and then started to tickle me. I doubled up, protecting my stomach, my most sensitive area. That was when Rick and Nat trundled down the street laughing and joking, until they saw me and Margie rocking back and forth on the swing. She was almost on top of me.

"What's going on? What's up?" yelled Nat in a gruff voice.

"She's tickling me to death," I yelled between giggles.

"Well, we'll see about that." He skipped up the steps followed by Rick. The three of them proceeded to tickle me, only Nat's tickles were more like rabbit punches.

Chapter Two

RICK AND I HAD TOTALLY DEVOTED OURSELVES TO SMOKING DOPE EV-ery day since we initially turned on in October of my senior year. We turned on our friends: Jim Behringer or J. B., as we called him, because of his close-cropped hair and businesslike demeanor. He carried a pocket-size notebook around in which he scribbled down notes, things such as the origin of the universe, model rocketry (his hobby), the stock market, and the various types of buzzes he at-tained from a joint of marijuana. He was very serious, never laughed at all. Unlike Hank Hipple, our skinny, goggle-eyed friend, who laughed all the time, especially when stoned. He bent over dou-ble, his eyes popping out of his head, his face turning beet red, tiny gasps escaping from his mouth. Sometimes he'd roll on the floor in silent laughter. Other times, Hank would rock back and forth in a chair, nodding in affirmation while we spouted out stoned ideas, one after another, until we realized Hank didn't hear us. He was sleeping with his eyes open. He was peculiar. So was Baby Huey, as we called him because he reminded us of the comic strip character, who was also easygoing enough to join into any mischief we might have had in mind.

One of the things we kicked around in our stoned-out reverie was what we were going to do after college. This was mostly my concern since I was the one facing the music. Rick and the others were juniors. They didn't have to worry as much about the draft. I had a plan for how to flunk my draft physical, but if this didn't work out, I thought maybe I'd hide out in the mountains in a com-mune or something. We all read about communes in *The Whole*

Earth Catalog. Maybe our own commune in the Rocky Mountains? Timothy Leary said, "Turn on, tune in, drop out." We were coming to that realization. We would drop out. We would aim to be self-sufficient. That was the plan, like mountain men in the old days. Live off the land, though in the modern sense. We threw out ideas. We could live somewhere in the Rockies near Denver—in the hills outside the mining towns: Idaho Springs, Cripple Creek, Central City. Bob Dylan had spent some time in Central City. That could be an ideal place. Or maybe Boulder. A college town. We could hire out as truck drivers and write novels on the side. (I was busily reading *On the Road* for one of my classes.) One of us would drive the truck while the other wrote the novel in the back. Then we'd change places. We'd finish our run, and another two guys would take over. Or maybe a guy and a gal. Then we could do more than write novels in the back of the truck. Another idea we kicked around was that we could write a syndicated column like Nicholas von Hoffman in *The Washington Post*, only more radical. Or invent a board game and make a million dollars. That was Nat's idea. We even went down to the theater workshop to design the board. Or we could farm the land of our commune. Sell vegetables at local farmers' markets. We didn't want to sell meat, though none of us were vegetarians. The idea of killing and cutting up an animal we raised was too much for us. The fact was we didn't want to be cogs in the big capitalist wheel. We didn't want to slog to work at eight in the morning, spend our days in meaningless, redundant work, and slog home at six at night too tired to play with the kids. We didn't even want kids. Well, maybe later, after we became self-sufficient.

But these brilliant thoughts of ours would have to wait, because right after we got back from Christmas break, the whole campus ran out of reefer. We pooled our resources—Rick, Nat, Baby Huey, J. B., Hank, and I. Rick and I hopped in the Mustang, a Christmas gift from my parents a year ago, and drove seventy miles southwest to Antioch College to meet a high school friend, Brinton Rowdybush.

The school's front quad was covered in plywood boardwalks. It had been raining for about a week, and the grass was soaked and mostly mud, though it was cold as shit and the forecast called for snow. The main building reminded me of the Cinderella Castle at Disney World, only the roofs of the towers were green not blue. The other buildings were standard Ohio college brick, though a few long, low-slung ones were multicolored metal siding.

At the end of one of these latter types in a glassed-in area a band of long-hairs played drums while their friends danced in a haphazard way, bumping into each other. Two men wearing Red Army caps were attempting the Russian squat dance. The women were dressed in various costumes: granny dresses, jeans like the men, one in cowboy boots, another in a muumuu waving a feather boa, and a very pretty dark-haired lady in starburst glasses and a miniskirt that showed her red underwear. She saw us staring and crooked her finger for us to come over.

Rick was tempted—he always was by the opposite sex—but I held him back. We were here on business. Seven hundred bucks burned a hole in my pocket. We climbed the stairs in the library and found Brinton sitting at a table surrounded by books that he was going through assiduously. He seemed tired, barely tolerating us. His smirk turned into a frown. It could have easily turned into a smile, and he could start laughing, but I sensed he wanted to get back to work, so I asked him where I could find some marijuana.

"Ask someone in Hashish Hall." He was looking at Rick, who was dressed in ridiculous orange bell-bottoms with holes in the knees, a white Mexican wedding shirt, and an orange scarf with red stripes.

"This is my friend, Rick Sager," I said. They shook hands. Rick had a far-off, goofy grin as if he were hatching a plan.

"Hey, man," Rick said in a whisper since this was a library, "why don't we go out to lunch after we finish here? You must have a union. This is such a funky college. I'd like to meet some of the students."

I knew what was on his mind: women. Rick's libido, I think, was supercharged.

"No, thanks. I have too much work, exams coming up and all," said Brinton, the smirk returning to his face. Brinton was ambitious. He had a gift for language. I thought he would join the diplomatic service. Nothing was going to stand in his way. Especially something as stupid as fun. Fun was a dead-end street.

We waved goodbye to Brinton and wandered off to Hashish Hall. There we ran into a gaggle of bearded pool players who directed us to room 707. We knocked on the door, and a preppy in a blue blazer, chinos, and loafers wrapped in duct tape answered the door. His hair was short like mine. He was singing along with Cream's cover of an old Skip James blues song.

"I'm so glad, I'm glad, I'm glad..." He eyed us suspiciously. "What?"

"Some guys downstairs told us that you sold marijuana," said Rick, leaning against the doorjamb casually as if this were an everyday occurrence for him.

"Oh yeah? What's their names?"

"I don't know," I said in a sincere fashion to put this guy at ease. "But I do know Brinton Rowdybush. I went to high school with him."

"Yeah, yeah," said the preppy, peering up and down the hall as if checking for narcs. "He's as straight as they come. But not a bad dude."

"So, you have anything?"

"Come on in." He grabbed Rick by the arm and yanked him in. I followed. He took one more look outside and closed the door.

In the corner of the room was an unkempt bed, a desk by a window covered with books, and a typewriter like he was working on a research project. His walls were covered with posters, mostly benign: a sunset in the Grand Canyon, a group of seals lounging on the rocks near the ocean—probably the Pacific, since he told us he was from California, though he'd gone to prep school in New England. Then a photograph in a black frame of our martyred president JFK in his rocking chair, smiling. What was he trying to prove with the heavy-duty music—now Ginger Baker in a drum solo—and his straight-seeming persona?

He looked at me, puzzled, and in an exasperated voice asked how much we wanted.

"A kilo," answered Rick.

"That will cost you seven hundred bucks."

"We got it."

"Show me."

I was reluctant to do so, but considering this was a college and not a back alley in a ghetto, and the guy looked like he'd graduated from Pencey Prep, I spread the money on his bed. He started to count it.

"You know, we'd like to test it before we buy," said Rick.

"Yeah, man, I understand," said the preppy, reaching in the pocket of his blazer and coming out with a joint. "But not in here. You go out in the woods nearby and have a couple of tokes. This is good stuff. It's enough to get you both high. Then come back here, and I'll have it all wrapped up pretty for you."

I was beginning to feel like a gangster, and it made me nervous. Maybe we were making a major mistake. Maybe the narcs would nab us. That was what we were afraid of. The narcs were all around us. They looked like us. They dressed like us. They said outrageous stuff so they could gain our confidence. They may even sell us weed. Maybe this preppy was a narc. I had been stoned on weed every day since I first turned on in October, except for Thanksgiving and Christmas breaks when I was home with my parents. I was getting paranoid.

Rick and I strolled casually out of Hashish Hall as if we were out to enjoy a nice intimate rendezvous with Mother Nature, only she was ugly, stripped down to the bare bones and blowing a cold, wet wind in our direction. We hopped behind a tree. Rick lit the joint, took a deep breath, and handed it to me.

"No, thanks, you test. I need to stay straight." It wouldn't do for me to be driving east on I-70 toward Denison all lit up. It would attract attention. The narcs again. Or maybe the state police. They had a reputation in Ohio for busting speeders. I didn't know what they did to slow drivers.

We returned to room 707. Mister Preppy was pulling on a weed of the tobacco kind. "Well, what do you think?" In his hand he was holding a book, *Candy* by Terry Southern and Mason Hoffenberg which seemed out of character for his disguise. I would think *Profiles in Courage* more appropriate.

"I think this stuff is groovy. Far-out." Rick was way ahead of the curve as far as picking up the lingo of the time. "What is it? Acapulco Gold? Maui Wowie?"

"Neither. It's pure as the driven snow," said the preppy.

"Cocaine."

"No coke. When I say pure, I mean it's clean. It's all keef, reefer, scuzz, shit. You get me." I could tell the guy was irritated. Rick was acting silly, so I knew for a fact whatever shit this was, it was working. I handed the guy seven hundred dollars.

"We get you," I said.

He handed me a Christmas bag with a picture of Santa and his reindeer flying through a holly wreath tied with a red bow. I looked inside at a whole huge block of tightly packed weed. I sniffed it. It was the real thing, all right.

We skedaddled out of the rain-soaked, funky, run-down campus of Antioch. Rick fell asleep immediately, and by the time we arrived in front of our apartment on South Main, he was totally downed out.

"Let's try some more," he begged, as if I was in charge of when he smoked.

"We will. We will." As matter of fact, I wanted to savor a taste of the stuff before we distributed it. I knew that once people caught on that we had found what everyone else was looking for, we'd be famous on campus. We hauled our Christmas goodies inside and turned the bag upside down on the bed. The brick of weed was the size of a cinder block. It awed and frightened us at the same time. We had pulled off the impossible—or had we? We were neophytes. How did we know that *They* weren't waiting for us outside? We had heard that the feds needed a warrant to search your home. Maybe right now one narc was in front of a judge pleading his case while the other kept an eye on us. Rick pulled the curtain back, and we peered out. The street was empty except for my Mustang, though the Granville cop car was parked behind it. That made sense since the police station was next door. It was turning dark. The rain changed to snow. The wind blew the snow sideways into the headlights of an oncoming car.

Rick closed the curtain. "You know we're way too freaked out. If the cops wanted to bust us, they would have pulled us over on the highway and searched us." The thing was that they never would have found it, since we hid the stuff in a compartment in the trunk that I only stumbled upon when I was cleaning the car one time.

"The thing is we need to find as good a place now," I said.

"Maybe we should've left it in the car," said Rick, scratching his head in a thoughtful manner.

He took out his pocketknife and cut a tiny nudge off the block of weed. "Roll some joints," he said. "I have an idea."

Rick took down his rucksack that was hanging on a hook beside the door. He poured out the contents: a couple of books, a notebook, pens, and a dog-eared copy of *Playboy*. Rick explained that he was interested in the Norman Mailer interview about his experience at the Pentagon march.

"I'll bet you were," I snickered.

He stashed the marijuana in the rucksack and tucked it under the bed.

I finished rolling the joints, and we smoked one down to the nub. The paranoia did not dissipate.

"I know a place where we can squirrel away the goodies, and no one would ever suspect," said Rick, running his hand through his curls thoughtfully. "I mean you can't bust a corpse."

I gave him a dumbfounded look until he pointed, and I knew he meant something down the street, and I caught his drift—the edge of town where the Old Colony Burying Ground rested at the top of a small hill behind a wrought-iron fence.

We'd go down there sometimes so Rick could show me the stars. He was good at that. Orion's belt. Gemini. One night when the moon had set, he showed me the hazy swirl of the Milky Way. To the right of the graveyard gate, on the highest part of the hill, were the twin sarcophagi of a husband and wife who died in the 1860s. The husband was a Civil War veteran. There was a crack at the bottom of the sarcophagus. We could pull out the stone and stash our excess dope inside.

We looked out the window. The snow had picked up. It was covering the street and sidewalk. "You know, if we go out there now, we'll leave footprints," I said. "Not only will they be able to find the stuff but they'll be able to trace it back to us."

"We'll take a broom along. Sweep away the prints."

"Actually not a bad idea," I said. I seemed to remember that from an old cowboy movie.

We went out on the porch to survey the wintery scene. The snow was falling in large clumps, covering my Mustang, the cop car, and the roof of the clapboard grange hall across the street. We wandered down the steps and up toward Broadway. We had forgotten our paranoia and were now suddenly famished. Aladdin's was still open, so we went in and ordered coffee and a brownie topped with ice cream and hot fudge. Yum-Yum, they called it. We wolfed it down, paid our bill, and headed back to South Main. A state cop car was parked behind the Granville car. We quickened our step and ran up the stairs to our apartment. We slammed the door and locked it.

"Oh, shit. Oh, shit," whimpered Rick as he ran around in circles trying to find another place to stash the dope.

A knock came to the door, and we both froze, a shared, foreboding fear in our hearts. They were going to lock us up and throw away the key.

"I guess we'll have to open it," I said.

"Guess so."

I crept over and opened the door a crack.

"Let me in. It's freezing out here." It was J. B. covered in snow. He had let his hair grow down to his ears in a bowl around his head. He looked like Prince Valiant, only blond. He stamped his feet and stepped in. He tossed a briefcase he was carrying on the bed and opened it. We'd forgotten he said he was going to come down about eight to help us break down our cache.

"You guys are acting weird," he said, smiling. "So, you must have the stuff."

"We do." I reached under the bed and pulled out the ruck, unzipped it, and dropped the block on the bed.

"Wow. Amazing. I would've never believed it unless I saw it with my own eyes. You must have some friend at Antioch."

We told him our story. He seemed even more amazed, us buying dope off a total stranger and coming out intact. We smoked the other joint and went about our work. Inside the briefcase was a small, flat scale that measured in ounces, a mortar and pestle, a wire brush, a wooden chopping block, barber's clippers, a chisel, and three dozen baggies. We divided up the goodies, thirty-five ounces in total, and smoked the excess. We didn't get up until two the next day, when we distributed our bounty and stashed what was left over at the bottom of the sarcophagus.

One night after the snow melted and the weather turned warmer, Rick and I wandered down to the Old Colony Burying Ground and smoked joints. The moon was at three quarters. It scudded across the sky like the sail of a ship blown by the wind. When clouds cloaked the moon for a moment, the graveyard turned black. All I could see was the shimmering red light from our joints and the blue outdoor light from the grange up the street. Then the moon poured out through a crack in the clouds and turned the graveyard silver. The black arms of the trees clacked together in the wind. Rick laughed. He recited two lines from an Andrew Marvell poem:

The grave's a fine and private place,
But none, I think, do there embrace.

I knew what he was thinking, thoughts that were not far from my mind. Rick had come to Denison an astronomy major but switched to English because the physics courses were too hard. He was a smart kid, but he had a belief—that I shared at the time and later regretted—that was tied up with that poem. We were ready-made for the sixties.

Chapter Three

I ENJOYED A BRILLIANT SENIOR YEAR AT DENISON. STONED EVERY DAY. Hardly lifting a finger yet receiving adequate grades. Enjoyed the courses. Asian lit was at the Bandersnatch, the student coffee house. We sat on mats on the floor in a circle with our guru, Professor Tony Stoneburner, spouting Chinese poetry, Tu Fu, Li Po. Deconstructing the intricacies of the *Upanishads, Dream of the Red Chamber*, and the Japanese Noh play. We smoked dope with Professor Holter. Howie to us. He taught Soviet Culture and turned me on to Vladimir Mayakovsky, the Soviet poster-maker and poet who wrote such lines as "Where cities hang and in the noose of cloud, the towers' crooked spire congeals—I go alone to weep that crossroads crucify policemen."

I spouted my own poetry at the Bandersnatch, one I remember, a poem I fashioned out of a perusal of a beatnik dictionary. It's called "create":

create a beat soul
like an existential bohemian poet
on that dharma road to naked joy
through the bop scene of lost humanity
forever a gas

Wow, we had finally arrived. Avant-garde intellectuals. Drug-buying heroes. Wild-eyed radical types. Rick and I cocks of the walk.

To justify our new status beyond a reasonable doubt, we joined a smoke-in at Monomoy, an independent dorm a few blocks from where we lived. Denison was 97 percent Greek. We were club members, not Greeks but geeks, dorks, dweebs, dings. In a word, nerds. We belonged to the American Commons Club though I quit during hell week when the brothers made us carry an egg in the crack of our ass across a room, drop it, pull up our pants, and then get down on our hands and knees and roll the egg back with our nose. My sophomore year I joined as a social member only. The point was that we were unacceptable on campus. We weren't invited to parties. We couldn't find a date, except maybe with girls of our ilk. But the times, they were a-changing, as Bob Dylan iterated.

So, we rolled the joints and invited everyone we knew who invited everyone they knew to the smoke-in on such and such a date in late winter 1968. Our notoriety was such that I knew we'd have a nice turnout.

For instance, I remember a Sigma Chi asking Rick and me if we had any stuff to sell.

"What stuff?" asked Rick.

"You know, you know," he whined, shaking his golden locks and circling his hand around as if he were trying to pull up the word. But he knew the word, and we knew that he knew.

"Oh, you mean marijuana," said Rick. "You want us to sell you an ounce of marijuana."

He blushed a deep red and looked around to see if anyone had overheard. He wasn't the only frat boy who assumed we were dealers. We weren't dealers. We were like Ken Kesey and the Merry Pranksters. Our aim was to turn on the whole world.

Though the campus was not exactly the Berkeley of the Midwest, the students were doing their part. I remember one warm day in late fall, a philosophy professor led a group of students on a march around the front quad. They waved handheld American flags. A few Viet Cong flags (red and blue background, yellow star in the center, in contrast to the red star of the Communist Chinese). Maybe two dozen students marching and chanting slogans such as "Hell no, we won't go." They settled under a tall oak tree that must've dated back to when my grandfather was a student and sang protest songs, Pete Seeger's "Where Have All the Flowers Gone?" The prof implored other students walking by on the way to one class or another to join in. Some of these students gathered in clumps, while others hurried by as if the protesters were contagious. It was the time of the Beta wars. I don't know the significance of the wars other than to make the Betas look asinine. They were the jock fraternity. They dressed in military fatigues. They carried toy guns. Normally they sneaked around shooting each other with their fake guns, *ratta-tat-tat*, *boom-boom*, like I did when I was a kid with my friends in the neighborhood. But now with the prof in the midst of his harangue, the frat boys crawled on their bellies, fired at him and the other protesters, and ran off laughing.

This was followed not long after by the Raccoon Creek Rock Festival where The Who, Johnny Winter, Spirit, and Dust blew us away. Rick and I climbed up to the rafters where we had a perfect view of the stage. Pete Townshend in his white jumpsuit jumped in the air and banged his guitar; Roger Daltrey turned his back to the audience and spread his arms out so the frills in the white jacket he was wearing spilled down like he was a bird about to take flight. "Tommy doesn't know what day it is," he warbled.

Then when Spirit came on, Rick slapped me on the back and yelled, "We've arrived."

I lost my balance and nearly hurtled down to the audience below.

Nat Koenig performed as a madman in *Marat/Sade*. Revolution was in the air. A traveling theater group from California stopped by to perform at the campus theater without their clothes on. A group of musicians with a psychological bent invited the audience up on stage to vent their anger with kazoos, tambourines, bongo drums, and castanets while they played backup music. A demonstration at the foot of the administration building led to one of the administrators promising to give us more free speech. He was pelted with flowers.

The planets seemed aligned for the Monomoy smoke-in. Only, as it turned out, some of the joints were laced with acid. I didn't know how this happened, but it was rumored the Moy Boys, as they called themselves, dipped the joints in liquid LSD like what you do with blotter acid. I smoked one of these weeds and ended up running around all night with my fellow students who had done likewise.

One of those students was the shy Sigma Chi dude who stuck closely to my side. "I don't know what's happening to me," he said in a shaky voice.

"Nor do I," I said. We both laughed and shivered at the same time.

We looked at each other. I noticed that he was outlined by an aura like a streetlight on a foggy night. "Your aura is golden," I said.

"Yours is purple," he said, sparks coming off his blond locks as he shook his head, "like you must be royalty or something."

I backed away from him and bumped into Rick, who was wondering why I was in this altered state. I told him my theory. He wanted one of those tainted joints. I reached in my pocket and pulled out a couple of bones. Rick took one and smoked it. It took him a while, but finally his eyes popped wide.

"Now I'm like you."

"You see my aura?" I asked him. Though we had never experienced auras as such, we knew the language. "What color is it?"

"Purple," he said, bending over. "I think I'm going to vomit."

But he didn't. We ran amok, staring at things as if we were seeing them for the first time. We came up to a maple tree and hugged it, feeling the bark like the wrinkled skin of an old man, looking up at a squirrel holding a nut, chattering, its tail twitching. We chased after a couple of stray dogs who were chasing each other until one caught up and started humping the other. This was a common sight on the Denison campus. The co-eds complained about it. There was even an editorial in the campus paper about how something had to be done about these dogs who seemed to be increasing the dog population by their carnal acts. But to us in our slightly altered condition, these acts were the miracle of conception.

We traipsed over to Shepherd Hall, the ROTC building, a one-story wooden structure in dilapidated condition. "Let's burn it down," said Rick, lighting a match, but then we saw the campus cops were moving up in a line to surround the building. The Sigma Chi frat boy blew out the match.

"What's the idea?" said Rick, shaking his hand. He had almost burned his fingers.

"I'm in Rotsee," said the frat boy.

We looked around and noticed that the downhill campus was full of students. Normally there was no one around here since most of the dorms and classes were located on the hill. Monomoy itself was disgorging students who were smoking joints while others were squeezing by to get inside to grab their share. *Hey,* I thought, *this is a happening.* No wonder the cops were here. Maybe they were afraid there were, among the smokers, revolutionaries lurking.

And sure enough, a revolutionary jumped out of the bushes and tossed a Molotov cocktail at Shepherd and caught the door on fire. The cops put it out but couldn't find the revolutionary, though our frat buddy saw a short guy scamper uphill and, thinking he might be the culprit, scampered up after him. We never saw them again. Well, I saw the revolutionary years later. He showed up at the campus of another school where I was getting a graduate degree. I rented an apartment that he was vacating. He was short, skinny, balding, nearly blind. He told me he had easily outrun the frat boy since he was on the track team. He was not my idea of a revolutionary. But neither was Trotsky.

Hank and J. B. joined us, as did Nat and Margie after they struck the *Marat/Sade* set. We smoked some more tainted joints and wandered around campus enjoying the mild weather before winter set in again. The campus police eyed us warily. How did they know we weren't wild-eyed revolutionaries? Bomb throwers? Raggedy-assed Che Guevera out to destroy their way of life.

Rick and I dragged ourselves home, the sun firing tiny beams of light across the horizon to jab us in our weary eyes. We crashed until midafternoon when we were rudely awakened by the jangling of the telephone. It was my mom calling to say that Dad was in the hospital and that he might die. I needed to return home immediately.

It took me two days to find a flight out of Columbus, but once I arrived, I took a cab to George Washington University Hospital expecting the worst, only to find Dad sitting up in bed joking with Ed Bronson, an old friend from his days as a newspaper reporter. Mr. Bronson kidded Dad about his mustache that he had recently grown. Accused him of being a hippie and that the next thing he was going to do was smoke grass.

"At least you won't grow your hair long," he said, winking at me. Mine was verging on long. Dad was bald.

I helped Mom get Dad settled back home. He was going to take a few weeks off and then return to work. We had a few serious talks about his ailment—kidney disease, though the doctor suggested that it might be worse. Cancer. I could tell they were both worried, and I thought about how weird it was that they were in this crisis that could mean the end of everything and here I was in another reality entirely.

I flew back to Columbus and tried to put it all out of my mind. Then came one last cold snap before the forsythia bloomed, and I realized that my reality may not be that far removed from my parents'. I was eligible for the draft once I left school. The ideal way to avoid the draft was to continue your student IIS status by attending graduate school. I found a better way, thanks to the Quakers who counseled us draft resisters: flunk the physical.

I had dislocated my shoulder playing football in high school. It was during summer practice my junior year. We were doing a punt-catch-and-pursuit drill. I was the catcher. The ball came at me high in the air, wobbly. It slipped through my fingers, bounced off my knee, and shot in the air. I caught it on the way down. A beefy lineman caught me under the armpit and pushed up. The shoulder joint popped out of the socket and rested against my rib cage. It took five hours to pop that joint back in due to the finicky coach who wouldn't take me to the hospital without my father's permission. The next year in a football game, the shoulder popped out again. Fortunately, there was a doctor in the house that time. Then it happened three other times, the last one when I was body surfing in Rehoboth Beach.

"You're a cinch to flunk the physical," said one of the Quakers. "All you need are letters from the doctors who treated you." That meant four letters from four doctors, which I collected during spring break.

Dad was back on his feet. Hard at work, though he came home early every day. He'd taken on a partner to lessen the burden on him. And Mom seemed happy. I didn't know what to think.

It was early April when the buses rolled out of the college to take us seniors to our physicals in Newark, the county seat for Licking County. We took the Granville-Newark Road, which I had taken a thousand times before on the way to one bar or another or even to the go-go club that had dancers in skimpy outfits in glass cages. I didn't look at this with any nostalgia; I hadn't been down this road since I turned on. Too many drunk drivers, though once I was here on foot near the edge of Granville and had witnessed the aftermath of an accident. Some drunken frat boy was hanging out the window when the car grazed a telephone pole and he lost his head, literally. This was what I thought about as we drove through the tunnel of trees that overhung the road. Maybe that could happen to me in Vietnam. I could lose my head, my foot, my hand, my mind. I could step on a sharpened bamboo trap with excrement on it and die a slow, painful death. Or get captured by the Viet Cong and rot to death in a tiger cage up to my chest in water. This, of course, is what I heard from the media, and it's all I knew about the war. I did have one friend in the neighborhood where I grew up who went to Vietnam. He wrote home to his family that he spent most of his time with a soldier he intensely disliked because this soldier was a survivor, and he figured if he stayed close, he'd survive as well. It didn't matter that I had my doctors' letters in my hands; I was still quaking in my boots.

We pulled up to what looked like a gymnasium and piled out of the bus.

I remember only a few of the more dramatic events in the physical. I remember they made us strip to our waist and form a long line. The doctors had different-colored magic markers that they stashed in the pockets of their white coats. They came down the line and checked us, and if something was wrong, they ran their marker across our chest. Different colors represented different problems. Like, one doctor checked my ears and ran a yellow marker across my chest. Maybe that meant I had too much ear wax, which was true. I had to have my ears blown out every year or so in order to hear properly. They checked my feet, and I got a blue marker. Flat feet. That was how my dad got out of World War II, that and an essential civilian job in radio censorship. Then they made us drop trou. They walked down the line in front and told us to turn our head sideways and cough while they grabbed our balls. No magic marker for me on this one, so my sex organs were intact. They told us to bend over and crack our ass by holding each cheek. They came down the line and inspected our assholes. I got a red marker—hemorrhoids. No way I was going to join this man's army. Maybe VISTA or the Peace Corps, no war for me.

After they finished with the group activity, they dealt with us individually. We went into glassed-in offices one by one. In one office, I handed over my recurrent-dislocated-shoulder letters. The man in the white coat looked over the papers and asked me a few questions.

"How did you first dislocate it?"

"Playing football," I said.

"How long was it out?"

"Five hours or so?"

"Why that long?"

"Well, it was a Saturday during summer practice when it happened. The coach took me into his office while the rest of the guys showered and dress..."

"Not so much detail. We don't have all day."

So I told the rest of the story in one sentence. He pulled out two magic markers. I got a green and a purple.

I visited the shrink who wanted to know if I had any personal problems that would affect my service in the armed forces.

"I don't want to kill anyone."

He laughed. "That's what they all say."

I got a gray marker. I guessed that stood for gray matter.

They gave us a battery of tests. The one I remember was for illiterates, I think, a series of pictures where we matched up a tool with its function—for instance, a screwdriver with a screw. Since I had problems with spatial relationships, I flunked the test. I got a pink marker across the chest. I guess I didn't qualify as an illiterate.

By this time, I had the following magic marker colors crisscrossing my chest: pink, gray, purple, green, red, blue, and yellow. I felt like one of the rainbow people. A soldier escorted me to a long line of benches against a wall. I sat down. I checked out my fellow bench-warmers. All undesirable in one way or another: nerds, minorities, long-hairs, ugly, ungainly, gassy, pimply, fat. It felt good to be a reject for once.

A few weeks later, I received a missive from Uncle Sam with my new draft card. I was classified 1-Y. That meant that I was qualified for service only in the case of a national emergency. I was lucky in two ways. I was lucky to be injured playing football. I was lucky because my draft board was located in Washington, DC, where 70 percent of the population was Black. There were plenty of bodies other than mine to fill the quota. I felt guilty about that in a way. My friends in Bethesda, where most of the population was white, had a harder time of it—Rick, for instance. He wrote a Conscientious Objector letter and had to wait until his board called him in to defend it. If they turned him down, he'd refuse to serve. Back then we wished everybody felt like us. Then we couldn't field an army, and we couldn't fight a war. We were just naive kids, you know.

Chapter Four

When I left for college a year after President Kennedy was assassinated, my parents moved from the house I grew up in to a brick colonial on a quiet street at the end of a cul-de-sac. The house I grew up in was a 1910 foursquare up the block from the playground where I played baseball, tag, and such with all the kids. We knew everyone in the neighborhood. We went to their parties, and they came to ours. I remember Mr. Wood, the neighborhood bully's father, at one of our Christmas parties got so drunk he put his coat on backward, and one of my best buddies, Pete Swindells, set off a box full of fireworks with a sparkler at a Fourth of July party to see what would happen. He nearly set fire to his garage. The houses in the new neighborhood were, at most, ten years old. I think my mom was tired of replacing the wiring and the metal plumbing, repairing the stucco that was cracking on the old house. She wanted something new. She wanted to start over since her kids had moved away. Only I was back.

Dad was in the hospital again. The prognosis was grim. But there was hope because he had been accepted into an experimental program at the University of Utah hospital. It was run by the inventor of the kidney machine, Dr. Willem Kolff. The idea was that they would rent an apartment in Salt Lake City for six months. Dad would undergo dialysis twice a week, and Mom would learn how to operate a kidney machine. I would keep the home fires burning until they returned.

The new house was on Twenty-Ninth Place behind my high school. It was on a hill that overlooked Cleveland Avenue. When

Martin Luther King was assassinated my senior year, I was home for spring vacation. I stood in the living room looking down at the cops who had set up a speed trap. They had cars lined up two or three at a time, handing out tickets. Then I went to the other side of the house and out the front door, where I could see the smoke rise above the treetops from the riots on Fourteenth Street. It was surreal. I felt like I was in a new world, a grown-up world. No more Howdy Doody and Buffalo Bob, no more Mamie and Ike. Yet I was a virgin.

My parents left for Salt Lake City. I was alone in a neighborhood where I knew no one and no one knew me. That was good. I did know Pie, Rick's sister, who was a senior at Walt Whitman High School in Bethesda. Her real name was Anne. It was Rick who gave her the nickname when she was still in diapers, referring to her as Humble Pie. That drove her to distraction. She was not the humble pie–eating type. We had a brief romance that was nearly consummated in the back of a friend's Dodge van the summer between my junior and senior years. She was a rabid Beatles fan. Her walls were covered with Fab Four photographs and an autographed photo of John Lennon that even I coveted. She was one of the screaming teenyboppers at the Beatles' first concert in DC at the Washington Coliseum in 1964. I think her attraction to me was that I had a sort of mop-head haircut. I looked like Paul McCartney.

Our romance ended when I told her she wore too much makeup. I was her elder by a few years and knew a few things about women—after all, I had a sister and mother. I also said her miniskirt was too short. It made her look like… I didn't finish the sentence because she broke into tears. Her makeup ran down her cheeks in two black lines that made her look like a sad clown. I tried to console her, but she would have none of it. She told me to buzz off.

By the summer after graduation, she had found a new boyfriend, Joe Johnson. He was a returned navy veteran she met while on vacation in Ocean City with her friends. Our romance was far in the past. She never mentioned my faux pas. I was once again in her good graces.

The fact was, even without Pie as my significant other, I was in an ideal situation. I worked for my dad, though he didn't like it.

"This will end badly," he insisted, knowing my lack of commitment and knowledge of his business, public relations. Most of his clients were broadcasters. He'd been in the business since its infancy. Things were changing, though. Cable TV was replacing over-the-air broadcasting. The FCC was changing rules limiting ownership. So, companies like Clear Channel could buy hundreds of radio stations. Dad was forward-thinking and offered John Barrington, a cable TV executive, a partnership. Dad did this because he was sick. He didn't like it that John wanted to hire me. But with Mom's cajoling, I was hired on a salary of $6,500 a year.

This would be seed money for starting our commune. Rick and I knew where we were going: Colorado, the mountains, hopefully. Pie had applied to Denver University. Early decision. She was a shoo-in, with her B-plus average and 1400 college boards. But even if she didn't make it, we'd still go there, and Joe planned to join us. I heard from Rick at Denison that a few of the women he knew who were graduating planned to move out to Colorado, as well as Hank and his new girlfriend, who he was madly in love with. Maybe they'd live with us. It seemed promising.

Meanwhile, I was a cog in the big capitalist wheel. Not that I minded that much. It was Dad's business after all, and he was sick. I was pulling off two things at once: securing my future while holding the fort until Dad returned home.

I was strictly nine-to-five, and even if I wanted to be later, Mr. Barrington was the same as me. Sometimes I'd find him slumped over his typewriter at three in the afternoon after a businessman's luncheon. He was not a happy camper. His family was still in New York. He'd spend the week at an apartment he rented near work and the weekend with his wife and kids. I got the feeling that his former boss, Irving Kahn, a cable TV mogul, had ordered him down here to help out Dad. Kahn was fond of my dad, as were all Dad's clients—or at least that was my impression. They were willing to hang in there until Dad regained his health.

In the morning, I'd wander into the office wondering what the hell I was doing here. I was nervous as a cat. I wanted to get high. That was when I took up smoking. Salem cigarettes. I'd light one up in the morning. Get off on a tiny buzz. Then it would take two cigs to get the buzz, and so on until I was hooked. I wrote press releases and a monthly newsletter for the cable TV association. I wrote several educational pamphlets. I can't remember what about or who my audience was or anything other than they were boring busywork.

Once I caught the train to New York to deliver some packages to Irving Kahn's office. Mr. Barrington took me to a fancy club where we proceeded to get a little tipsy. I stayed at the Gladstone Hotel on East Fifty-Second and Lexington. It had seen better days. I remembered going there when I was a kid with my dad. Our hotel room had been on the top floor. I cracked open the window. I could hear the roar of the traffic below us and looked down at the tiny cars and people so far away it was frightening. It took forever to ride down the elevator to the ground floor, where Dad took me to a restaurant. We chowed down on big, juicy steaks. I couldn't finish mine, but I did manage to inhale my favorite dessert, ice cream topped by butterscotch sauce sprinkled with chopped peanuts. Dad pointed out a famous movie star a couple of tables away. Ginger Rogers. She was beautiful. I was in heaven. But not now. Now I was a hippie. New York was dirty and crowded. I couldn't wait to get home.

Nights were the ideal time at home. I'd light a joint, and people would visit. Joe's friend Bill Barbour when he could get away from Quantico. He was a marine. Pie's numerous friends, mostly classmates of the female variety.

The only downer was our drug dealer. Normally you don't make friends with your dealer. But this one was an old buddy of Rick's from Walter Johnson High School. His name was Quayle Smith. In high school, he had tooled around in an MG sports car. He was happy-go-lucky, popular with the girls, a tall, lanky dude with beautiful, silky blond hair down to his shoulders, a sharp-featured face, and pale-blue eyes. But then he traveled to Mexico and delved into drugs like Nat Koenig had, but unlike Nat, Quayle delved too far, or so it seemed to me. Now he lived in the basement of his house on Kirby Road. His main companion was his black lab, Thumper. He barely spoke a word. The girls were afraid of him, and so was I—not for what he'd do to me but what he could do to himself.

I remember before Rick left for college that fall we picked up a couple of lids at his house. Quayle followed Rick and me upstairs after the transaction because he wanted to show us something. We wandered into the dining room, where Mrs. Smith was sipping a cup of coffee.

Rick introduced himself.

"Oh, I remember you," she said. She was thin and sharp-featured like her son, though her eyes were black as coal. Her hair was in a carefully coiffed bouffant. She wore a dark suit and a tired expression, as though she needed to catch up on her sleep. She was as spooky, in her own way, as her son. "You were one of Quayle's best friends. Are you in college?"

"I'm a senior," said Rick.

"I wish Quayle went to college." She cast a doleful glance in her son's direction.

But Quayle was busy opening the top drawer of a mahogany buffet against the wall. He pointed at the contents. "I want you to look here," he said.

We sidled over and peered down at the silverware neatly stacked in a wood container and, in a corner, an American flag folded in a triangle.

"That flag was on top of Dad's coffin. He was a war veteran."

"Your father died?" asked Rick, taken completely by surprise.

"Yes, we buried him in the military cemetery in Culpepper, Virginia."

We attempted to express our condolences to Mrs. Smith, but she had vanished into the kitchen, or at least that was what I surmised from the swinging door swishing back and forth. Quayle checked her out as well, a smirk curling up his lips. The guy was weird, I thought. Rick thought it wasn't the guy—it was the situation. Living at his ticky-tacky suburban home with his mother. It was like he was stuck in a time warp. All he needed was some fresh air. That was why we invited him to my place. He spent most of the time sitting alone in a corner of the basement room while we hung out getting stoned. He wouldn't get stoned with us. He would sometimes smile to himself as if he were having a conversation in his head or nod to the music like in the Doors song about faces coming out of the rain.

I think I would have gone nuts if it was not for Pie and her friends. Well, not Celia and Janet, whom she had known since elementary school, I think. They put together a folk music trio and sang at local coffeehouses for teenagers. I didn't think they liked me—or Rick, for that matter. But that was all right.

Besides, I was more attracted to Pie's newer friends, like Josie. I remember a photograph of us. We were at Seneca, a park on the Chesapeake and Ohio Canal by the Potomac River twenty or so miles west of Washington. This was one of our places to smoke dope in nature. I was sitting on a log, bent over, rolling a joint, wearing sunglasses, laughing. Josie straddled the log. She wore black tights and a leopard-print jacket. She was a blond. Her skin was pale. She was staring at me rolling the joint. But that was it. I don't remember kissing her or doing anything else other than giving her a back rub once.

I didn't think Josie was attracted to me, but Sally Russo was. She was a year older than the rest of Pie's friends. I didn't really think of them as women, which was kind of embarrassing since I considered myself a man. She was nineteen. She was headed for the University of Wisconsin in the fall, but that summer she worked as a secretary at the Spanish Embassy and seemed to spend every night at my place.

Pie saw my interest in Sally and suggested I entice her with a gift. I took Sally out to dinner and pinned her with my old ACC badge, which I had held onto in case it came in handy. She asked me what it meant. I told her it was a way of saying that you cared for a girl and that the next step, if things worked out, was an engagement ring. When we left the restaurant, she told me that was the prettiest gift anyone had ever given her. It was a triangle outlined by white seed pearls with a small ruby in the center. At the top corner was an *A* and at the bottom two corners, two *C*s. We climbed in the Mustang, and she leaned over and kissed me.

"I think I like you an awful lot," she cooed. On the way back after dropping Sally off at her home in Bethesda, I thought about how I was living a double life. Here I was a dope-smoking college graduate who dodged the draft. I wanted to move out west to start a farm with my buddies, but I was also a good boy holding down my dad's business, a good boy who pinned a girl in the old-fashioned way—though I had salacious ideas in my head. But you got to start somewhere. The fact was that I was confused. But you know, it was the sixties. I rejected my parents' materialistic values. I wanted to live a more meaningful life. Yet I wasn't sure what that meant or if I meant what I was saying. Was I simply echoing the mantra of my generation? Or was I a true believer?

Sally told her family about me. They wanted to check me out, so I was invited to a party one Saturday afternoon at her house. I think it was a Jewish holiday because the extended family was there. I was introduced around. I knew I was nervous because my face felt hot as a griddle.

Finally, I came to Sally's grandfather, a distinguished old gentleman leaning on his cane as he stood to shake my hand. "So, when are you going to marry Sally?" he asked with a wry smile as if he knew exactly what I was up to.

Sally and I drove to Seneca and sauntered down the Chesapeake and Ohio Canal towpath, found a bench in an isolated spot, sat down, and smoked a joint. Then we climbed up a hill along a meandering path to a deserted farmhouse at the edge of a cornfield that I had found years ago when I was in high school. The walls were scrawled with graffiti: "Jack loves Jill," "John wants Mary," "Ted kissed Catherine." On the second floor up a rickety stairway was a threadbare mattress beside a big gap in the wall that revealed not only the canal but the Potomac beyond it. We sat down on the mattress, and Sally embarked on a long conversation about what she planned to do when she entered college. I think she was nervous.

"You know what my major will be in college?" she asked rhetorically. "Spanish. I want to spend my junior year abroad in Spain. Then, if I like it, I'll move there forever."

"Why would you want to do that?" I knew she had a thing about Spain, but why leave our country when things were about to get better?

"Oh, I don't know. I can speak Spanish so well," she said, brushing a dark-brown curl out of her eye, "that it seems like it's in my blood. I'm a Sephardic Jew, you know."

"So was Levi Strauss, the guy who invented blue jeans," I said, having read it somewhere. Maybe in one of the business magazines I perused at work.

"I didn't know that. You're pretty smart, Jeff." She leaned forward and kissed me on the cheek, as a reward, I suppose. "You know the Jews were kicked out of Spain by Ferdinand and Isabella, the same as the Moors." She went on and on in this vein, in a nervous way, as if she were trying to put off the inevitable, until I put my arm around her. She leaned into me. She let me kiss her and reach my hand under her bra without her jumping. Finally, she said, "Not here."

I took that to mean, not here but somewhere else. I checked out our surroundings, the graffiti on the walls, the threadbare mattress where many a couple must've borne out their desires. How disgusting to think of what they left behind. How unromantic. I took Sally's hand and pulled her to her feet.

"Let's go," I said.

SALLY'S BEST FRIEND was Robin Gran. She wore black from head to toe like a fifties Greenwich Village beatnik. Her hair was black, her eyes were black and catlike, sometimes she wore black lipstick and red rouge to highlight her high cheekbones. Her breasts were pear shaped. Her rear was pear shaped. She was almost as thin as Twiggy and as well-proportioned as Marilyn Monroe. She was perfect, but she had an abrasive personality. We'd sit cross-legged in a circle in the basement living room at my parent's home on Twenty-Ninth Place and pass joints around. Then we'd play board games. The women preferred *Life*, or they'd watch the men play *Risk* and look disgusted. Only Robin would play with us. The idea of *Risk* was to take over the world, and how she played it was to make alliances with one or another player until she had all the players in contention with each other, and she'd sneak in and win. She always won, except for one time I beat her.

She said, "I let you do it. You're cute."

I think I blushed and said something stupid like "So are you."

I didn't have the slightest idea why she was showing an interest in me since she had a boyfriend, Kevin. Kevin was a cutup, always ready to entertain us with a joke like the one I remember: "One day, a little boy wrote Santa Claus, 'Please send me a sister.' Santa wrote him back, 'Okay, send me your mother.'"

The thing was that Robin kissed me on the cheek when she saw me or rubbed up against my body like a cat. "Meow, meow," she would purr.

I thought she was trying to make Kevin jealous. But that wasn't it at all. Sally and Robin were rivals, lookalikes—the same height, the same coloring, though Robin's hair was straight. They had fought over Kevin, and now they were fighting over me. That made me feel good.

I think the last straw was when Sally wandered into the basement one time after a hard day of work pushing papers at the Spanish Embassy. She caught Robin going through her ritual of greeting me.

"How would you like it if I did this?" she addressed Robin, tossing her curls. She marched over to Kevin, kissed him on the cheek, and rubbed up against his body. "Meow, meow," she purred.

"I would say you were being immature," said Robin, smiling and gritting her teeth in equal measure. I didn't know what to make of this. A few hours later, they were pals talking about a shopping trip to Hecht's department store, where they each purchased the mini mod dresses they now wore. Same size, different colors. Robin's dress was black, and Sally's dress was lemon colored.

"You look better than me," admitted Sally. "That's because black makes you appear thinner."

"You're saying that I'm not thin."

"No, no, no. I'm saying that if I wore black, I would appear as thin as you."

"That's true. That's very true," admitted Robin. They looked over at me listening in to their conversation. They changed the subject.

I guess they came to a kind of truce, because Robin never again greeted me in that affectionate, meowy fashion, and the next day Sally told Pie she wanted to sleep with me.

A few days later, Joe, Pie, and our other friends headed off to see *2001: A Space Odyssey* at the Uptown Theatre. I wanted to go as well, but Sally declined, and I didn't want to leave her alone.

"We'll go sometime later," I said. The Uptown was our widescreen theater. I could imagine what fun it would be, but there were other things that were more fun, or so I'd been told.

We waved goodbye to our friends. We smoked a joint. We listened to some music, and then I asked Sally if she wanted to go upstairs. She nodded solemnly.

I escorted Sally into my sister's room. I could've done it in my room, but I had two single beds. Susan's was queen-size, so we had more room to move around. Sally was no help. She told me she was a virgin. I didn't tell her anything because I didn't want to appear like an idiot. We took off our clothes and climbed under the covers. I was worried that we wouldn't get this over with before the movie was over, but I needn't have.

We made love again over that summer, I don't know how many times—she still had a month before she left for Wisconsin, and to be honest, I thought that I was madly in love with Sally. Maybe she should stay in Washington, transfer to GW or American University, where Robin was applying for next year. But she told me she'd been accepted in an advanced Spanish language program at Wisconsin. I could follow her to Madison, but that was impossible as well after what I had promised my parents.

We spent one last day together.

"I'll come home for the holidays," she said. We were in the garden in back of my parents' house, surrounded by a high wooden fence. We heard the low hum of traffic on Cleveland Avenue. The wind rustled through the trees above us; the birds sang. The sun was setting. It didn't feel like fall was around the corner.

"You know I could be gone when you come home for the holidays. I could be in Colorado scouting out a place for us to live." That was what Rick and I and the rest of us planned, though I doubted it would be that soon.

"Then I'll visit you in the summer. I'll get a job." She took my hand and squeezed it.

That was the way we left it. I drove her home, and a few days later, she left for college.

I DIDN'T HAVE much time to mourn her loss because Susan and I flew to Salt Lake City to see our parents.

Dad was confined to his bed in an apartment they rented near the hospital, but sometimes I took him out for a drive. Once I took him all the way to Park City, where we sat in the car at the bottom of a ski slope watching the skiers. Dad asked me for a cigarette.

"I don't have any," I said, though he could see clear through my white shirt to the green pack in my breast pocket.

"You don't have to lie to me." He reached in my pocket and pulled out the pack.

"Mom doesn't want you to smoke. It's not good for you."

"Yes, your mom is right, but I need some pleasure in life."

I lit the cigarette for him and one for myself. Dad was concerned about his business. He asked me if John neglected the broadcasting clients in favor of the cable ones. I said no and told him we still renewed his clients' broadcast licenses and that at one luncheon meeting at the Capitol, Senator Magnuson, the chairman of the Commerce Committee, asked how he was.

"What did you say?" Dad flicked his ashes in the ashtray, nearly setting the carpet on fire with an ember. I stamped it out.

"I said you were fine. And he said you're a great man and I should be proud of you."

"You're kidding," Dad rejoined, almost blushing. I'd never seen him do that before. He changed the subject. "How's Sandy?" Sandy was Sandy George, my dad's fiercely loyal bleached-blond secretary, who knew more about the office than John and me combined.

"She's fine," I said. "Working hard."

"If anyone can save the business, she can," said Dad. He turned quiet as he settled back to watch the skiers. There was one weaving back and forth around the others, his scarf flying in the air behind him. "Ah, I wish I could do that," he said, taking a puff of the cig and laughing. "But I never learned how to ski. There aren't any mountains in Ohio, though I cross-country skied on barrel staves with your Uncle Tom. That was fun."

I knew that Dad had a fatalistic streak. He told me more than once that he wasn't long for this world because he had had scarlet fever when he was a kid. I looked it up in a medical dictionary, and sure enough, one of the long-term complications of scarlet fever can be kidney disease. Maybe I should've kept my big mouth shut (I didn't want to jinx his chances), but after we poked out the weeds in the ashtray, I said, "Don't worry, Dad, you're going to be all right. You'll get back to work. I swear to God."

"Okay, you're probably right," he said, patting my knee. "Maybe I'll find a new kidney and live twenty or thirty years more. That's when I'll quit smoking. One thing at a time."

When I returned to Washington, I found a small package from Sally Russo in the mailbox. I opened it. Inside was my ACC pin and a letter from Sally. She said she was returning the pin because she was in love with someone else. An exchange student from Barcelona. She might marry him, she said, though she tried to soften the blow by telling me how much she thought of me as a friend.

A few weeks later, in late October, I drove along River Road with Pie and Joe. We were headed for Seneca. The leaves were turning red and brown, and I was feeling devastated. I didn't know what to think. Even though I could see that Sally needed to go on with her life, I felt crushed, an unloved human being in a lonely universe. Then "Hey, Jude" came on the radio.

Annie Pie sang along with the music, and I followed haltingly since I didn't recall all the lyrics. We turned down the radio when the song was over but kept up the singing. Joe joined in. I was amazed that the Beatles knew what I was feeling. Not that I had anyone to let into my heart, but I had a sad song and there was a possibility I could "make it better."

I parked the car, and we wandered along the towpath. It was

Saturday, cloudy, a chill in the air. Seneca was deserted. We found a secluded spot along the river and sat down on a log. We passed a couple of joints around like I had on that long-ago day with Sally and watched the gray water of the Potomac race by us on the way to Great Falls.

"Beautiful, isn't it," said Pie.

I looked at her. She seemed to be surrounded by a golden aura like an angel. "Yeah, beautiful," I said and flicked the last tip of the joint into the water.

MY PARENTS ARRIVED home in January, the day after the kidney machine arrived. They assembled it in the basement bedroom. Mom operated the machine. They had put two shunts in Dad's wrists: one to carry the blood out to be cleaned by the machine, the other to carry the cleaned blood back in. Dad was like the Incredible Shrinking Man, except that he didn't get smaller and smaller. He got skinnier and skinnier, until he was a skeleton.

In mid-March they moved him to GW Hospital, and every three days, Mom gave him a dialysis since the technique was so new that no nurse was trained to operate the machine. In April, Dad died.

Chapter Five

I HAD A DREAM A FEW WEEKS BEFORE I LEFT FOR COLORADO TO START my new life. I was six years old at a horse show in the country in a big crowd, and I was scared. I was all alone. I scanned the crowd but didn't recognize anyone. A bunch of horsey men and women in jodhpurs and felt hats. Nasty looks on their faces. Then I heard a familiar cough in the distance. Mom. She was a smoker. She was moving closer. The crowd parted. She walked up, leaned down to where I was sitting on the ground, and lifted me in her arms. I woke up. This had really happened; it was a memory, not just a dream. I hadn't thought of it in years, but it bubbled up from my subconscious and spooked the hell out of me.

It was one month after my dad died. I clumped downstairs yawning and thinking about my dream. Mom sat alone at the dining room table sipping coffee, staring out the window. Her cereal lay untouched in front of her, turning soggy. Her eyes were red rimmed, her mouth turned down. But when she saw me, she smiled in a distracted, careworn way that made me want to burst out in tears.

I fixed a bowl of cereal and coffee for myself and sat down next to her. "Hey, Mom," I said, "why don't I stay here another year until you're settled down."

"No, thank you," she said, patting my hand. "I've got to get used to being alone, and you've got to get used to being on your own. I made a rhyme." She giggled in a not-too-convincing way. "Besides, I have more than enough help."

What she meant was that she had help in closing down Dad's business and selling his interest in two radio stations he owned with a partner. She was more than settled down financially. Emotionally, I guess, she had my sister. Susan and her husband lived on the campus of a prep school near Dyke, Virginia. Porter was assistant headmaster. The stone cottage they lived in was large enough to accommodate Mom when she visited, which she did often since the birth of her first grandchild, Porter—Po, for short. My father, two weeks before he died, snapped a photograph of Po sitting on the front lawn of the house on Twenty-Ninth Place. Po was wearing a yellow playsuit and a yellow newsboy cap. He was staring at the camera. Dad's shadow was on the lawn next to his grandson. He was holding up the camera. I could see the shadow of his skinny arms, his gaunt face, and the funny Tyrolean hat pushed down over his ears. That photo gave me the creeps, and I supposed, when Po grew up, it'd do the same for him.

To be honest, I felt guilty that my sister would be there when my mom needed her and I wouldn't. But I was five years younger than Susan and unattached. I pictured myself ending up like Quayle Smith if I stayed. Besides, I was champing at the bit. It was only natural for me to leave.

Susan and her family drove to Washington to pick up Mom. She planned to stay a couple weeks at their stone cottage. I ordered Chinese food from the Moon Palace the night before they left (one of our Thursday night rituals when I was growing up). We sat at the dining room table passing around the paper cartons. Susan cut up sweet and sour chicken and vegetables and fed Po, who was trying to squeeze out of his high chair. He paused to take a bite. Took the vegetables out of his mouth and threw them on the floor. Giles, their French poodle, gobbled up the tiny pieces. Po was getting such a thrill out of how Giles scampered around that he threw all his food on the floor until Susan stopped feeding him. Then he went back to trying to squeeze out of his high chair.

"He's such a devil, like you were," said Mom. She launched into the story about how one night when Dad was on a business trip, she was tucking Susan into the crib when the little devil pointed behind her. "Who's that man over there?" baby Susan asked.

"Of course there wasn't any man. But she scared me to death." Mom launched into other stories such as when I was two, Susan wiggled one of her baby teeth out of her mouth and placed it in my mouth to see what I looked like. I swallowed the tooth. And once Mom let her push my baby carriage down the sidewalk. Susan let go. I flew down the street toward the busy intersection of Thirty-Fourth and Macomb. The carriage hit a tree and tipped over. I fell out but didn't cry, I was so traumatized.

Susan reveled in these stories about her devilish behavior. There were many more that Mom didn't delve into. But the point was that Dad was a devil when he was growing up and Mom was Miss Perfect. I took after Mom. But now the situation was reversed.

The next morning, I waved goodbye to my family as they drove around the corner on Twenty-Ninth Place in Susan's red Oldsmobile station wagon she inherited from Dad. I waved goodbye a lot lately, I thought to myself, as I wandered back in the house, hands in my pockets, feeling dejected. Mom told me once that I had a morbid personality. I dwelled too much on the past. I decided she was right and the best thing for me to do was dwell on the future.

One week after Mom left and a month before the Denison contingent graduated, Joe Johnson and I waved goodbye to Washington, DC. We drove Pie to her home in Bethesda. She waved goodbye to her boyfriend, tears in her eyes. We hopped onto the Beltway and got caught up in bumper-to-bumper traffic until we reached Interstate 70 in Frederick. We followed 70 all the way west. We were in a hurry to find a place to live.

We met Baby Huey in Denver. He had graduated early and was driving in from Steubenville in his dad's Plymouth Valiant. We sniffed around the Rocky Mountains a couple of weeks, sleeping at campgrounds, checking out realtors and small towns like Idaho Springs, Central City, and as far afield as Cripple Creek and Gold

Hill. We had a grand time sightseeing but didn't accomplish much in the practical sense. Finally, we found a motel in Nederland to spend the night. Then we found the local realtor, a short, fat guy who rubbed his hands together constantly like he was closing a deal. I don't know how many places he showed us, but there was only one we could afford. It was an A-frame on top of a hill. Somebody had chopped about five trees down to the west so we could get a partial view of the snow-covered Continental Divide. There were three major drawbacks: No water. No septic system. No electricity.

"Only a few thousand dollars extra to get those in," the realtor informed us. I'll call him Ray.

Then there was the fact that the only access to our property was through someone else's land.

"We'll draw up a thirty-year contract with this fellow," said Ray. "For five hundred dollars a year, you'll have exclusive access. No problem; he's a good man."

It was ten acres of land. Not much of it flat, except around the A-frame there was a good-sized field full of wildflowers.

"How long is the growing season here?" asked Joe.

"The growing season?" asked Ray with a perplexed look. "You can't grow anything up here unless, I don't know, you grow marijuana. A lot of these hippies grow marijuana. But it's illegal. You're not going to grow marijuana, are you?"

"No, no, no," I said. "We want to be self-sufficient."

"What's that mean?"

"That means we want to grow our own vegetables. Build a barn to house livestock," said Joe. "You know, things like that."

"Welllll, I guess you could do that."

We returned to Ray's house, and I relaxed in a recliner. Outside the window, two hummingbirds were hovering around a glass bird feeder, sticking their long beaks in a hole and darting off in a circle before they came darting back for more.

Ray was sitting at his table going over figures, making calls to the electrician and the well and septic company until he seemed satisfied and showed us his results. "Here's how I figure," he said, pointing at the paper he scribbled on. "The house and property cost you ten thou, improvements another eight—I forgot to add in the heat, windows, wiring, and insulation. That's eighteen with a down payment of $3,600; that leaves you paying $186 a month on a ten-year mortgage at prime, 8.6 percent times twelve equals $2,232 a year plus $500 for access plus one thou for utilities. That comes to a total of $3,732. That's how much you'd have to raise a year. That's $311 a month. Then, after ten years, the house and property are yours."

He paused for us to take this in. "How's them apples?" he asked, waving his hands. "All you have to raise is $311 a month, and in ten years you'll probably be able to sell the house at three times what you paid for it. That's forty thousand bucks."

"Sounds good," said Joe, pulling on his mustache, grinning abstractly. He had this twinkly look about him that reminded me of a downed-out Santa Claus, only he was as skinny as a rail. It drove me crazy. It didn't help that he was Pie's boyfriend and seemed to be a freeloader.

"Where do we sign?" Joe asked.

Ray's eyes lit up.

"I don't know, 311 bucks is a lot to pay every month on top of groceries and everything else. I imagine since we're out in the middle of nowhere, it'll be hard to find jobs," said Huey, putting in his two cents' worth. His boss where he worked in his hometown had arranged a job for him in Denver. My guess was that he didn't want to live here. Too far to commute. Besides, he had a point.

"My friends and I need to talk," I said quickly before Ray could answer.

"Okay," he said. "I'll go in the next room. Make you fellows some coffee. Cream and sugar?"

We said yes, and Ray danced into his kitchen. I told Joe that we didn't know much about buying a house. We should probably consult somebody who did. That meant parents. Joe's dad was a narc in Fairfax County, Virginia, and hated his guts because he smoked dope and was against the war. I wasn't sure about Huey's parents. I volunteered we call my mom, though I didn't like it. She had enough on her plate. But when Ray danced back in the room with the coffee, I asked to use his phone.

I sat down in the recliner and watched the hummingbirds hover and dart away and hover again while I dialed Mom's phone. She answered in two rings. I explained to her what was up. I could hear her gasp. I asked her if she was okay.

"I'm fine," she said, "but I'm wondering about your mental state. You're barely out of college. You don't have a job. And you want to buy a house. You don't need to saddle yourself with so many burdens."

That was all I needed to hear, and after some pleasantries, I hung up the phone and turned to Ray. "We'll think about buying the place. I mean, it's a big commitment."

Ray looked crestfallen but nodded slowly as though he were accepting the inevitable.

"You call me as soon as you decide," he said, escorting us out of his house to the Mustang. "These mountain A-frames sell like hotcakes."

We spent the night at the motel in Nederland wondering what we should do next and woke up in the morning with headaches. There was a funny smell in the air. Gas from the propane heater. We twisted the knob until the gas was off. We grabbed our clothes and our bags and stashed them in my car. Then we hustled to the front desk to tell the clerk what happened. We asked him if we could use another room to take showers before we left.

"Sure," he said with a casual shrug, as if this was a common occurrence. He handed us a key.

"My brain is about to explode," complained Joe, holding his head delicately.

The clerk, a skinny cowboy type in fancy boots and straw cowboy hat, directed us to a convenience store down the street where we purchased aspirin. When we returned, the door to our old room was open. We went to the new one. Took aspirin. Took showers. And waited until our pain subsided before we even spoke.

"What do we do now?" I asked.

"I don't know," said Joe, pulling on his mustache and thinking. "Two weeks of bad karma. Maybe we shouldn't live in the mountains."

"Then let's move to Denver. We'll rent a place. Everyone will join us. And then we'll figure out what to do," said Baby Huey with a look of relief.

I was reluctant to give up so easily. Didn't we come out here to establish our own commune? Weren't we disciples of Timothy Leary? We were already turned on and tuned in. Now it was time to drop out. That was the plan—to be like mountain men in the old days. Live off the land, though in the modern sense. But how do you implement our ideas in a way that would work? We were college boys, wet behind the ears, so I felt Baby Huey was right. We needed to figure things out rather than act on impulse.

We ended up in a run-down row house on Thirteenth Avenue. Huey started his job at a vending machine company. He drove to work early in the morning, and we wouldn't see him until the evening. I didn't know about Joe, but I felt guilty, even though it was my sixty-five hundred dollars that I earned working for my dad that supported our meager lifestyle and, you know, we were hippies. We were against the work ethic.

But that didn't mean I was unwilling to work. The house was a mess. Trash left over from the last tenants, three baseball-sized holes in a wall in the front living room, the third stair to the basement missing. I swept and patched up. I wanted the place to look presentable for Rick and Pie, but even more for Hank Hipple and the Denison women. I mean, who ever heard of a commune without women? I was giddy with anticipation, but Joe wasn't. He was in a deep funk and wouldn't help out. Probably because Pie was delayed in getting out there.

However, Joe was willing to snoop around the neighborhood with me. The rest of the block was divided between poor people of various extractions, that includes hippies, but not Chad, a ski bum and the son of the owner of the houses on the block. He collected rent.

Next door on one side was a Mexican family. They were quiet. Sometimes I'd see the father on the front stoop. Once I said hello. He looked up and smiled. Then the bus came by. He sprang to his feet and dashed down the street to the bus stop.

On the other side was Butch the Speed Freak. We could hear him rattling through the house day and night, singing to himself. He'd do that for maybe three days, until he crashed. Then the next day he rattled around again. It was rumored that he was once the drummer for Iron Butterfly—the drummer you never heard of.

At the end of the block was a country rock band. They banged on their instruments for hours on end, and when they went past ten in the evening, the cops visited to suggest they shut down the "motherfucking noise," as one of the neighbors called it.

Sam, Chad's girlfriend, called on us three times in the first week because her boyfriend was sleeping with another woman. We said we were very sorry but there was nothing we could do. She said she knew that, but she needed someone to talk to who wasn't insane like everyone else on the block.

I think one of the things that might've driven people insane was the traffic. It started at five in the morning and lasted well past ten. Thirteenth was a main one-way artery into town. Colorado drivers liked to gun their engines, honk their horns, and drive too close to each other, so there'd be a fair number of fender benders. Cops loved to barrel ass down the road in the middle of the night, sirens wailing. Semis stopped at the light at the end of the block, their airbrakes screeching.

It was brain-numbing experience for Huey and me, who slept in the front bedroom. Joe thought he was nice to take over the back bedroom where there was a hole in the ceiling. It was not aesthetically pleasing, and when a heavy vehicle rumbled by, dust drifted out of the hole. Joe would sweep it up the piles in the morning. But if Joe opened his window beside his bed, he could hear sweet silence in the trash-filled courtyard that extended the length of the row houses. He sometimes heard cat yowls and the pitter-patter of rats on the trash. But not to the degree of the traffic noise under our window.

Rick and Pie pulled up a few days after July Fourth when the temperature was close to ninety. They had hitched a ride from Joe's friend, Bill Barbour. Bill had been discharged from the marines and was on his way to Fort Lewis College in Durango to give college a try. He was flush with cash and happy to get on with his life. He treated us to tacos at the Taco Bell on Colfax and a movie, *The Illustrated Man*, I think. Rick loved Ray Bradbury.

Bill was going to stay for a week, but I think the writing was on the wall. Not only the money, but the tension in the air. I was pissed at Joe for not helping me out with the house. Even Huey, when he wasn't at work, gave me a hand. Joe was pissed off at Pie for taking so long to get here. He wondered if there was another guy. He came up with two names: Kevin, Robin's boyfriend, and Quayle, the drug dealer. Pie was not pleased by his insinuations. And Rick, though he wasn't pissed off, was intensely excited about the moon landing on July 20, even packed a portable TV in the back of Bill's car so we could watch. He informed us about the three-stage rockets each with their own fuel supply that would push the command module free of the earth's atmosphere and on and on, ad infinitum, driving all of us sort of wacko.

The next morning, Bill left for Durango. We decided to paint the house—even Joe—at Pie's insistence.

The house was a shotgun style, skinny and long, with a dusty basement made of crumbly rock walls painted white. We left that alone. We painted the living room bright yellow, the banisters that led to the second floor green like the grass—a nature motif—the middle room psychedelic purple, the radiators black and red. The kitchen we left alone. It was a nice doctor's-office green, the room where we could calm down after going through the purple room. We painted an accent wall in each bedroom, one was blue, the other pink, and the bathroom we left as it was. Pie painted flowers in one corner of the kitchen and the bedroom she shared with Joe. She hung her Beatles posters in the yellow room so people would know that we were into peace and love. In the purple room, we hung the psychedelic pictures that Rick brought from college—Jim Morrison bent over his microphone, Jimi Hendrix bent over his guitar, a field of marijuana with the caption "This Bud's for You."

THE DAY BEFORE the moon landing, we finished our work on the house. Rick and I purchased two bottles of cheap prosecco at a liquor store on East Colfax. On the way out of the store, we were accosted by a short guy, maybe five feet tall, muscular arms, pinched face, and a swagger about him that reminded me of someone—I don't know, Napoleon. He dropped his rucksack at our feet and opened it. Inside were about half a dozen bananas and a couple bunches of grapes.

"You want to buy?" he asked. "Cheap."

"No, thanks," I answered.

"It's fresh food. Bananas still green. Grapes right off the vine," he said, laughing. "That's my name, Grape. I once had a girlfriend who claimed she was going to make a raisin out of me. Ha-ha."

"No, thanks," I said, but this time in a louder voice. He scowled. We stepped around the ruck, crossed the street, and headed down Corona. Rick noticed the little bugger was following us. When we reached our door, he came skipping up the stairs.

"I tell you what," he said, catching his breath. His ruck must have been heavy. "I need a place to crash for a couple of days. You let me stay with you, you don't have to pay a cent for this stuff. It's free." He smiled hopefully at Rick as if I weren't there. "I'll buy you more stuff tomorrow."

"Okay, come in," said Rick, stepping aside.

THAT NIGHT, WE got stoned, except for Huey who had to work the next day.

"Later, we'll trip. Big surprise in that direction," said Rick, bouncing up and down like a kid. He turned on the TV, but we couldn't find a signal. Rick was upset in a huge way, like he was about to put his foot through the screen, so I duct-taped the rabbit ear base to a windowsill. I moved the antenna around until the signal was perfect. We waited for hours for the great moment when the door opened to the Eagle landing module. Neil Armstrong bounced gingerly down the ladder in his bulky space suit. He stepped on the moon. He said his famous words: "That's one small step for man, one giant leap for mankind." Rick jumped up and cheered.

We followed Rick outside. He wanted to show us where they had landed on the moon. It was a cloudless night. I could see the outline of the moon, but much of it was in shadow. A crescent moon.

"If you look halfway up beyond the shadow," explained Rick pointing to a place I could only imagine, "that's the Sea of Tranquility, where the module landed. That big crater."

I couldn't see the crater.

"The first human beings on the moon," said Rick, shaking his head. "Unbelievable."

"Yeah, unbelievable," said Huey, yawning. He'd been burning the midnight oil at work and losing weight. The starvation diet we'd all been on was taking effect.

We crawled inside and gathered around the television, but the show was over. We were bushed. Too much dope. Too much bubbly. But we were hungry. We ate the grapes and bananas, dipped them in a jar of peanut butter we found in the kitchen. Grape dug in his ruck, pulled out two hubcaps off a Cadillac he said he found along the highway and offered them to us. Rick hung one of the hubcaps on the wall and put another on the table to use as an ashtray.

Grape curled up on the couch and fell asleep.

"I don't trust that guy," I said as we climbed the steps to our bedroom.

"Oh, you're just paranoid," said Rick.

Maybe I was, but the next morning Rick and I were sitting out on the stoop watching the traffic rush down Thirteenth Avenue when Grape came swaggering up the skinny sidewalk whistling, his hands in the pockets of his dirty jeans. He was weighed down by his rucksack. He motioned for us to come inside.

He turned the ruck upside down on the kitchen table and out poured a cornucopia of candy, bananas, lunch meat, a pack of bacon, a loaf of bread, mayo, mustard, sliced cheese, instant coffee, creamer, and a dozen sugar packs. "Breakfast," he said.

"Where did you get that?" I asked.

"What does it matter where I got it?" he said defiantly, though with a touch of hurt feelings in his voice. "I promised I'd get you more food, that's all."

I stood my ground.

"Okay, at the convenience store down the street."

"Did you pay for it?"

"Of course I paid for it."

I had been to that convenience store before to buy Salem cigarettes. The clerk, a sad-eyed older man with a bushy mustache and a mole on his cheek, handed me my cigarettes with a weak smile. He wore a World War II marine veterans cap with "Iwo Jima" in red letters embossed across the front. It sent shivers up my spine, and I hoped that Grape wasn't lying.

I suspected later that he probably was, but we enjoyed the bounty he shared with us, disposing of all that food and candy in one day. He exacted a promise out of us that he could stay a couple more days. That was when I noticed four of my records had gone missing—two Rolling Stones, a Donovan, and Pink Floyd's *The Wall*. I asked Grape if he'd seen them.

"No, haven't seen them." He shrugged, smiling innocently and scratching his stomach. He didn't look me in the eye.

A week or so later, Rick and I were trucking down East Colfax talking about the burritos we planned to enjoy at Taco Bell when we spied Grape sitting on a stool at the end of the block under a tree selling LPs out of a crate. I wandered up to take a gander, but he jumped in front of me, blocking my view.

"You don't want any of those records. They're all scratched up." He grabbed me by the arm and tried to drag me away, but I pushed him aside.

I leafed through the albums, and there was *The Wall* and Donovan and a bunch of other LPs I bet he stole from people in the neighborhood, but no Rolling Stones.

"You dirty little bastard. You sold my Stones albums," I growled. I felt like taking a swing at him, but I tried to keep the nonviolent demeanor.

He didn't. He squared off with his fists raised. "Nobody calls me little."

I stepped around him and picked up the crate. "I tell you what. Don't ever come by our house again, or I'll pound you into the pavement with help from the neighbors, who you probably ripped off as well."

By that time, we had attracted a crowd of long-hairs and bums of all sorts, male and female, anxious to see what happened next.

Nothing happened. Rick and I marched down the street. Grape still squared off but was not at all threatening. I think I saw tears in his eyes.

A few days later, Hank Hipple drove up in a van with his girl-friend, Edie, and the three Denison ladies who planned to join our commune. They checked out the rush hour traffic, the shirt-less, pasty-skinned Butch the Speed Freak lounging on his stoop, a couple of leather-clad thugs strutting by, and our small, not clean enough but colorful abode, and decided to move to Boulder.

Chapter Six

RICK LIKED TO THINK OF HIMSELF AS A LAID-BACK GUY WHO TOOK A positive outlook on life, the Meher Baba of our dwindling commune. "Don't worry, be happy" was his motto. Okay, he said, so Hank and the ladies who planned to join our commune decided instead to move to Boulder. So our record collection was somewhat diminished. So we lived in a dump in the middle of the ghetto. So what. The moon landing was a success. The big surprise he promised us was still waiting.

Rick opened a tin that he kept locked in his luggage. Inside were twenty or so purple-colored blotters of Owsley acid. Purple Haze, he claimed it was. Owsley Stanley was a legendary chemist in Berkeley who concocted, it was rumored, the very same Purple Haze that Jimi Hendrix dropped when he burned his guitar at the Monterey Pop Festival.

I had tripped only one time before, my senior year at Denison at the smoke-in, and that, a mild one. Rick had tripped fifty-seven times, he told us, but never on Owsley.

"I think we are in for a mind-blowing, out of sight spiritual experience," said Rick, sighing. On the way west, he had read Aldous Huxley's *The Doors of Perception* and wanted to share the epigraph with us, two lines from William Blake's "The Marriage of Heaven and Hell." He pulled the Huxley book out of his luggage and read: "'If the doors of perception were cleansed everything would appear to man as it is, Infinite. For man has closed himself up, till he sees all things thru narrow chinks in his cavern.'"

Rick closed the book and looked at us as if he were the teacher and we—that is, Pie, Joe, Huey, and me—were his pupils. He informed us that what we were about to experience when we dropped the Purple Haze was the Infinite, the world as it truly existed outside our limited vision. "We will perceive the spiritual oneness of everything in the universe."

"Bullshit," I said, though I didn't know as much as Rick as far as acid was concerned. What I perceived as a possibility was that the drug fooled your body into seeing things that weren't there in the same way that aspirin fools your brain into thinking your pain isn't there. That didn't mean I disbelieved Rick. It meant that I needed proof that there was something beyond the drug controlling my perception. A magic hand. God. Whatever. This exasperated Rick. We argued back and forth until he came to the conclusion that the only way I could accept his point of view was to take a leap of faith. I said I'd keep an open mind.

"So, are you going to drop the drug?" he asked.

"I never said I wasn't."

Huey, however, did say he wasn't. He had to work. His parents were flying out to pick up his dad's Plymouth Valiant, and he needed to buy a car of his own if he expected to keep working.

"I'll trip with you guys some other time," he said, making me feel like a real chump. Guilt rearing its ugly head.

The plan was that we were going to drop the next day, so I trudged upstairs to catch a few winks. I awoke at two in the afternoon to a siren. A police car screeched to a halt in front of our house. He was ordering a motorist out of a car. I went downstairs. Joe and Rick were at the window delivering a running commentary about the events outside to Pie and three neighbors—Chad, Sam, and Butch the Speed Freak. Of all things, Shostakovich's *Symphony No. 5*, a gift from my parents in the desire to expose me to the finer things in life, was spinning on my Philco.

"The cop's gone," said Rick. He looked at me. "You know, you're surrounded by a green aura."

"That makes sense since that's my middle name," I said.

"The color of grass," he said as if he hadn't heard me. He danced around in a circle. He was wearing bell-bottoms, a blue Mexican shirt, and a red bandana around his head. His curly, sandy-colored, afro-type hair stuck out below the bandana like Mickey Mouse ears. "The walls are breathing," he said. "They're making music. I can see the notes."

"I can see the notes too," said Pie.

"So can I," said Joe. He wore a red bandana too, but it was around his neck in cowboy fashion. He put his arm around Pie. She pushed him away.

"I don't want to feel your skin."

"You guys dropped without me," I said in a disappointed tone.

"Here," said Butch, handing me a tab of acid. "They dropped half an hour ago. It comes on fast."

"How about you?" I asked.

"Oh, not me. I don't touch the stuff." He didn't need to, the way he whistled under his breath in monotone like a tea kettle at boiling point and looked at me with unfocused eyes. I think I picked up the tune "In-A-Gadda-Da-Vida," the essential psychedelic anthem when whacked out on drugs of all sorts.

I went in the kitchen, turned on the faucet, and washed the acid down my throat. I said hello to Sam, who was staring out the kitchen window and shaking her head.

"What's wrong?" I asked her.

"It's Chad. He's in a deep funk," she said, sniffing. "The girl he was sleeping with ditched him. And that would make me happy, except that now he hates me even more."

"Why don't you ditch him?"

"I could never do that."

I wandered into the living room where Chad was sitting on the couch, sipping a Coors and glaring at the wall as if it was his worst enemy. Sam sat down beside Chad. She leaned close to him. Put her hand on his thigh. He pushed her away. A shadow crossed over her face. I looked over at Pie and Rick. They were staring at Chad and Sam like they were a daytime soap opera.

"Hey, Chad," Rick said finally. "You're bumming us out. Why don't you drop?"

"I don't want to," he said. "Besides, I thought you gave the rest to everyone in the neighborhood."

"No, I have one left," said Rick, reaching in his pocket and pulling out a lint-covered purple tab. He handed it to Chad.

Chad took the tab, brushed off the lint, stuck it in his mouth, and swallowed it with a sip of beer.

I had to leave these human beings when I came on because they started to look threatening, changed color, grew hair, snarled. I went to the backyard, knee-high with weeds and trash. On the far side of the block behind the band house, Chad had parked his Corvette. The rest of us used the street. A rusted Volkswagen engine and the rusted body of the car up on blocks, all the windows smashed in, graced the middle of the backyard field like dinosaur bones. I didn't see any rats, but I restricted myself to the back steps. A cat came up and nuzzled my leg.

My whole body tingled like warm lava was flowing through my veins. I looked across the lot at an apartment house. The windows were mostly dark except a few, one with a man cooking, another with a woman writing at a desk and being bothered by her pooch that she tickled behind the ears on occasion and finally pushed away, and a third window full of people who breathed in and out in unison. As a matter of fact, the whole building started to breathe in and out. I didn't see notes, because I couldn't hear music, but I heard a buzzing noise like a bee had crawled into my ear. I realized that I was humming deep in my throat, so I stopped.

In the movie *X: The Man with the X-ray Eyes*, Ray Milland discovers eye drops that improve his vision way beyond the normal. He goes to a party and sees people in their underwear, though he knows they are fully clothed. He takes some more drops and sees them naked and then through their skin to the blood coursing through their veins, to their palpitating organs, their skeletons. A whole room full of moving, breathing skeletons holding drinks like a horror show. They swallow the drinks. He can see the digestive process. He can see through walls, through a series of walls, through cities, through the earth until he's taken so many drops that everything seems to run together like the paint melting on a canvas. He wanders out in the country in a state of shock until he staggers into a tent where they're holding a revival meeting, to the podium where he yells at the preacher, "My eyes! My eyes!" The preacher consults his Bible and, with arms outstretched, yells back, "If thy eyes offend thee, pluck them out!"

What I saw wasn't real, or at least I didn't think so. What I had to do was split myself down the middle, play the role of Ray Milland's character on the one hand and play the moviegoer on the other. That way, if the drug battered me with an excess of stimuli, I could pull back to the safety of the audience. *This is only Hollywood*, I could say to myself.

The two of us stumbled in the house. Shostakovich was still on the record player. Now I saw the notes come out of the breathing wall. No one else was in the room. I panicked. I yelled. Someone yelled back from the second floor. I took the stairs two at a time and fell flat on my face at the landing. I banged my knee on a stair and felt a sharp, tingling pain climb up my leg, encircle the pelvic region, and move up my spinal column to my brain, where it registered in such a massive rush I thought I'd pass out. I made a burping noise. I saw stars. I saw the whole cosmos. I got to my feet and limped into Joe's room. The others were looking at the hole in the ceiling.

"What do you see?" asked one of them.

"I see bouquets of roses flowing down. I tried to catch one."

"We see that," they said, "but we see birds too."

I saw the birds—red birds that intermingled with the red rose bouquets down to an amorphous red stain suspended in midair.

We gravitated to the sheik's tent that Joe had constructed over his bed out of India blankets and closed the blinds so we couldn't be seen from the outside. We took off our clothes. We looked at each other's bodies clinically. The skin's like silk, said one of us. Freckled silk. That referred to me. Pigskin. Wineskin.

"I hope we don't spring a leak."

Chad pawed the women, first Sam, who reacted with uhs and ahs, then Pie, who screamed, "You're disgusting."

She put on her clothes and marched downstairs. We put on ours and followed to the front porch stoop to watch the traffic.

The cars seemed like huge, squat monsters, with two white eyes each and engines that roared like dangerous metal animals. Herds of them, hurtling by, switching lanes, honking, the drivers inside with their own eyes intent on the road, swallowed by the machine and as much in control as Jonah inside the whale. Across the street, a one-armed man puffed away at a cigarette, waiting for a hole in the traffic. He seemed two-dimensional, a shadow against the brown brick wall, his skinny legs bent, his skinny torso, an overlarge square ass and head, a Zap cartoon character. The light turned red two blocks up, and he trucked across the street, legs still bent.

We decided to go to Cheeseman Park a quarter mile away in a quiet, well-kept part of town. I walked beside Rick, who seemed to be trucking too. I trucked with him. We turned skinny, square assed, square headed, like the one-armed man. Rick pointed to the electric wires above us that appeared to throw off sparks.

"Oh, Jesus," I gasped.

"Oh, Christ," he responded.

"*Wow.*"

"*Wow* is *mom* upside-down."

I'd heard him say that before, but now it seemed so full of wisdom, like a Zen Buddhist riddle, but I couldn't quite figure out what it meant. I was so addlebrained by my senses, the way they intertwined and crashed into each other, that I couldn't put one thought in front of another.

At Cheeseman, a drunk leaned against a tree. He fell down. He got up. He fell down. He got up. He trucked rubber-legged across the street and fell down on a trim lawn in front of a well-kept house. He melted into the grass. Rick watched me.

"I don't feel good," Rick said, sitting on the grass and leaning up against a tree. I noticed that his lips were blue and that a sliver of silvery spit dribbled down his chin.

"Physically," I said, leaning down beside him.

"No, no, no," he said. He pointed at a woman sitting on a bench reading. "Don't you think she's beautiful?"

In this condition, I wasn't sure of looks, but then the woman looked up at me with big, dark, moist eyes that seemed frightened. "Yes, she's beautiful, but what's your point?"

The woman stood up and hustled past us so close that I could tell she was a wisp of a thing with a turned-up nose and a creamy complexion. Black hair, almost exotic, like she was a belly dancer or something.

"My point is that I'm at the spiritual center of the universe and I feel lost," he said, choking as if he were about to cry. "I need a woman."

"Why do you need a woman?"

"A woman is like an anchor that would hold me down so I wouldn't float off into the universe and explode into a thousand pieces."

"That's interesting," I said, not in the least aware at what he was getting at.

"What I mean is that I could marry that woman. We could have babies together. That's the kind of anchor I mean."

"That's called responsibility," I informed him.

"Ugh!" he exclaimed, looking up at me, then over at the empty bench. He jumped about a mile. "That woman, she disappeared," he gasped, rubbing his eyes as if she had been an apparition. "I think I'm on the verge of a bad trip."

I dragged him to the playground in the park, followed by the others. We interlaced ourselves in the bars of a jungle gym like we were kids again. Across the street near where the drunk had melted into the grass, a well-heeled couple walked their dog. They paused to look at us. The man in a tweed jacket, a feather in his hat, sucked on a pipe thoughtfully. The woman rocked her head. I couldn't tell whether in approval or disapproval, though I was afraid her head was going to fall off.

Rick unlaced himself from the jungle gym bars and sat down on the ground, crossing his legs. He looked morose.

I sat down beside him, put my arm around his shoulder. "Are you okay now?"

He shook me off. He didn't like physical touch. "You see that couple across the street with the dog? Are they real?"

"They're real."

"Was that woman on the bench real?"

I told him she was real and he must not have seen her leave. This seemed to calm him somewhat.

Pie came up and put her arm around Rick. "How are you doing, little brother?" She asked.

"I'm fine," he said.

The row houses, when we returned, were infested with people in our condition. They were on the stoops. They climbed out the second-floor windows to the roof, jumped from roof to roof, in and out of windows. The band at the end of the block played country rock in their front room with the door open, so I could hear them from our house when the traffic didn't drown them out. I leafed through my albums looking for *Sgt. Pepper's* but couldn't find it nor, for that matter, *Rubber Soul*, so I settled on an oldie, the Kingston

Trio's *Hungry Eye*, but Rick put Shostakovich back on. I couldn't take that, so I went upstairs alone.

I checked out the bathroom. The fixtures were so highly polished that the light from the overhead reflected off them, blinding me. I quieted a drip from the faucet, sat down on the toilet and flushed it, then stared between my legs at the water as it was sucked down in a vortex. I felt like I was going to be sucked down as well, like an insect going around and around toward a dark hole. I jumped up and fled to my room.

The same cat that had nuzzled my leg in the backyard was curled up in a ball on my mattress. I pet her. Sparks flew from the fur. She reached out and clawed me in the gap between my thumb and index finger. I felt a sharp pain that climbed up my arm to my head. I felt a massive rush. Saw stars. The cosmos. I wanted the drug to go away, but it had a mind of its own.

I jumped up and wandered into Joe's room. I opened the sheik's tent and saw Pie pressed against the mattress as though imprisoned by gravity.

"Hi," I said.

"Hi."

"Do you mind if I lie down next to you?"

She made room. I lay down, put my hands behind my head, and stared at a line of light that came through a tear in the blinds and sparkled—seemed, in fact, to sprinkle pixie dust all over the inside of the tent. Would I start flying now?

"Wow," said Pie.

"Huh."

"Wow. This is something."

I turned over on my side and stared at her. She had round, dark eyes that sparkled with the dust and satiny, soft skin. She stared back at me.

"You don't have any lips," she said. "Your chin's too small."

Not the words I wanted to hear.

She reached up and touched my dimple, which, if I might say so myself, was more attractive than Kirk Douglas's, whose dimple reminded me more of a deep scar left by a pimple.

I took Pie's hand. We intertwined fingers. I leaned over and kissed her. She opened her mouth, and my tongue slipped in, ran over her tongue, the ribs at the roof of her mouth.

"That was good," she said when I moved away. "Do it again."

Somewhere in the audience that I placed in my brain, a voice reminded me that this was someone else's girlfriend. Should I surrender to this uptight, repressive voice or liberate myself, sleep with any consenting adult, eat, drink, and ingest whatever? I already ingested whatever. Why should I stop there? Not that Pie would consent, but, you know, Joe didn't own her and all was fair in love and war. I kissed her again. She turned on her side and pressed her body against mine.

Behind me I heard the tent rustle, and yet another disembodied voice asked me, "What's going on?"

"Oh, hi, Joe," I said. I brushed the pixie dust off me and stood to take a beating I knew would not come. Joe took seriously this thing about peace and love. Once he caught his baby sister in the embrace of an older man. He gave the old man a piece of his mind, for which Joe was severely beaten. He was practicing passive resistance.

But I think I'd driven him over the edge because he took a fistful of my shirt and popped off a couple of buttons. He was on the verge of slapping me with his open hand—perhaps he wanted to challenge me to a duel—when Pie stepped in.

"We didn't mean anything," she said.

"I don't understand," he sputtered. "You didn't want me to touch you earlier. Why did you want him?"

I didn't wait for her answer. I loosened his grip on my shirt and staggered downstairs to the breathing walls and Shostakovich. This drug was getting to be a monkey on my back. I went to the basement, where I heard voices. There was Rick, Chad, and Sam sitting cross-legged in a circle in the middle of the room.

"Sit down," said Rick. "What do you feel?"

They broke the circle to let me in. I sat down, looked about the basement. A mushroom grew out of the wall. The wall itself was moist and crumbling. Dust motes flew about in the air and collected in a thin film on the floor and so thick on the only window that I couldn't see outside. The pipes above our head were knocking. They, too, were dusty.

"Dusty," I said.

"Damp, dusty," said Rick. "Rub your hand."

I watched Chad and Sam do this and tried myself.

"How does it feel?" asked Rick.

"Flaky. Like I'm rubbing off dead skin," I replied.

"No, dusty," said Chad. "Keep rubbing and rubbing, and tomorrow morning they'll come down and find four piles of dust in a circle. That'll be us."

"I saw a *Star Trek* once," said Sam, "where these three aliens had a machine that would change you into a square block, and if they liked you, they'd turn you back, and if they didn't, they'd step on you. There'd be nothing but dust left."

I rubbed my hand raw until I saw some red rise up.

"Blood." I shuddered. "I've rubbed through my skin."

"Let me see," said Chad. "That's not blood. That's dust. Red dust."

I felt myself crumbling like the wall and got to my feet. "I've had enough of this dust."

At three in the morning, we all huddled closely together on the small roof outside the second-floor window. The streets were empty except for an occasional cartoon character, no doubt fellow row-house denizens who, like us, were in the slow process of coming down. We saw one gentleman wander up and down the street, knees bent, rubbing his chin thoughtfully; another two played Frisbee and bounced the disk off the hoods of parked cars; and a group, five I think, dashed out of an alley, knees bent, in tennis shoes, untied laces trailing behind them. They circled the Frisbee players—all running abreast in perfect step with each other, the Four Horsemen plus one—then they disappeared down another alley. The thoughtful gentleman hopped on a traffic control at the end of the block. The players stopped playing when they saw a car come down the street. The thoughtful man banged the traffic control. The light turned red. The car screeched to a halt. He waved at the occupants. The car ran the light. This happened twice more until a man in a shiny blue suit jumped out of a car and chased the thoughtful one off the traffic control. He waved to us as he ran past.

We climbed back through the window and crawled to our respective beds, where we crashed until late afternoon. After a hearty meal of Big Macs, fries, and fried apple pies—we hadn't entirely cast off consumer culture—Rick and I retired to the front stoop.

The sun was setting behind us, the shadows edging up the brown brick wall of the apartment building across the street. Butch the Speed Freak stood in the shadows with his hands in his pockets waiting for a break in the traffic. He was whistling "In-A-Gadda-Da-Vida" for all he was worth. I didn't know where he disappeared to after we dropped, but here he was like an apparition. When he finally crossed over, he gave us a friendly nod and bounced up the stairs to his house.

"Well, you know, now that we've had our fun, so to speak, we've got to turn serious," said Rick, turning serious. "First off, there's the little matter of my conscientious objector letter that I have to defend in front of my draft board. One day they'll summon me, and I'll have to return to Bethesda. Second, we need to work on this commune thing. We need to recruit women. Right! I mean who ever heard of a commune without women, unless you're gay or something."

Chapter Seven

WE WERE NOT GAY OR SOMETHING. WE MAY HAVE WANTED TO START a commune with women, but first we needed to find the women. To accomplish this, we needed to lighten up on the psychedelics. Rick understood on a certain level that if he continued dropping acid, he may end up like Ray Milland. "We need to stay straight in order to stay sane," he said as he cupped a joint on the front steps of our abode.

He handed the joint to me. I took a puff and handed it back. "Yes," I agreed, enjoying the high but paranoid the cops might see us. "It's difficult to get anything done when you're insane."

What we needed to get done first was to deal with Joe Johnson. It started with his anger at Annie Pie for finding her and me in his sheik's tent embracing and grew from there. We weren't sure where it was going, but we could hear them bickering through their closed bedroom door. Joe's voice was loud enough that we caught the haughty tone, though too low for us to distinguish the words. Pie sobbed. Her unrefined adolescent voice gushed from her heart like a fountain and through the door's keyhole, down the stairs to my ears, where it forked into tiny rivulets and trickled into my own chest. It reminded Rick of the emotional stew he used to come home to in high school, his sister and mom at loggerheads. To me, it was like a mating call. I was, I admit, immensely pleased as I watched the degeneration of the relationship.

Pie would run away and hide when it got to be too much for her. I don't know where, but Rick said she stayed with Sam at the end of the block. Joe hid out in his room playing a blues song on his bottleneck guitar. We all came to know it well because he played it over and over again. Night and day. Now, I don't remember his voice or the lyrics, but the twangy sound of the guitar as he ran the bottle down the frets still vibrates in my ear like the far-off whine of a chainsaw. Whenever he left his hermitage, he wandered around the house like a ghost. He barely spoke above a whisper. He never looked at us but rather through us, as though he glimpsed the far shore of the River Styx.

This went on for two weeks. We couldn't stand it, not even Huey, because sometimes Pie and Joe argued through the night, and Huey needed his rest for work. So we consulted Pie, who cried like a river but agreed that we should talk to Joe. Maybe he had to leave. He was spoiling our happy home. Our talk involved giving him a hundred dollars and driving him out to Interstate 70. It was mid-July when he stuck out his thumb, and where he headed we didn't know, though later we heard it was Minneapolis.

Pie went berserk. The very night that we returned from dropping Joe off by the highway, she enticed the first male she found off the street. They spent the night together. I was shocked. But this was the Age of Aquarius, so I couldn't be too shocked. I had to think. Would I as a male entice a female off the street in this grungy part of the city where we lived? A part of the city full of bums and dope peddlers? At first, I thought no. I wouldn't want to risk a social disease. Then I thought of the person Pie selected. He was a pale, blue-eyed, curly-haired, tall, lean individual. Smiled in a secretive way. I think he was drugged. Maybe he had escaped from the local VA hospital. He was handsome in a Paul Newman way. Would I sleep with a female of comparable beauty? No doubt I would. So, I had to forgive the lady. Besides, I knew this relationship wouldn't last long.

It lasted a week, until she found another victim outside a movie theater on Colfax that I noticed appropriately enough was playing *Succubus*. Then another at a Mountain concert at Red Rocks. I don't think she slept with these last two guys. They weren't as handsome, but they served a purpose, I think, as an insurance policy until someone worthwhile turned up. I developed a theory. Pie was looking for a reincarnation of her father. I had seen a photo of the family standing in front of their home on Bradmoor Drive in Bethesda. Rick was in a cowboy outfit, Pie in a Minnie Mouse sweater dress and pink socks, their father towering over them in a gray suit and red tie, crowned by the same curly, brown hair as the rest of the family and a big smile for the camera. His shoulders were squared, his hands steepled in front of his chest as though he were about to deliver a Dale Carnegie speech. He seemed to exude confidence. His wife, Joan, smiled up at him, as did Pie, as if he was the center of their universe. Pie was only twelve years old when he died suddenly of a heart attack.

So, yes, that was my theory. These men fit the father figure bill in the physical sense. They were tall. Lean. But they weren't perfect. Joe was not tall. He was lean. But I figured he must've been perfect until he disparaged her, or at least that was what I assumed he did. I mean, that was how I fell out of her favor. Disparaging her for using too much makeup and wearing miniskirts. I was not the physical specimen she wanted, but I figured if I kept my cool, she could overlook that as she had with Joe.

Soon after I came up with my theory, Pie dropped her boyfriends and moved into the room across the hall. I wanted to move in with her but didn't have the nerve to ask, so what I suggested was that we take a road trip to Taos, New Mexico, to see the communes. That was what we wanted: a commune in the country rather than what amounted to a crash pad in the city.

Annie Pie thought about it for a day and told me she couldn't wait to leave town for a while. "We'll have an adventure," she said.

I knew that only Pie and I would be available for this adventure since Rick had found a part-time job on the night shift at the Wonder Bread factory and Huey worked overtime to pay back a bank loan. After his parents left with the Plymouth, he gave into his weakness for sports cars to purchase a Fiat 124 Spider, a little red beauty that sat out front catching the eyes of passersby, along with my Mustang convertible and Chad's Corvette. You would think we lived in Cherry Creek. Then there was the matter of J. B.'s rumored arrival. He had been working for his father in Tempe, Arizona, and was flush with much-needed cash. I figured we had to make a quick getaway.

Both Rick and Huey thought that us checking out the communes in Taos might be a good idea. I guessed they suspected I might have an ulterior motive, though it was none of their business. Pie was her own person. Besides, she was a woman, and we needed women in our commune, went my logic back then.

I still had a couple thousand bucks squirreled away in the bank, more than enough to pay for gas and food. We drove down I-25, and I don't remember much except that I had this wonderful desire inside me that I knew would soon be realized. We stopped outside of Raton, New Mexico, in a park. Raton is high up in the mountains, and there was a cold wind blowing. We didn't last for long in our sleeping bags. We climbed back in my car. It was a tight fit. This was a 1966 Mustang convertible with bucket seats in front and a skinny backseat where we spent the night because I insisted. We made out. The windows steamed up. I touched different parts of her body in an effort to work down between her legs. She took my hand away three times. She finally moved to the front seat in disgust.

She turned around. "I don't need this," she said. "I only want to be your friend."

We visited the communes in Taos. I remember one, New Buffalo, on a hilly stretch of barren land north of town. They wouldn't let us stay overnight.

"Everyone wants to stay overnight. Then they want to stay a month," said one bearded fellow who looked like a goat. New Buffalo was very popular at the time, a sort of model for the communes of the future, though I didn't find it that appealing. I went inside one of the huts where they were preparing dinner—basically beans and rice with a few vegetables mixed in, a hunk of bread, and a glass of water. The hut was made of adobe brick. The floors were dirt. There were only three windows, so most of the light came from an open door and a kerosene lamp that hung from the rafters. I peeked in one of the bedrooms. Two hammocks hung from a wall. That was all. No indoor plumbing, except for a sink with a hose attached to an outdoor spigot. There was an outhouse behind the hut. The kids were playing in the mud. They were all dirty. There were other huts along the line of hills. I didn't bother to check them out nor the teepees wrapped in canvas at the top of the hill. Nor did I check out the fields where they were growing vegetables.

I backed up against a fence, shaking my head sadly. A goat crept up behind me and started to eat a hole in the seat of my pants. Pie pointed this out, and I jumped away. She was laughing. "I guess I'll have to change my pants," I said as we headed back to the Mustang at the bottom of the hill.

We pulled out of New Buffalo and headed north to the D. H. Lawrence Ranch, where the writer once lived with his German wife, Frieda. We drove a long, winding road to the top of a mountain. We parked in a lot and checked out what must have been his house. It was after-hours, so we didn't get inside. We followed a long path to his grave, which overlooked the valley below. We could see New Buffalo and beyond that Taos spread out like a toy village. We watched the sun turn the valley golden.

"I have to pee," said Pie as she jumped from one leg to another like a little girl. I followed her behind the white stucco shrine where Lawrence's ashes rested below a statue of a phoenix. She didn't mind my watching as she lowered her pants and bent down next to a pine tree. I could see the dark forest of hair between her legs, and it filled me full of desire as well as doubt. I decided that I needed to pee, unzipped my pants, and let go with a thin stream. It was a difficult process considering I was hard. I could see her looking at me out of the corner of her eye, and I thought this was a moment that D. H. Lawrence could have related to. But nothing came of it. Pie finished her business, lifted her pants slowly, and skipped down the hill, where I found her looking at the grave of Frieda Lawrence Ravagli.

"Why do you think she's not in there with her husband?" She pointed at the shrine.

"Maybe they had a fight," I kidded.

"Maybe it's because she married again after Lawrence died. Or why else would she have Ravagli at the end of her name?"

"If that's true, where's Ravagli?"

"Maybe he's still alive."

We spent the night at a campsite in the mountains above Taos. Pie allowed me to zip the sleeping bags together because of a chill in the air. We climbed in together. I usually slept bare assed. But she frowned upon that. I jumped in my jean cutoffs sans briefs. I'd thrown away my briefs because, well, they were extra pieces of clothing I didn't want to lug around. Pie was in her bell-bottoms, but the heat of our two bodies in that confined space caused her to strip down to her underwear. I had a flashlight that I used to read from a book of D. H. Lawrence quotations that I had purchased at a bookstore in Taos.

"'Love is the flower of life and blossoms unexpectedly and without law, and must be plucked where it is found, and enjoyed for the brief hour of its duration,'" I read as I lay on my back.

"What do you think he means by plucked?" she asked, lying on her side facing me. I turned toward her. I could see the shadow across her face lift as the moon came out from behind a cloud. Her chestnut-colored hair covered one eye, and she winked at me with the other.

"You know exactly what he means."

"Okay, well, if you pluck a flower, it soon dies. If you leave it alone, it thrives."

I shrugged, turned my flashlight on the book again, and read, "'The fairest thing in nature, a flower, still has its roots in earth and manure.'"

"That's the truth."

"'I shall always be a priest of love.'"

"That's disgusting."

"'If a woman doesn't have a tiny stick of harlot in her, she's a dry stick as a rule.'"

"If a man has a tiny stick, does it matter whether a woman is a harlot or not, as a rule?" Pie answered back.

I slammed the book shut. "Enough," I said, stifling a laugh. I wanted her to take me more seriously, as if I were trying to woo her with fancy thoughts, which I was. At the same time, I worried that the tiny stick she referred to was my own. She had seen it today. I reached out and touched her cheek out of a kind of desperation.

"Please, Jeff." She grabbed my hand and squeezed it. "All I want is for you to be my friend. I have enough trouble as it is." She turned in our sleeping bag, away from me. "Let's go to sleep. I'm tired."

"Before we do, I have one last question."

She turned her head and gave me a hard, exasperated look.

"Oh, never mind." I was thinking about my stick but also that I didn't want to embarrass myself more than I already had managed.

In the morning, we visited the hot springs in Ranchos de Taos that the bearded fellow at New Buffalo told us about as a place to stay while we were in town. We drove up a gravel road and parked the Mustang between a red-and-white Volkswagen Bus covered in paisley flowers and rainbows and a battered Ford truck covered in dents. We trudged up a hill to an adobe hut. The door was wide open. Beside it like a sentinel stood a man in a wide-brimmed cowboy hat and white jumpsuit. He checked us out and bowed slightly. "Have fun," he said as we entered the hut.

Inside, ten freaks were either milling about, leaning against the wall smoking dope, or dancing to Dylan's "Mr. Tambourine Man" on a battery-operated tape deck.

We wandered outside and stood next to the sentinel, squinting our eyes. It was a bright day. We were in the high desert, and the flowers on the cactus were in bloom. The wind picked up. It blew the leaves of the aspen trees, a nice, dry, bell-like chime.

Below us in a small ravine were the hot springs. Steam rose from the water. The water glistened, as did the naked bodies of those who were cavorting in and around the pool. On a hill overlooking the pool were about ten men, Mexicans and Pueblo tribal members from the village north of town. They were sitting on crates and leaning against rocks, drinking beer and pointing at the naked ladies and laughing and poking each other like they were having a great time.

I heard later that the pool was sacred to the Pueblo, though it was owned by a Mexican rancher who had recently died. That present ownership was in doubt—whether it would revert to the tribe or go to the descendants of the owner. Meanwhile, the hippies moved in, and neither the tribe nor the descendants seemed to mind.

"Let's take our clothes off and jump in the pool," suggested Pie as we followed a path down the hill. This was something I could not object to. We removed our clothes, but before I could catch a good glimpse of Pie, she jumped in the pool. I jumped in after her. The water wasn't that deep, but it was over our heads and warm as a cat in the sun. She held on to the side of the pool. I held on next to her. I moved closer. She moved away until she bumped into a blue-eyed man with a blond ponytail at the end of the pool.

"Oh, hello," he said, shaking her hand and looking down at her with a satisfied smile as though he could see all her body even though the water was murky. "What's your name?"

"Anne," she smiled up at him.

"I'm the guru," he said, rubbing his hands together. "I live here. I assume you have come to visit. You can stay here for a while. I can teach you some lessons. Hatha yoga. Kama Sutra, perhaps."

"Sounds interesting," said Pie, looking into his eyes as if mesmerized.

I felt like I didn't exist, so I swam to the other side of the pool where there were about ten other naked freaks treading water. One was a woman who seemed to be all alone. I swam over to introduce myself. She said she was Betsy from California.

"Where in California?"

"Malibu."

"Hey, the beach. I bet it's beautiful there."

She looked like Robin Gran, whom I'd met back when I'd moved back home after graduation. Betsy's hair was black, and her eyes were black, catlike. She wore black lipstick and a gold chain that ended at her pear-shaped breasts. She put her hands on my shoulders and moved closer. I was about to succumb to desire when I remembered Pie.

"Wait a minute," I told Betsy and swam over to where I'd last seen Pie. She was sitting at the edge of the pool. Her legs dangled in the water. I saw all of her from her beautiful long legs up her shapely torso to her tiny breasts with the taut goose-bumped nipples. My mouth was watering. I felt like Pavlov's dog. I almost forgot my new love Betsy until I saw that Pie still eyed the blond guru with a longing she'd never shown toward me. The fingers of his hand like spider legs inched up her thigh. I swam back to Betsy, but she was with another man.

I paddled around for a while more in search of another woman, but they all seemed to have paired off. I was beginning to see what this was all about and what an idiot I was. I looked at the men on the hill, laughing and poking each other as they drank their beers and pointed at the naked ladies. One randy old fart in a red bandana pointed at Pie holding hands with the guru as the two of them disappeared around the hill.

I waited there a few minutes wondering what I was to do. I felt so alone and abused. What was wrong with me? I didn't have an answer on the edge of my tongue, so I scrambled out of the pool and chased after Pie and the guru, unclear about what I would do if I caught up. I scrambled around the hill, but they weren't there. Neither were her clothes, thank God. I turned around and ran up the hill to the hut. As I passed the sentinel, he quipped, "Nice outfit."

I looked down. I was naked.

"Oh yeah," I said as I backed off. I wandered over to my clothes and put them on. And then I started to think: *What is wrong with me?* I was not her lover. I was not her brother. I was her friend, or at least that was what she wanted me to be. And what were friends supposed to do in a situation like this? *This is the Age of Aquarius, right?*

I was sort of trudging up hill, talking to myself, thinking that, you know, maybe in the hut I could find some hippie chick of my own, when the sentinel in the floppy cowboy hat grabbed my arm.

"Hey, man, that red Mustang down there," he said, pointing at my car. "That yours?"

"Yes."

"You wouldn't mind giving me a spin into town? My buddies left me behind."

"Not at all," I said, thinking to myself: *This would be a good thing to do. Get my mind off my troubles.*

We scrambled downhill to the car. He introduced himself. "Wavy Gravy's the name," he said.

"Jeff Richards," I said, shaking hands wrist to wrist, as was the freak custom.

We jumped in the Mustang. I lowered the convertible top. He took off his cowboy hat and enjoyed the wind blowing through his hair as we sped down the highway. He didn't say much, but he thanked me as I dropped him off at the square in Taos. He donned his hat and leaned back toward the car so close to me that the hat brim knocked against my forehead.

"I saw your lady friend wander off with that buff guru cretin," he said, shaking my hand. "But that shouldn't worry you as long as you remember one thing."

"What's that?" I asked him.

"Laughter is the valve on the pressure cooker of life."

I watched him wander off to a crowd of hippies lounging around a fountain sunning themselves while the tourists wandered by looking at them like they were the scourge of the earth. Wavy Gravy turned around and waved as I drove off.

I felt somewhat better. I even tried on a laugh for size. But it didn't seem to fit. I parked the Mustang next to the banged-up truck at the hot springs, and there was Pie holding up the wall in front of the hut, looking perturbed.

I ambled up to her. I wasn't going to give an inch.

"Where have you been?" she asked in a frosty tone.

"Oh, I drove somebody into town. How about you?"

"You know where I've been."

"With the guru," I said in a calm voice as though I didn't care.

"You know what kind of lessons he wanted to give me? It wasn't Hatha yoga. It was Kama Sutra. He wanted to fuck me fifty different ways. The son of a bitch."

"Oh, that's bad."

"I wish you were there to protect me."

"I wish I was too," I said, thinking I blew it. I could've been a hero.

We spent the night in the hut curled up in our sleeping bags, me wondering the whole time what was up with Annie Pie. It even came to the point that I inched over to her—we were in separate bags. I considered her state of mind and asked if I could make love to her. No strings attached. I promised to be very kind and gentle.

"You're very sweet, Jeff, but you know how I feel," she whispered in my ear so my whole body tingled. "Besides, I don't think I want to be with a man again for a long, long time."

We returned to Denver a few days later. In our absence, J. B. had arrived and moved into the basement. Within a week, Pie moved in with him. I should've known. J. B. was tall. He was lean. He was blond and blue-eyed. When I first knew him, he wore black horn-rimmed glasses and his hair was in a buzz cut. He was into model rockets, and I remember us going out to a field to watch him launch his rockets way up in the sky until they reached the apex and floated down dangling from a parachute. He had been as calm as those skies. Now, in the interim between college and the present, he had remade himself. He had grown his hair down to his shoulders and exchanged his glasses for contacts. He had made himself into the perfect specimen. A confident warrior. All he needed was a sword, a shield, a wing-tipped helmet, and leather clothing. My theory was correct. She was looking for her father, and I might as well forget Pie as far as any intense relationship was concerned.

Chapter Eight

HUEY AND I WERE RELEGATED TO THE BACK BEDROOM WHEN PIE moved to the basement. The reason was that Gina the Euglena had wandered off the street and into Rick's bed. It was weird that she named herself after a one-cell animal but understandable since most of the time she was totally blitzed out beyond comprehension—hers or ours. She carried a bag full of multicolored pills that she would partake of and on occasion mumbled how the mafia was out to kill her.

Huey and I could hear Rick and Gina fucking their brains out in our former bedroom across the hall. The walls must've been thin. Sometimes we would hear Gina shriek. We didn't know whether it was a hallucination or an orgasm, but whatever it was, it happened enough times during the night to interrupt our sleep patterns, which was bad for Huey, since he had to work in the morning. I was annoyed and maybe a bit jealous, though I got to know Gina in her more lucid moments. She would visit me when Rick was working at Wonder Bread or during the day when Huey was likewise occupied. I had a way with women. They all wanted to be my friends: Annie Pie, Margie Walker, and now Gina.

I remember one time I was under the sheik's tent perusing a pile of comics that J. B. brought with him from Tempe, namely the *Fabulous Furry Freak Brothers* and *Zap Comix*. The cat I had met in the backyard when I tripped was curled up in my lap, purring. I named him Freddy because he was a tabby like Fat Freddy's cat in the *Freak Brothers*.

"What are you reading?" Gina asked. I told her. Freddy woke up and meowed. He tiptoed over to her lap and settled down. Back to purring.

"A stray cat like me." She smiled and stroked Freddy. She had a feline look about her, large, hazel-colored eyes, button nose, chubby cheeks, and a pointy chin like Rick. Black hair in disarray. And a rough-hewn, generous Viking body. A mixture of looks that made her seem both innocent and menacing.

Gina leaned over to see the comic book. It was R. Crumb's *Whiteman*. The character was the archetypical white man of the era, dressed in a business suit. He was polite to women. Lifted his fedora as he passed by. Patriotic. When he saw the American flag, he came to attention and saluted. But underneath his calm exterior was another person. I noticed that Gina was reading the balloon in the last panel where Whiteman, foaming at the mouth, revealed this other person as a "raging LUSTFUL BEAST that craves only one thing! SEX."

"This is news." She laughed, launching into a story about her own Whiteman. She grew up in a fancy part of Memphis, and as soon as she was old enough, she and her friends drove into town to visit the clubs on Beale Street. "I love music, any kind, blues, folk, rock. So, I went to the clubs. That's where I met Whiteman, an older guy who turned me on to drugs. I was only seventeen, and my parents, when they found out, sent me away to the McLean Hospital in Boston as far away from Whiteman as I could get. My parents are rich." She giggled. "You know who I met there? James Taylor."

She sang a folk song in a soft, appealing voice about how she's gone to Carolina in her mind and seeing the sunshine and some guy from behind.

"I should've married James on the spot. He'll be be famous one day," she said, sighing. "The doctors let me come home for a visit, but I was so hooked on drugs that the first thing I did was visit Whiteman. I was a year older. No longer jailbait. I let him do his *lustful beast* thing on me. Well, I fooled him. I stole his drugs and ran away as far as I could."

She held up her bag of multicolored pills. "He has connections with the Memphis mafia."

I found her story suspect, especially when Rick informed me that she once worked on a dude ranch in the Wet Mountains of Colorado. Whiteman, in this case, was a handsome wrangler named Phil, who looked exactly like Rick only his curly hair was cut short. He turned her on to drugs. They did the *lustful beast* thing, and she ran away with his drugs because a couple times he beat her up. She told Pie that she worked at a hospital in Lakewood. She ran off with some of their drugs, but not to worry. She had been in charge of inventory.

Gina disappeared for a few days, probably to refuel on drugs. In the interim, Rick found her purse in a corner of his room below a pile of her clothes. He found her expired driver's license inside a pocket and showed it to me. The license read:

Gina Leigh Jackson
142 W. Wyandotte Parkway
Memphis, TN 38114

"I guess that means the story she told me is the true one," I said, scratching my head.

"She could've also worked at the dude ranch and the hospital."

"She ever tell you how old she is?"

"Nineteen," he said, doing some calculation in his brain. "That means she didn't have time for those other jobs. She came straight from Memphis."

"Maybe not." I pointed at the birthdate on her license. "July 5, 1939," I said. "That makes her thirty years old."

"Jesus, I've been sleeping with an old lady," he said, snickering. "But what the heck. She's pretty. She's nice in bed. I don't plan to marry her. I don't know what her story is, but who cares."

We all should have cared, but especially Rick. He started to notice that his crotch itched like crazy, that it hurt to take a piss, and that sometimes there was a white, watery discharge out the tip of his penis.

"Maybe you've got the clap," suggested Huey. J. B. and I agreed.

"She's a stray cat like Freddy," I said. "No telling what she'll pick up along the way."

We were all grossed out at the thought, Rick so much that he made an appointment at a clinic down the street. The doctor confirmed that he had a sexually transmitted disease, but it wasn't too far along. It went away with a heavy dose of antibiotics.

When Gina returned from her travels, she was relegated to the couch in the purple room. I returned to the front bedroom. Huey had the back room to himself, which made sense. He had to wake up earlier to head off to work in his little Fiat Spider.

Along with the comics, one night I was reading a book that J. B. bought from Tempe, Herman Hesse's *Siddhartha*, and thinking about samsara, karma, and stuff. I was tired, so I shooed Freddy off my stomach and turned on my side. He curled up in a ball behind my legs. I nodded off and was in dreamland in a matter of moments, meditating beside a river, when Freddy rudely awoke me, yowling for all he was worth. I jumped up, startled. I could smell something in the air—smoke—drifting up the stairwell.

I dashed down the steps to the living room, followed by Rick. The couch was on fire. We ran into the kitchen. There was a bucket under the sink. I filled it up and tossed it on the fire. Rick found a huge pitcher. He filled it up with water and did the same. J. B. came up from the basement to join the fire brigade. We managed to put out the fire and clear the smoke by opening the windows and waving blankets in the air. We stashed the couch in the backyard. It was a charred ruin, burned down to the frame. We thanked Freddy the cat, who was rubbing up against our legs, meowing. We could've died if he hadn't alerted us.

Later we found out it had been Gina the Euglena. She was popping some of her multicolored pills when she dropped a smoldering cigarette between the cushions and forgot about it. We should've kicked her butt out right then, but she begged us to stay. She'd be more careful. She'd smoke outside.

We let her stay, a big mistake, as it turned out. A dozen of my records went missing, including Shostakovich. That didn't bother me. But there was also *Rubber Soul*, *Their Satanic Majesties Request*, *Highway 61 Revisited*, and other favorites. We had another Grape on our hands.

Huey told me that one night when he was coming home from work, he caught Gina taking the records down the street. He asked where she was going. She said to the band house at the end of the block.

"I watched her go in the front door, so I suspected she wasn't lying."

I hustled down to the house and asked the bug-eyed bassist if my records were there. He said he hadn't seen my records, but he'd ask the other band members as soon as they got back from the grocery store.

I decided to go directly to the source. Gina the Euglena was still in the purple room on a funky mattress she'd found in the backyard. She was lying on her back, arms outstretched, mouth open, staring blankly at the ceiling. Her bag of pills dribbled out on the mattress.

I shook her gently. "You okay?" I asked in a soft voice.

She looked at me but didn't utter a word. She seemed pale, but it was hard to tell in the faded light that came from the dirty window. Maybe she was sick. Maybe she had overdosed. Maybe she was playing possum, afraid that I would deliver the fifth degree, which was exactly what I intended. But why take chances? I mean, what if she died? Would we toss her out back with the rest of the trash? Or would we call the police? That could be worse. I found no option other than to seek out help. I rushed upstairs to the back bedroom, where Rick, Pie, and J. B. were playing *Parcheesi*, our second-favorite game behind *Risk*. I told them what was up. They acted disgusted.

"We got to kick that bitch out," said Pie. She had caught Gina making a play for J. B.

"Yeah," said Rick.

We rushed downstairs. Gina was gone. But later in the evening, she wandered into my room. I was leaning against a pillow in the sheik's tent reading *Siddhartha* when she toppled on top of me. I raised my hands to protect myself—she was a hefty woman. I felt a twinge in my shoulder as she landed. She started to tickle my chest with her sharp fingernails and ran her fingers down to my stomach, my most sensitive area. I jumped and twitched like a puppet at the end of a string. I didn't know what her intention was, nor would I ever find out. As I jumped and twitched, I must've raised my arms, and somehow she got underneath and pushed up. She dislocated my shoulder. I screamed bloody murder.

Gina jumped up and ran out of the room yelling for help from J. B. and Pie, who were fixing dinner. They ran up the stairs just as I clambered to my feet, holding my arm to my side. I didn't want to go to the hospital and wait three hours in the emergency room for someone to help. Besides, this dislocation didn't seem as bad as the others. The shoulder bone seemed to be lolling at the corner of the socket, not banging my ribcage as it usually did. Pie and J. B. helped me downstairs. Rick wandered in from the front porch. After a few tentative tries, I managed to hang my arm over the banister above the newel post. I asked Rick to take my hand and yank down hard toward the floor, but not too hard because I didn't want my arm to fall off. I was making a joke, but no one was laughing.

Rick yanked, and my shoulder bone popped back into the socket. I felt this huge sense of relief flood through my body like I had died and gone to heaven. I sat down on the stairs, holding my arm. The pain was gone, though I could feel a twinge. I knew my tendons were loose and rubbery. I didn't want it to pop out again. So, I put on a sling and wrapped an Ace bandage around my body to keep it in place for a week or so until the tendons tightened.

I told my compatriots what happened.

"She's more dangerous than Grape," complained Rick. "Not only does she steal but she almost burned down the house and dislocated your shoulder."

"You forgot what she did to you," I said.

"I don't want to think about it."

"She made a move on me," groused J. B., "but I wouldn't let her get within a mile."

"I saw her in the basement with you when I came down the other day," countered Pie. "She was closer than a mile."

They glared at each other until I asked whether anyone knew where the miscreant had wandered off to.

"Oh, she ran past me down the street just as I was coming in the house," said Rick, shaking his head. "She was in a big hurry."

We all laughed as if it was a big joke, but it wasn't the next morning when I found that she had pilfered not only my record collection but the Philco record player itself. Or maybe it wasn't her. Maybe some robber jimmied the window during the night. Or picked our lock. You could never tell in this neighborhood.

"We should leave here," I said to Rick as we sat out on the front steps watching the traffic. "I mean, if we're really going to start a commune, we need to be in the country or a small town like Idaho Springs or Boulder where there are fewer druggie-type strays to drag us down, steal our possessions, and such. Maybe even murder us."

Rick suggested a more philosophical view. "The fewer things you have in your possession, the happier you are. Do you understand me?" He wagged his finger as if he were my guru. I found this annoying. "These druggie types are doing us a favor by stealing our possessions. Now they are the ones burdened with worries that what they stole from us will be stolen from them."

"These druggie types will sell our possessions on the street to support their habit," I countered. "They won't have anything to worry about but their next fix."

"That might be," said Rick, "but look at it this way. The more they steal from us, the less we'll have. The less we have, the more mobile we will become and the happier we'll be."

This was whacked-out logic that made my stomach turn, especially since none of his stuff had been stolen. What if they stole his portable TV? Would he be singing the same tune?

An ambulance raced by, weaving through the traffic, siren wailing. Rick continued, "There is only one possession that I consider sacred: my body. They can steal the clothes off my back, I don't care, but not my body. I truly believe one thing you said, Jeff. There is always a possibility that we could be murdered in a sketchy neighborhood like this. So, I agree with you, we should leave here."

This was about the time of Woodstock, and a couple of friends were traveling through on their way to New York. They asked us if we wanted to come along. We thought about it. We thought about the intensity, a million drugged-out hippies blitzed out on music on a small parcel of land. We thought of Rick's clap and the burning couch. The city of Denver in general. We'd had it with intensity. We wanted someplace quiet. We thanked our friends from Denison and settled on Baja California. We felt bad that Baby Huey could not come along. He didn't want to get behind on his car payments. But, you know, he was a big boy. He could take care of himself. We were leaving, if only for a while.

The next day, we hopped in J. B.'s blue VW Beetle, J. B. and Pie in the front, Rick and me stuffed in the back seat with the backpacks. There was no air-conditioning. We were driving through the desert with the windows down. The hot, dry air blew in our faces. We were miserable and couldn't wait for the cool breezes coming off the Pacific when we reached Baja.

We crossed in Tijuana. It turned windy. Trash blew down the

highway. There was not much vegetation except for tall cactus, yucca trees, mesquite, and knurly oaks. There were small mouse-like creatures with long, white tails and big eyes leaping around the rocks at the bottom of the cliffs where we camped out. The first thing we did was search for firewood, but it was mostly low-lying vegetation infested with lizards and what sounded like rattlesnakes. No firewood.

We jumped in the car and drove down the road to where we saw a sign that said "Lena" with a crude painting of a campfire under it. We drove up the dirt driveway. A man came out of a small hut with a big smile. Before we could even ask him for what we were there for, he raised all the fingers of both hands and said, "Yanqui." We tried to argue him down, but it was no use. He went around back of his hut and came out with a small bundle. We gave him ten bucks. But it didn't matter. It rained that night, and we retreated to the tent we had pitched. We ate gorp, three cans of tuna, and bread spread with peanut butter and drank from a bottle of tequila con worm I had purchased at the border. Then we smoked some dope. The Mexicans didn't care, we figured.

In the morning, the sun was out. It was a beautiful day, big, fluffy cumulus clouds that floated in a sky that was so sparkling blue it hurt our eyes to look at it. We were on a wide beach that curved around with the cliffs. At each end of the beach, there were rocks you had to climb over to get to the next beach. The sand was a grayish-white color and sparkled like the sky. It was covered in seaweed. We were the only people on the beach. So, we took off our clothes and dived into the waves. This was a difficult time for me, watching Pie running around all day, the water glistening on her skin, laughing as J. B. chased her. They were in the first throes of romantic love, and I was jealous.

Fortunately, I was deeply into *Siddhartha*. I had just reached the part where he left the concubine. He was totally satiated from immersing himself in the world of earthly delights. Now he lived the more austere life of the boatman ferrying tourists across the river.

The river represented eternity. I sat in front of the tent trying to imagine myself as Siddhartha, only my river was the ocean and the roar of the waves as they broke against the shore. It was a nice feeling, imagining eternity, and sad as well. Yet I was neither satiated nor enlightened. Though I did put Annie Pie out of my mind, I contemplated other pleasures that awaited me.

We drove to Ensenada the next day, where J. B. suggested that we forego any fruit or vegetables at the farmers' market. "They're probably contaminated. You know they use human crap for fertilizer." We accumulated instead a grocery bag of canned food and a case of Mexicali and headed back to the campsite. After a swim to work up an appetite, we prepared our feast then sat back to enjoy the sunset.

J. B. had a shortwave radio, and he turned it on to a station out of Hawaii that reported there was an earthquake in the Kuril Islands, north of Japan.

"You know what that means," said J. B.

"Tsunami," said Rick, who was sipping a Mexicali. "I don't think there is much between us and Japan."

"Exactly. If you draw a straight line east from the Kuril Islands, the first significant landfall would be Baja California. There's a possibility that a thirty-foot wave could come crashing into this beach. With the cliffs behind us, there's no chance we could survive that."

"Oh, come on. That earthquake's thousands of miles away," I said.

"It doesn't matter," said Rick, furrowing his brow as if searching his memory. "There was an earthquake off Chili a few years ago that produced a tsunami that hit Hawaii and then went on to Japan, where it killed hundreds of people."

Pie wanted to know what a tsunami was exactly. J. B. explained that it was like you were sloshing around in the bathtub and the water spills over the side.

"Okay," said Pie, looking doubtful.

"How long would it take?" I asked, slowly warming to the possibility.

"A week maybe," said Rick, lighting a joint and passing it around. We were from the East Coast and thinking in terms of hurricanes and how slowly they moved.

"I think a shorter time," said J. B. "Maybe a day or two."

"That means that we should get out tomorrow at the latest," said Pie, "and leave this wonderful paradise."

"Yeah, I don't want to leave," said Rick, who commented on how cheap the food was. If only we could manage free firewood, we could stay here for a month and still have money to get us back to Denver. So, for the night, we forgot the tsunami and got totally wrecked.

In the morning, we were lounging around what was left of the campfire when Pie spotted a tiny figure hobbling over the rocks at the end of the beach. We watched as the figure turned into a scraggly-haired dude with a doomed gaze in his eyes. He wore a walking cast up to his knee and supported himself with a walking stick.

When he got even with us, he yelled, "Got to get out of here. The federales are arresting all the hippies and putting them in jail."

Pie was watching him carefully. He was as skinny and knurly as his walking stick. "You want something to eat?" she asked.

"No, gotta get out of here."

"We could drive you."

"No, safer this way." A rucksack was strapped to his back. I don't think it was stuffed with clothes but with something else. Maybe illegal.

He hobbled over the rocks at the northern end of the beach.

"Did I imagine that guy, or was he real?" I asked.

"I think he was real," said Pie hesitantly.

"I don't know," said Rick, voicing what we were all thinking. "This may be a beautiful place, but it's full of negative vibes."

"Yeah," said J. B., shaking his long locks, "first the tsunami. Now this."

We packed up all our gear and stuffed it in the Beetle. We drove north at a fast clip—but not too fast, for fear that the federales would arrest us for speeding and stuff us in jail with the rest of the hippies. We weren't stupid. And before we reached the border crossing, we tossed all the dope out the window. We knew there was something worse waiting on the other side if we did not.

Chapter Nine

THINGS WERE FALLING APART. PIE MOVED OUT OF OUR ROW HOUSE and into the dorms at the University of Denver. J. B. was upset. He found work at the vending machine company with Baby Huey. His job was to operate a machine that applied the state and city tax stamps to the bottoms of the cigarette packs. He didn't care for the job. It didn't pay well, and he found it unsavory that he was a co-conspirator in wrecking the health of millions of his fellow Americans. J. B.'s plan was to work at the warehouse until he raised enough money to move to Boulder.

Huey planned to quit as well but not for altruistic reasons. He made one hundred bucks a week. His Fiat 124 Spider cost thirty-five hundred. The bank was crazy enough to give him a loan that he paid back at the rate of one hundred forty-three a month. It came to the point that if he remained in Colorado, he'd either lose his car or starve to death. Already he'd lost enough weight that he could no longer pass as Baby Huey. He felt like there was no choice but to move back to Ohio. He called his old boss. He said Huey could have his job back anytime he wanted it.

Then Hank called us from Boulder to tell us that his girlfriend, Edie, was pregnant. She was flying to Mexico City to get an abortion.

"I love her. I want to marry her, but she wants to go through with it. I mean, I could accept that, even though it's my child as well. I'm paying the money. But she won't let me come with her. A high school friend is taking her instead," he blubbered over the wire. "Can I move in with you?"

I suggested that it might not be a good idea since he already had a job in Boulder. "Besides, you're living with a bunch of women. Why would you want to leave that?"

"I love Edie. I can't stand it here without her."

I painted a dire picture of our state of affairs, meaning that we were like a sinking ship. We were reduced to dinners of beans and rice like those freaks at New Buffalo. Sometimes we ate Kraft Macaroni & Cheese or Rice-A-Roni. We drank Tang and Kool-Aid. Peanut butter went a long way. We were always low on marijuana. We had to save money for gas to get to work. Rick found a station near the Wonder Bread factory where it went for nineteen cents a gallon. We could barely pay our monthly rent. Soon we'd be out on the street. Maybe I was exaggerating, but you know, we were college graduates. We were not supposed to live this way. I was beginning to wonder what I was doing. I knew it was the sixties. I knew I rejected my parents' materialistic values. I wanted to live a more meaningful life. Yet I wasn't sure how you live a meaningful life when you're starving to death.

I told Hank a version of this, and he had to agree that, if anything, it was we who should move to Boulder rather than he to our humble crash pad on the seedy side of the Mile High City. By the time I hung up, I was feeling extremely downtrodden, thanks to my own way I'd depicted our dire straits. We needed to escape, like Huey and J. B., before Rick and I drowned in sorrow. But how were we to pull it off with our limited resources?

Thankfully, I didn't have to drown too deeply, because we were rescued by Uncle Sam and Mom. Uncle Sam mailed Rick the summons he expected. He was ordered to appear before his draft board in Bethesda to defend his CO application. Mom called a few days later with a job offer after I hinted to her that we were starving to death. She would pay Rick and me fifteen hundred dollars if we sifted through my dad's files to see what to keep and what to throw away. It was costing a fortune to keep it in storage. Hey, I thought, we would arrive on the eve of two major antiwar rallies. It was like the planets lining up. A harmonic convergence. How could I say no to Mom?

We decided to hitchhike. We handed Huey the keys to the Mustang and asked him to drive us to I-70.

"I don't understand. Why are you hitchhiking when you have a car?"

"Money," I said.

"Gas money. Are you kidding? I could lend you that," he said.

"Thanks, Huey, but, you know, you've done enough. Besides, we never hitchhiked that much before. It might be fun."

"Yeah, I'll bet."

He let us off at an underpass twenty miles outside of town. We bear-hugged him goodbye because not only was he a generous soul but we guessed we'd never see him again. Steubenville was somewhat off the beaten track.

We stuck out our thumbs.

It took four rides to reach Limon. The sun was on the horizon. In the distance, about a hundred yards off the highway, was a long line of cottonwood trees following the meandering course of a stream. We hiked over there through the tall grass and took off our backpacks, sat down against a tree, and watched the sun sink lower until it turned the tall, wavy grass in the endless field a golden color. We dug in our packs for our dinner: tuna sandwiches, Fritos, and defective Hostess Twinkies that Rick carried off from the Wonder Bread factory after he quit his job.

After dinner, we cut a nib off a block of hashish the size of a marble we kept in tin foil. We thought it would be easier to hide and last longer than grass. We lit a pipe, lay back against our backpacks, and argued Buddhism—in particular, samsara, and how Rick thought he needed to get a grip on where he came from and where he was going. He had read *Siddhartha* as well, but he was far more serious into this thing and sometimes called me Doubting Thomas for my reluctance to fall for all this sweetness-and-light Meher Baba bull-shit. We listened to the lulling of the cows and the burbling of the stream. Then we chanted, "Ommmm," Rick with fervor.

"What do you think the Buddhists say about war?" asked Rick.

I laughed because I knew this was a rhetorical question.

Rick grinned. He pulled a piece of paper out of his breast pocket and read, "'All are afraid of the stick, all hold their lives dear. Putting oneself in another's place, one should not beat or kill others.'"

"Interesting," I said, nodding, not knowing where he was headed with this but thinking it might have something to do with his CO application.

The next morning, we stuck out our thumbs. We waited forever. It was chilly. We put on our sweaters. But when the sun reached its zenith, it turned hot. We sweated like pigs. Waves of heat rose from the highway, and the silos in the distance flapped in our vision as though printed on a sheet in the wind. Just before we were about to give up and turn around, a green-and-white Plymouth blowing smoke from the tailpipe pulled over. We jumped in the back seat. Two geezers grinned at us, one with his left arm missing below the elbow. He showed us how deft he was by taking out a book of matches, sticking it in a gap at the end of his stump, and striking a match to light his cigarette.

The driver, skinny with a turkey neck and a golf-ball-sized Adam's apple—Adam, I'll call him—leaned over his seat and winked at us. "We'll take you as far as Omaha, where we're stopping over to see my daughter for a week before we head off to Florida for the winter."

The other said, "We're bums living the high life." He advised us never to get married like his buddy, though he admitted it was nice stopping off to visit the daughter and grandkids. "They're good people. Treat us fine. His wife, though," he said, pointing his stub at the driver, "kicked him out of the house because he lost his job."

They were veterans of World War ll. "Fought with Patton," said Adam, whose eyes were half-turned toward us as he drove down the highway. "l drove the tank. Shorty was the gunner."

We pulled over in Colby, Kansas, at a gas station next to a farm stand. The stand was unguarded, so Adam headed in the gas station and engaged the attendant while Shorty stole the produce in the stand and tossed it in the back window, where we caught it.

Adam wandered out of the gas station with two Snickers bars. "Had to buy something," he said as he jumped in the Plymouth. We sped off.

Ten miles down the road, we pulled off in a park next to a river. We sat at a picnic table under a willow tree. The driver pulled out a switchblade and cut a watermelon in four pieces. He cut the remaining Snickers bar and passed it around. We shared our Hostess Twinkies.

"The rest goes to my daughter once we arrive in Omaha." The rest included two more watermelons, a dozen ears of corn, six or so apples, and four jars of jam.

"You know, l don't like to steal, but you gotta eat," said Shorty, shaking his head sadly. "Adam and l were in Paris after the liberation. We wanted to see Versailles, which was outside of town. So, we hitched a ride in a US Army truck full of food. A block or two before we reached our destination, the driver pulled over and told us this was as far as he went. We jumped out, and a Frenchman came up, exchanged a bunch of cash with the driver, climbed behind the wheel, and drove off.

"We asked the fellow what was going on. He said the people of Paris were starving. The US Army had food. The French had francs. So, you know, the people of Paris wouldn't starve. He waved at us and walked away. And that's what l mean—you gotta eat. Those were rough times."

l didn't see the comparison since these times weren't as rough. But, of course, l wasn't in Shorty's head, nor had l been through his experiences, so maybe he was right. These were rough times.

We drove maybe ten more miles down the road then pulled over to pick up another hitchhiker, a tall, crew-cut guy with close-set eyes, hefting a duffel bag, which he put on his lap as he climbed in next to us. He had a big smile.

"Where you going?" asked Adam as we pulled out on the road.

"Omaha."

"That's exactly where we're going," he said. "You a soldier?"

"Was a soldier," he said, a look of suspicion coming to his eyes.

"That makes you a vet like us," said Shorty, looking in the rearview mirror to check out the guy. "We were in the Big One."

"We were with Patton in Bastogne. That's where I got this." He showed his stump. "It was one hell of a ride. You in Vietnam?"

"Yes."

"How was it?"

"It was one hell of a ride," he said, and then he stared at us for a while, as if we were aliens from outer space.

Around the Kansas state line, we were pulled over by a state trooper. I stuck the hash and pipe between the cushions behind me. The trooper strolled up and looked in the window. He ordered all of us out.

"You know you're blowing smoke out of your tailpipe," he said nonchalantly.

"Yes, sir," Adam said. "I plan to get that fixed once I reach my destination."

The trooper's eyes passed over all of us and came to rest on the soldier.

"You in the army?"

"No, sir. I was discharged."

"Can I see your papers?"

The soldier hesitated for a moment and opened the duffel. He took all his clothes out and laid them carefully beside the road. The trooper told him to hurry up.

"I'm going as fast as I can." At the bottom of the bag, he found his discharge papers.

The trooper thumbed through the papers carefully and handed them back, satisfied.

"Okay, you fellows can get back in the car, and you"—he pointed to the driver—"fix that tailpipe." He strolled back to his car and sped off.

We watched the vet repack his clothes in the duffel, carefully folding each item. He was cursing under his breath. We jumped in the Plymouth, and about ten miles down the road, we crossed into Nebraska. We all breathed a sigh of relief, especially the soldier, who said to no one in particular, "Thank God, I'm almost home."

The vets let us off in downtown Omaha, and it wasn't long until we found another ride. Rick and I arrived in Washington two days later.

It was the fall of 1969, and Nixon was nine months into his presidency. The war in Vietnam was not over, as he had promised. I guess it was hard to put the brakes on a war, especially a stupid one. We took over the fighting for a colonial power on the pretense that we were fighting the Communists. I mean, Ho Chi Minh's hero was George Washington. His mortal enemy was China, not the US, until we came along.

Rick and I parted ways, he off to stay with his mom in Bethesda, me with mine in DC. He told me about his visit to the draft board that happened two days after we arrived. He waited for hours before being ushered in. He sat in a chair. The draft board members sat behind a table. They stared at him like he was beneath contempt, except for a gray-haired man in dark suit and gray string tie. He looked like a Madison Avenue ad exec.

"Mr. Sager, I agree with your premise that we hold all our lives dear," he said, leaning forward so Rick saw that, according to the gold Naval Academy pin in his lapel, he was the class of '43. "And I agree also that we should respect the other man's right to live. But I have a question for you. What if this other man does not respect our right to live? What would you do?"

"I would protect myself."

"Let's say, for instance," another draft member chimed in, "someone attacked your mother, and the only way to save her was to kill the attacker. Would you do it?"

"Yes, of course I would," said Rick. "But nobody is attacking my mother."

"That may be true, Mr. Sager, for now," said the Madison Avenue exec. "But who knows what the future will bring unless we protect ourselves from those who do not respect our rights. Request for conscientious objector status denied."

They didn't have a gavel to bang, but they all gave Rick the evil eye, or so he said.

Rick was so downed out by the verdict of the draft board that all he wanted was to smoke dope. Since we didn't have any, we drove out to Quayle's house on Kirby Road in Bethesda and knocked on the door, but nobody answered. Perhaps Mrs. Smith was out getting her hair done. We turned to leave, Rick cursing under his breath, when I spied Quayle. He was sunning himself on a lawn chair behind the box elder bushes to the right of the door. He was invisible from the street, and I suppose that was the way he wanted it.

"Hey, Quayle," I yelled. He looked up startled and put his hands on the arms of the chair as if about to push himself up and run. But then he saw Rick.

Rick asked him if he had some dope. Quayle said no, but we could drive him someplace where he could buy some. He insisted that we take his black Labrador along, so we put the two of them in the back seat. Thumper stuck his head out the window, his ears flapping in the wind. He sniffed the air. Wagged his tail.

Quayle directed us to the Dupont Circle area to a group house on Seventeenth Street across from Paramount Steak House.

We parked the car and cracked the window so Thumper would be comfortable while we were inside. The house was dark except for a strobe light that flashed on and off. There was the Rolling Stones'

"Satisfaction" on a record player only it was skipping and came out "we don't wantwantwant...." Barely a stick of furniture in the house. A weird place—scruffy-looking freaks sitting on the floor, backs against the wall, brains in another time zone. Quayle disappeared. He returned with a couple of ounces of marijuana stashed in his satchel. He carried a haunted expression in his eyes like he was feeling trapped or something.

"I got to get out of here," he mumbled. "This is dangerous."

We followed him back to the Mustang. Thumper jumped up and down as we opened the doors. Licked his master's face. "Good old doggy. Good old doggy," said Quayle, the haunted expression dissipating.

When we arrived at Quayle's ticky-tacky house in Bethesda, Rick asked him if he'd like to join us for dinner.

"No," he whispered as he squeezed out of the back seat of the Mustang followed by Thumper. "Me and Thumper are tired."

We watched him teeter up the front steps and into his house like an arthritic old man, mumbling to himself. He stared at us through the curtains on the other side.

"You know, I think Quayle is cracked in the head," I said as we drove off.

"Yeah, maybe a little. But I think the real problem is too much dope," said Rick. "One day he'll come out of it." Always the optimist.

A few weeks later, we joined the March Against Death: Rick and me, Bill Barbour and Joe Johnson, who were visiting their families but had come specifically for the demonstrations. They were, after all, vets, so their stake in this was greater than ours. I also invited Robin Gran. She was a student at American University, and her cut-up boyfriend was somewhere in college on the West Coast. They were still dating, she insisted.

I remember I was standing on the steps of Arlington House looking down on the crowds crossing the Memorial Bridge and moving beyond that, toward the Lincoln Memorial. The crowd split and went to either side of the memorial. It looked like a million people, though I'm sure it was much less. There was a slight breeze coming up, blowing the leaves off the trees and sending them scuttling across the cement walkway. Directly below me was the Eternal Flame, where both assassinated Kennedys were buried, and the Tomb of the Unknown Soldier, guarded by soldiers in blue uniforms marching back and forth in perfect cadence. I was thinking the obvious. *Jeez, I'm surrounded by dead people, and before long, if we keep it up in this country, we'll have to build skyscrapers on the grounds of Arlington Cemetery to house more dead people. I mean, how many wars do you have to fight to make the world safe for democracy?* I didn't answer that because I didn't think I could, but I had a creeping suspicion that we already fought too many. Anyway, I tried to focus on the individual dead soldier because that was the purpose here. We each were supposed to yell out one of those names as we passed in front of the White House so President Nixon would get the idea from the living yelling out names how many dead people there were as a result of his policy. We walked down the slope of the hill and took our place at the end of the parade.

It was twilight. We lit candles and held them aloft. I let the candlewax drip down on my hand. It dried quickly, and I let more drip down until it covered my hand down to the palm. It took three or four candles to do this, but we had plenty of time because it took three hours to get from the Virginia side of the Memorial Bridge to the front of the White House, maybe one mile. I handed the name I was supposed to yell to Joe Johnson because there weren't enough names to go around, and he deserved it more than I. He was a veteran. Robin held a candle that she kept waving back and forth. She chanted, "Peace now! Peace now!" along with the rest of the crowd, mostly long-hairs like us but also parents with their children, grandmas and such. Rick was waving the candle as well. He put his arm around Robin's waist. She hip-butted him. They both laughed. He skipped forward and gave Bill a name to yell out.

"You see, he's from Springfield, Virginia. Just like you."

When we reached the black wrought-iron fence in front of the White House, we were joined by two men in black suits. They weren't Secret Service. They were drunks.

"What's *thish?*" said one of the drunks.

"I don't know, a parade?" responded the other.

"Itch a Halloween parade."

"Halloween wash two weeks ago."

"It's a march against the war in Vietnam," I told them.

The two men straightened up as if they were trying to act more dignified. They tried to march with us, but they were marching more sideways than forward and bumping into people in the crowd.

Joe and Bill yelled out the names of their soldiers who died in Vietnam, and we marched on, craning our necks to see if we could spy Nixon standing at a window in the White House.

At the Treasury Building, we spiked our candles on the metal fence. We turned around as we marched down Pennsylvania Avenue to see the lower perimeter of the building all lit up like a birthday cake and the marble edifice reflecting the dark, flickering shadows. I took the melted wax off my hand. The wax fingers were green, arranged in a grip as if they were clutching a knife. I thrust the hand at Robin. She jumped back as if frightened and laughed.

Two days after the March Against Death, the five of us met in downtown DC for yet another march. We followed the crowds toward Lafayette Square. Green DC transit buses were lined up front to back to block the demonstrators from getting near the White House. We stopped by St. John's Church on the north side of the square, an imposing yellow church with a white steeple and six white columns in front. Blayney Colmore, a friend of my sister's, was standing in front of the church. He was an Episcopal priest in long black robes wearing a silver cross, a handlebar mustache, and a toothy smile. He gave me a big hug. Susan had told him I was coming.

"You be careful," he said. "No telling what the police are up to."

"They won't be up to anything," said Rick with a goofy grin. He was stoned. "Too many of us."

"Five hundred thousand," said Robin, raising five fingers.

"Could be. Could be," said Blayney, rubbing his chin. "Then you be careful you don't get trampled to death."

We circled around the buses and down toward the Mall, where the main gathering was to take place. We were inching down Fifteenth Street past the Treasury Building. We saw a puff of smoke followed by a band of raggedy, long-haired freaks exiting F Street and scattering in every direction. One blended into our part of the crowd. I swear it was Abbie Hoffman.

"Tear gas?" I asked him.

"Smoke bomb," he said, catching his breath. "We were burning an American flag when the cops showed up, so we set off a smoke bomb to screen our getaway."

He laughed and jumped on the steps of the Treasury Building, waving his headband, a Viet Cong flag.

The crowd was tightly packed, like an anaconda twisting down Pennsylvania Avenue. We were forced to follow. I checked out the signs that the protesters were holding:

SILENT MAJORITY
FOR PEACE

MAKE LOVE
NOT WAR

IMPUDENT SNOBS
FOR PEACE

I was sure this last sign was inspired by Spiro Agnew, the vice president, who said in some speech, "A spirit of national masochism prevails, encouraged by an effete corps of impudent snobs who characterize themselves as intellectuals." We all knew at that time that the real intellectual was Agnew with all his big words and such.

I checked out some more signs:

HELL NO

WE WON'T GO

I DON'T GIVE A DAMN FOR UNCLE SAM

I'M NOT GOING TO VIETNAM

BOMBING FOR PEACE IS LIKE

FUCKING FOR VIRGINITY

STRAIGHT MIDDLE-CLASS TYPES

FOR PEACE

DROP ACID

NOT BOMBS

We broke from the crowd on Pennsylvania Avenue and snaked our way toward the Mall near the Washington Monument, where a bandstand was set up. Pete Seeger was singing Lennon's "Give Peace a Chance," and the crowd was picking it up. They interspersed the lyrics with phrases like, "Are you listening, Nixon...Are you listening, Agnew...Are you listening, Pentagon...." The chant roared up and down the Mall from the Capitol to the Lincoln Memorial in an echoing wave. And as far as you could see in every direction, a sea of protesters. It was mind-blowing.

On the way home many hours later, I saw a middle-aged woman leaning against a tree, a fur hat askew on her head, a blue cotton coat with big blue buttons open to the wind. She was shivering, but I didn't think it was from the cold air. Beside her was a sign that showed the photograph of a young man in an army uniform and below it the caption:

MY SON WAS KILLED IN VIETNAM. WHAT FOR, AMERICA?

I pointed her out to Robin, and Robin thought we should comfort her. But as soon as the woman saw us heading in her direction, she narrowed her eyes and gave us such a nasty look that we turned away.

Chapter Ten

MOM AND I HAD A HEART-TO-HEART TALK.

"Do you have any goals?" she asked me.

"My goal right now is to goof off." I was being a wise guy, and I was also taking advantage of my mom, who was soft-hearted. If I had said the same thing to my dad, he'd probably have taken a swing at me.

"How long do you think you will goof off?"

"Until I'm tired of it, I suppose."

She went into a long story about when she graduated from college, she didn't know what to do. Three men proposed to her, and she settled on the basketball player from Denison. Her father had also played basketball at Denison, and she thought maybe she didn't love the guy, but she missed her father, who had died her senior year. She took a job teaching at the elementary school in her hometown, where she worked for five years until my father rescued her from the suitor.

"I loved teaching. I loved your father. I loved my children. But, you know, I didn't want to embarrass your dad. People would think if I worked that he didn't make enough money to support his family."

"I'm not sure what you're getting at, Mom."

"What I'm getting at is that I had a hard time figuring out what to do until I realized how difficult it was to buck the system. That's what you're doing," she said, smiling. She had a gap between her front teeth, a flaw, I supposed, like the freckles across her nose. She was otherwise perfect looking—at least, that was my impression, the way men groveled at her feet. But she was my mother after all, and I shouldn't have an opinion about her looks.

She brushed her fingers through my hair, and I squirmed like I did when I was a kid. "You goof around as much as you want to," she said, sighing. "But one day you'll get tired of goofing, and you better start thinking about what you want to do with your life."

We finished our work cataloging my dad's files. I wrote Mom a memo saying I'd divided his papers into three categories. First was the early part of his career, when he was a crime reporter for the *Cincinnati Post*. I collected his clips, including a black widow case. A lady poisoned four of her husbands before she was caught and electrocuted. Then he was a radio reporter at WSPD in Toledo, Ohio. He wrote *The Diary of Captain Reckless*, that were broadcast over the station as a series of seventeen radio plays. Then midcareer during World War II, Dad was head of radio censorship for the federal government. After the war, he worked in the executive end of broadcasting until he started his own business in 1954. Mostly what I filed in this last category was one speech after another that he wrote for broadcast executives and politicians. Governor Collins. General Medaris. Harold Fellows. McCollough and Quaal. W. D. "Dub" Rogers. Senator Griffin. Senator Potter. All were just names to me except Senator Potter. His daughter, Wendy, was my age. She once came to a baseball game when I was maybe twelve years old. She sat in the stands. I totally ignored her. When I got home after the game, I asked my mom what Wendy was doing there. "Maybe she likes you," said Mom.

Going through Dad's files dredged up a lot of memories, and I think that was part of what Mom intended: to see what a wonderful life she and Dad had led and how I could lead the same kind of life.

When we were about to leave for Colorado, Mom said, "You know, the only thing we have in this world is each other. When we die, there's nothing left behind except our children, their memories of us, and these." She pointed to the boxes where I stored Dad's files. "Pass them down to your children."

Maybe Mom was feeling her mortality. I couldn't blame her for that. But I had to admit, this little speech gave me the creeps.

Not Rick. He leaned toward the positive side. "Your mom's a Buddhist," he said after she dropped us off on Interstate 70.

We stuck out our thumbs. We decided to take the northern route, even though it was coming on to late fall and it was getting colder. We both had warm jackets and sleeping bags. Besides, this route was faster, we thought. It was an uneventful trip. Rick and I fantasized about our move to Boulder and what we would have to do.

Get jobs. That was a downer. Cogs in the capitalist wheel. But then we thought jobs were a means to an end. We could quit anytime we wished and live off the proceeds. Then find other jobs once the money ran out. "We have to pay the piper" was the way Rick put it, and that didn't seem so bad, until we thought of the other piper on Rick's tail, Uncle Sam. By the time we reached the Midwest, we were in a deep funk.

One of our rides dropped us off at the student union at the University of Nebraska in Lincoln. It was about four in the afternoon. We had fifty bucks between us that we were saving for necessities. The rest of the money we made from organizing Dad's files I had asked Mom to deposit in our bank accounts. We didn't want to get robbed while we were hitchhiking. To raise our spirits, we decided to splurge. We found a cafe down the street and ordered meatloaf, mashed potatoes, green beans, and gravy. Ten dollars gone. We wandered back to the union. Our hope was that we would sit down on a comfortable couch until some long-hair asked us if we'd like to spend the night at his digs. We once spent a night like this at the University of Illinois when a fellow freak picked us up outside of Champaign, and we thought this could happen here. At the worst, we could sleep in the union.

About an hour into our sojourn, we spied a bony-faced guy in thick glasses and long hair handing out pamphlets. He came up to us.

"Would you like to come to a Buddhist meeting?" he asked.

"Can we crash there after the meeting's over?"

"Sure, sure. Why not?"

We followed him out to a step van where about six other characters in disheveled clothing like us waited. On the way out, the driver introduced himself as George.

"I'm a shakubuku Buddhist," he said proudly.

We came to the edge of town, about the last apartment house before the prairie, piled out of the van, and went up a flight of stairs to the apartment.

"Welcome to our home. It is a humble place, but we are just starting out," he said, ushering us inside, where we were greeted enthusiastically by the other Buddhist devotees.

The leader of the group was a black-haired man with a hairy black mole on his chin. He called himself Taki, but he reminded me more of a New Jersey transplant from the way he rolled his Os.

He asked us to gather in a circle for confessions.

The first came from George. "I am in love with a beautiful woman who paid no attention to me until I chanted *nam-myoho-renge-kyo* a thousand times in front of the Gohonzon, the sacred scroll, and then she came to my room." He didn't tell us what happened in his room, but he put his arm around the woman next to him, who was attractive in a rabbit-like way. She had buck teeth.

"We are to be married next month," she said, smiling radiantly.

The devotees clapped their hands together and cheered lustily like their team scored a touchdown. We did likewise, though I looked over at Rick, who raised his eyebrows as if to say, *Jeez, weird.*

The next to confess was Gregory, a middle-aged man with a pot belly and salt-and-pepper hair. He was jealous of his neighbor who owned a flashy car. He wanted a flashy car as well. But he needed to get in the proper frame of mind to call forth his Buddha nature, and it took many more than a thousand chants in front of the Gohonzon until he found a new job that paid him enough money that he could afford his flashy car, a Cadillac.

There were other confessions that I only half-listened to: one about ending nuclear proliferation, another about cleaning up the rivers, and a third about winning the lottery. Rick poked me in the side. I was nodding off.

Taki, the head guru, raised his hands—one empty, the other with a rolled scroll wrapped in a red ribbon. "We are the shakubuku Buddhist. We believe the pursuit of happiness is the goal of life, and to do so, we must create value. We chant *nam-myoho-renge-kyo* a thousand times in front of the Gohonzon"—he shook the scroll in one hand0—"and from these chants, we call forth our Buddha nature, and from our Buddha nature, we create value, whether it's ending nuclear proliferation, owning a flashy car, or marrying the woman of our dreams."

Taki opened the scroll and thrust it in front of us so we could see the foreign letters printed on the fake parchment paper. He asked us to chant. We did, stumbling through the words as the devotees were in full-throated chorus.

"Myoho-renge-kyo, myoho-renge-kyo, myoho-renge-kyo, myoho-renge-kyo, myoho-renge-kyo, myoho-renge-kyo, myoho-renge-kyo, myoho-renge-kyo, myoho-renge-kyo."

We didn't make it to a thousand because Taki closed the scroll. I think this was a demonstration to show how it was done, because next he told us we could all have our own personal Gohonzon. We didn't have to go to a Buddhist meeting. All we had to do was chant in front of the open scroll and we would attain our own personal happiness.

"Does this cost money?" I asked Taki.

"Oh, we couldn't give it away for free. We have to cover costs." He laughed.

"How much?"

"Ten bucks would do, but if you want to contribute more, that would be appreciated."

Rick fumbled through his pockets and came out with a five, three ones, and change. I hesitated, but then I thought it was cheaper than most motels. I forked over a ten. Taki handed the scrolls to us and gave us a beatific smile worthy of the old master himself.

We wandered over to George, who was gathering up the raga-muffins to take back to the union.

"You know we're spending the night," I said.

"I'm sorry. I talked to Taki. He said there was not enough room."

"That son of a bitch," I said, kicking the wall before I left the apartment.

George looked genuinely shocked, but he didn't say anything. He drove us back to the student union, and we piled out of the step van. The building was dark and the doors locked, so all us ragamuffins scattered in different directions. Rick and I went down a side street, thinking of crashing behind a bush in a yard next to a big foursquare. We passed a Lutheran church with a high steeple that rose above the trees. Above the basement door I noticed a battered orange sign that said, "Shelter."

"Do you think that means air raid shelter?" I asked Rick.

"No."

We rushed down the stairs and knocked on the door. It was opened by a big, burly man who looked like the state trooper who had stopped us on the highway on our way east. "Come on in, boys. You look bushed." We followed him through a long hallway to a huge room. There were ten mattresses lining one wall, mostly empty. "We don't hold to no ceremony around here. Just flop down and go to sleep. I'll keep an eye on your sacks."

I nudged Rick before we crashed out. "Glad they don't hold to no ceremony," I whispered. "We've had enough as it is."

Rick laughed and looked around at the other snoozing bums,

who seemed to be twice our age, raggedy old drunks. "Yeah," he whispered back, "you're right."

In the morning, the pastor drove us out to the highway, and it wasn't long before we hitched a ride.

TWO DAYS LATER we arrived at 1109 East Thirteenth Avenue determined to leave, finally, for good. J. B. had moved up from the basement to the back room after Huey left for Steubenville. Al Stroman, another Denison alum, had moved into the basement while we were gone. He was doing his CO work at a local hospital. We thought J. B. would be strapped for cash, but no. Not only was he still stamping taxes to the bottom of cigarette packs but I think he was dealing dope. He had some connections that I was unaware of in Boulder. Maybe that was why he wanted to move there. He shared some fine stuff with us.

"You know," said Rick, relaxing in the purple room, "I think we're going to love Boulder because that's where all the girls are."

But we weren't quite ready for the move. We had to deal with the draft lottery.

We gathered in front of Rick's portable TV on the appointed day and watched two silver-haired men in black suits and an old black-haired lady with a scowl on her face. They sat behind a table taking tabulations. Behind them was the American flag. In front of them was another silver-haired man with silver glasses that reflected in the camera lights. He stuck his hand in a wide-mouthed glass jar and pulled out a blue capsule that he handed to the lady. She opened the capsule and looked at a piece of paper inside then handed it down the line to first one then the other man behind the desk. They peered at the paper. They handed the paper to the announcer behind a microphone who announced the number as "258." That stood for anyone born on September 14 between the years 1944 and 1950. They were first in line for the draft.

There were ten of us in the room, and we sighed in relief. But this was only the beginning of the painful experience. I think they did 366 drawings, the last one for leap year. These codgers were so slow in going through the process that when we came to the fourth date, February 14, ten minutes had already passed. Chad, the resident manager, jumped up waving his hands, but he didn't seem too upset.

"That's my birthday," he said, snorting happily. "Valentine's Day, 1952."

"Awww, jeez," complained Rick. "Then why do you bother watching this dumbass boring show when you're not even eligible for the draft? To make us feel bad?"

"No, it's not that at all. I wanted to know what it feels like to lose the lottery." He laughed and looked around at our grim faces.

"Don't worry," countered Rick. "When this lottery is over, there'll be another one. Maybe then you'll know what it feels like to win."

Nothing else happened until the 117th drawing, when the bug-eyed bass guitarist in the band down the block groaned, "October 22. I'm waxed."

"If that was my number, I'd shoot myself," said Butch the Speed Freak. "That is, shoot myself up."

"I'm not going to do that. I'll hide out in the mountains. No one will find me."

"Sure, sure," said Butch. But as it turned out, his number came up not that far down the line at 141, I think, August 18. Not that it mattered with what happened to him later.

The rest of the lottery was not that bad. Rick figured that they would not draft men beyond two hundred. "I mean, how many men are born between the years 1944 and '50? Probably close to a million. We are the baby boom generation."

The others agreed, and as it turned out, they didn't draft beyond 195. Rick came in at 256, me at 237. Not that it mattered. We were safe, though I felt sorry for the bass guitarist.

That night we celebrated Rick's new draft status, and the next morning we sat on the stoop watching the morning traffic race by on another warm day. Rick and I felt blitzed out and somewhat guilty about our move to Boulder. We were leaving J. B. behind and maybe some other friends from Denison who were planning to come out to join our crash pad commune. But this guilty feeling quickly dissipated when an unmarked black van pulled up in front of Butch's house. About half a dozen feds piled out in chinos, red ties, and blue jackets with the FBI logo printed in yellow on the backs. They sprinted up the steps and banged on the door. Butch opened right away, as if he had been expecting them. One of the agents handed him a piece of paper. Butch looked at the paper briefly and slammed the door. They waited patiently for Butch to return, but when he didn't, they twisted the doorknob. The door flew open. They backed away from the entrance, pulled out their handguns, and one by one entered Butch's house. We backed up to the porch, afraid that a stray bullet might find us. But no shots were fired. We heard a scuffle going on inside, and then we saw Butch in handcuffs dragged down the stairs and into the back seat of a sedan that had just pulled up. Two of the agents scooched in the back seat, one on each side of him. The sedan drove off.

The rest of the agents returned to the house. They put up crime scene tape. They rummaged through the contents. They tipped over lamps. They ripped open a bean bag couch and pulled out the stuffing. One of them yelled, "I found something." He held up a tightly wound bag of what looked like moth balls. He sealed it in an evidence box and carried it out to the van. This went on all day, the feds searching every nook and cranny of the house. They must've carried out twelve boxes or so, and we were beginning to think old Butch the Speed Freak must've been sitting on top of a drug warehouse.

Chad and Sam came by to enjoy the festivities. One of the agents handed Chad a notice.

"What does it say?" I asked.

"It says no one can enter the house under penalty of law until otherwise notified. Shit," said Chad, shaking his head in disgust. "My dad's gonna kill me."

When the last agent closed the door and padlocked it, he marched down the stairs and turned in our direction.

"You guys are next," he said, smirking. He skipped down the rest of the stairs and scooted in the passenger side of the black van. He rolled down the window and saluted us.

Chapter Eleven

RICK AND I MOVED TO A ONE-ROOM APARTMENT ON TWENTY-FOURTH Street, a few blocks from Folsom Field. We were on a month-to-month lease. The thing I remember about the apartment was that you could open the sides of the bathroom vanity, look in the mirrors, and see your face repeated thirty times over, moving away from you in a parabolic curve, your head growing smaller and smaller until it was a pinhead—a perfect setup for dope fiends such as ourselves.

We found jobs, Rick in Boulder Canyon at the Red Lion Inn, me at the Hungry Farmer. I bused tables, but the customers complained about my long hair, so they put me in the back. I wore a hair net. They fed me the cheap food on the menu. They paid me minimum wage. I worked twelve-hour days. I wanted money, money, money. I was the dishwasher, but the manager insisted that I help Carl, the backup cook, a relative of his. The manager was a short guy with sandy-blond hair and a red pencil mustache. He wore madras shirts and wide paisley ties, green pants, and pointy shoes. He screamed at me because Carl wasn't fast enough. It wasn't my fault, I told him. I was the dishwasher.

On Christmas Eve, the place was so packed and Carl so far behind that the manager totally lost his mind and accused me of trying to ruin his business. I told him I was doing fine. The dishes were all washed and ready to go. "It's Carl over there. You either fire him or find him an easier job."

I checked out Carl. He was on the verge of tears. He was a bald, pudgy guy. His pants ended at his ankles. "I'm sorry, Carl. I didn't mean to hurt your feelings," I said. I put my arm around his shoulder.

"It's not your fault," he said, glowering straight at the manager in an accusatory way.

I was fired on the spot. I threw my apron on the floor and told the manager to go fuck himself. I strolled out of the Hungry Farmer feeling righteous for losing my job in a good cause, but then I wondered, *Hey, where's the next paycheck coming from?*

I needn't have worried because I found another job in three days. It was at a laid-back Italian family restaurant. The food was great, and I was treated like one of the family. One night while I was shoveling down a plate of spaghetti and meatballs after we closed, Dean Angelo, the restaurant owner, told me his life story. He was born in a small town in Italy in the mountains in a wine-growing region. His father left for the United States, where his uncle owned a restaurant. The plan was to save enough money to send for his family, but the war intervened. They were stuck in Mussolini's Italy. When they strung up el Duce and his mistress in the square, the Germans marched into his town. His family hid in a cave where they kept the wine. The Americans marched in. They came out of the cave and moved to New York City.

"I played high school football. We won the city championship. I sat on the bench at one of the Giants games with Y. A. Tittle." He had been a big guy with a bushy mustache. A linebacker, he said. "Now if that isn't an American immigrant story, I don't know what is."

He slapped me on the back so hard I nearly choked on a meatball.

I told him I played high school football, though I didn't say a word about how it got me out of the draft. Seems to me that immigrants, like religious converts, are more patriotic than the rest of us, and I didn't want to lose his respect.

He gave me a dollar raise, made me backup cook, and hired a down-and-out cowboy who must've come in off Larimer Street.

"This is the best job I ever had," said the cowboy. The reason he felt that way was that the customers sometimes didn't finish their wine. He would funnel the wine from each glass into an empty bottle until, at the end of his shift, he would push out the back door with a smug smile on his face and a full bottle of blended wine in his satchel.

Rick made more money than me because the Red Lion Inn was a classy eatery. The waiters took in one hundred dollars a night on tips alone. That was a veritable fortune for Colorado, where things cost half as much as they did on the East Coast. You could buy gas for nineteen cents a gallon and groceries that would last a week for twenty bucks. But we weren't doing that. We ate our main meals at the restaurants where we worked and popcorn the rest of the time. I loved popcorn. So did Rick. Our only extravagance was that we loved to smother the popcorn in margarine. We'd pour on the salt and spices. Sometimes we'd buy beer. But mostly we'd chase down our popcorn with water. We were saving up for something big. We didn't know what at that time, but it must've been important.

Meanwhile, Rick was toiling through another Buddhist phase that came about as a result of visiting an Orange Julius to quench his thirst one day and wandering into a nearby Buddhist store. He purchased two T-shirts, one with the *om* symbol written in Sanskrit, another with Buddha meditating under the Bodhi tree surrounded by the words "Inhale the Good Shit...Exhale the Bad Shit." He also purchased a pair of loose-fitting white pants tied by a drawstring, a purple bandana, and a knurled walking stick. He looked more to me like a samurai warrior than a devotee to the peaceful path. He showed me a pamphlet that was titled *The Noble Eightfold Path* to right understanding, right thought, right speech, right action, and so on.

I kidded him about the shakubuku Buddhists in Lincoln who took our money.

"I'm more interested in Zen Buddhism," he clarified. "I'm trying to accept the duality of the universe. If I can accomplish the goals in this pamphlet, I will be at peace with myself. I won't feel hassled by earthly concerns. I will live by example. People will admire me."

"Jeez, Rick, you got it bad," I said.

He was in a deep funk, and I knew why. One night after work, I had wandered into the apartment exhausted, and there was Rick with a friend of one of the Denison women on the Hill, the same ones who wouldn't stay with us in Denver because we were slobs. We talked for a while, and then I fixed my dinner of popcorn, which I chased down with a Pabst Blue Ribbon (we had purchased a case on sale, 50 percent off). Then I nodded off. In the middle of the night, I awoke to the faint grunts of my roomie and his bedmate. I could see their silhouettes across the room moving up and down like a couple of slinky toys mating. This went on for a week, until one night when I slogged into the apartment and Rick was alone.

"What happened to your girlfriend?" I asked him.

"She went home to her fiancé."

"Her fiancé?"

"Yeah, the bitch."

Rick told me that he was falling in love with her and then she sprung this thing about getting married. "How would you feel?"

"I guess I'd feel bummed out."

I was bummed out when Pie shacked up with J. B. rather than me. And I felt the same draw as Rick had, pretending like I was Siddhartha, an ascetic who didn't need to immerse myself in the garden of earthly delights.

On one of our nights off, we went to the band shell in Boulder's Central Park for a free concert. They were handing out peyote buttons, and we took three each. We chewed on them. Drank water. Chewed some more. After a while, our stomachs started to churn. We lost interest in the concert—it was a local band, mostly bongo drummers and an off-key singer. We found the closest bathroom and tried to vomit in the toilet. It was mostly dry heaves. A long-hair with a ring in his nose, red-and-white-striped pants, and a bare chest told us to hold it in "if you want to have fun."

He exited the bathroom. The door banged behind him. We held it in. We stumbled outside. Our stomachs settled down. We started to see fireflies like tiny Tinker Bells flitting through the air and heard a roar in our ears that we figured was the roar of the universe but was, in truth, the roar of Boulder Creek that spilled down off the rocks from the mountains and through the park. It was a spiritual high. The Yaqui used peyote as part of their religious ceremony, to see visions and such.

But whatever it was, Rick was blabbing on endlessly. I could hardly understand what he was saying, but I was fascinated by how purple his lips had turned. His teeth sparkled like diamonds. He was saying something about Shiva and Krishna, and I was wondering if he wanted to join those fellows in the orange robes.

"No, no way," he said. But we danced around to their chant:

Hare Krishna, Hare Krishna,
Krishna, Krishna, Hare, Hare.
Hare Rama, Hare Rama,
Rama, Rama, Hare, Hare.

"Who's Rama?" I asked.

"I don't know. Maybe he's like Shiva the Destroyer. We have the creative and destructive forces, you see," he said, making a prayerful sign under his chin and smiling with his sparkly diamonds.

We woke up the next morning curled up next to Boulder Creek, a cop standing over us snapping his baton against his hand. He poked Rick in the side. "Get your butts in gear," he snarled. We struggled to our feet, blinking at the sun.

"What's the matter, Officer?" I asked in my polite voice as if I didn't know.

"This park is closed from dusk to dawn."

"It's already dawn," said Rick, smirking disdainfully.

"You think I don't know that," said the cop. He was about our age, skinny as a rail, tiny eyes, big nose. "I know you been sleeping here all night, and I could just as well run you in."

He banged Rick in the elbow. Not too hard, a love tap. But it must've hit his funny bone, the way Rick jumped around, cursing under his breath.

"You leave this park right now," said the cop, raising his baton.

Rick was in the process of grabbing the baton, but I dragged him out of the park. The cop stood there with his hands on his hips and a wicked grin on his lips.

"Don't be a fool," I said to Rick. "He's got a gun."

"Oh yeah. You're right. Bad karma," he said.

We limped back to our apartment.

Rick threw his clothes in the corner. "Fuck this Buddhist shit."

But a few days later, he started to wonder. "Maybe what I need is karmic fine-tuning. You understand what I mean," he said between tokes from a bowl of hash. "Maybe I need an event in my life that will alter my brain cells, steer me away from samsara and down the road to enlightenment." That event came in the form of Steve Falsack, who we met on one of our visits to Denver on our days off.

Rick and I had been sitting on the stoop at 1109 when Steve's Dodge Dart died in front of the house. We helped push the car over to the curb. He thanked us and sat with us on the stoop. He introduced himself. We shook hands.

"Aren't you going to get the car fixed?" I asked.

"It's no use. I don't have any money. She stole it from me," said Steve, stroking his bushy mustache, his eyes tearing up. He put his head in his hands. His shoulders shook.

"Hey, take it easy, man," said Rick, patting his back. "Who's 'she'?"

Steve said that "she" was his girlfriend. He had visited his parents for a week in the Bronx—I could've guessed that from his whiny nasal accent—and when he came back, his apartment was bare. No TV, no furniture, not a stitch of clothing, no girlfriend, no money he had loaned her to tide her over until he returned.

"I start a job in a week. How am I going to show up if I don't have any clothes?" he said, tearing at his hair. I'd never seen anyone do that except in cartoons.

Steve stood up, walked down to the car, and kicked the tire. "Can you believe my luck? I mean, the Dart isn't a beauty, but it only had sixty thousand miles on it, and I put a brand-new stereo in. Cost me an arm and leg." He locked the car and turned to us. "Do you mind if I spend some time with you until I get on my feet? Can't go back to the apartment since I owe rent."

Rick and I looked at each other and shrugged, thinking, why not. It wasn't our place anymore. "We'll have to ask our friends," we said.

J. B. didn't care, nor did Uncle Al, as we called him. He had moved up from basement to the front room that we had vacated. "The more the merrier," he said, though he exacted thirty bucks a month from Steve.

Steve begged us to drive him around town to look for his girlfriend. He was convinced that he'd catch her traipsing along the street or at some flea market selling his goods. We drove straight down Broadway to Santa Fe near his apartment and damned if we didn't find her selling his clothes off a rack. Steve told us to wait, jumped out of the car, and ran after her. She was showing a customer a madras shirt when she looked up and saw him. She scurried off but didn't get more than twenty feet before Steve grabbed her by the arm and swung her around. He shook his finger in her face. He yelled at her. She yelled back. I couldn't hear what they were saying, but after five minutes, I guess, the guy holding the madras shirt—a weathered-looking Marlboro man in cowboy boots and hat—sauntered over to join the argument. It reached the point that Steve shoved the cowboy away. The cowboy shoved back. Then Steve shoved. They were yelling at each other the whole time, until suddenly the shoving stopped and they peered up the street as Steve's girlfriend disappeared around a corner. The cowboy shook his head and slapped Steve on the back. Steve handed him the madras shirt. He wandered back to the rack and grabbed what was left of his clothes. Not much.

I drove up. He put the clothes in the back seat and climbed in next to me.

Now Steve was as happy as he could be. He stored his clothes in a corner of the room in a crate that used to be Joe's bedside table. He looked up at the photograph of a smiling Meher Baba that Rick hadn't taken with him to Boulder. He read the caption:

DON'T WORRY—
BE HAPPY.

Steve ripped the photo off the wall, stared at it for a while, and broke into laughter.

"What's so funny?" asked Rick in a puzzled tone.

He showed the Indian avatar to Rick then to me. "That's the spitting image of my dad, mustache and all. But you want to know what's funny?" he asked rhetorically. "My dad never smiles. The reason he doesn't smile is that he isn't happy. The reason he isn't happy is that he worries all the time." Steve sent the postcard sailing across the room, where it landed at Freddy the cat's feet. Freddy batted it around for a while.

A few weeks later, we sat on the roof of the row house. Smoking dope. Watching traffic. It was a gabled roof, pitched at a forty-five-degree angle no longer than eight feet from end to end. Steve was excited about his job. He paced back and forth in front of us. Up the roof. Down the roof. He turned to us.

"You know what I like about the job? It's only a mile from here, a nice walk down Thirteenth Avenue and I'm there," he said, tweaking his mustache. "No reason to get snarled up in rush hour. I mean, it's the perfect location. Maybe I could live here longer."

We didn't pay much attention to what he said, being too concerned that he'd fall off the edge of the roof.

"You know what else?" he said, as he turned to us. He was on the front edge of the roof at a funny angle, his legs spread apart like a sailor on a pitching ship. "I'm one of six people in the office, the only one with a college education other than the boss. And the boss is about to retire. You know what? I think they're grooming me to take over his position."

He raised his hands, all excited about the possibility of a huge pay raise. He lost his footing. He flailed his arms and toppled backward. We were ready for him. We reached forward and grabbed what we could—me his shirt tails, Rick his belt—and yanked him toward us. He fell into our laps.

"Shit," he said, giggling nervously. "I could've died. But at least I'd have died happy."

He called us in the middle of the week a few days later to tell us that his Dodge Dart had been stolen. "Well, not stolen. Impounded by the police. It's in a lot in southwest Denver, and I was wondering if you could come by on your day off and take me there."

We took him to a lot on Saturday and cooled our heels waiting for the cashier to finish lunch. Steve was doing a slow burn, and when the cashier handed him the bill, he exploded. "Shit, two hundred bucks. That's more than my whole week's salary."

"Not my fault," said the cashier, shrugging.

Then a guy in uniform with a patch that said, "Security Police," escorted us to Steve's Dodge. Steve wiped the dirt off the window and peered in. "Holy crap," he said, crooking his finger at the security guy. He shuffled over with his hands in his pockets and peered in.

"What do you see?"

"Looks to me like somebody stole your radio."

We peered in and saw a bunch of cut wires sticking out of a square hole where the radio should be.

"That's a brand-new piece of equipment. It set me back three hundred bucks," he whined. I could see he was on the verge of tears. "Weren't you supposed to be guarding it?"

"Not my fault."

"What do you mean? Aren't you the guard?"

"Yep, but look around you," he said, gesturing. There were about five hundred cars packed tightly together. "Too many cars, not enough security."

Steve beat us back to the house in his Dart. We parked our car and went over to see how he was. He was leaning against the steering wheel. We knocked on the window. He rolled it down and looked up at us. There were tears in his eyes. "I can't stand it," he said, blubbering. "I give up."

Rick and I drove back to Boulder. Something to do, I don't know what; otherwise, we would've stayed to comfort poor, hassled Steve Falsack. A few days later, J. B. called us to say that Steve had quit his job and called his parents. They sent him an airline ticket. "I drove him to the airport this morning. He handed over the keys to the Dodge Dart and said you could have it."

When we next made it into town, I let Rick do the honors since it was going to be his car. He got behind the wheel and turned over the engine, but it wouldn't start. He tried it three more times. Same result. We tried a jump start. No luck. We put gas in the carburetor, a trick Rick had learned from a mechanic friend for when the gas was low. Who knew whether the gas was low or not. Finally, we gave up.

Rick kicked at the tire but missed. Hit the rim with the end of his foot. He was wearing sneakers with a flexible toe and must have damaged himself. He limped back, sat on the stoop, and rubbed his foot.

"You okay?" I asked him.

"I wanted that car."

"Maybe we could take it to an auto repair shop."

"No way, too much hassle," he grimaced, took a few deep breaths, and sighed. "I don't want to be hassled. I don't want any trouble. I don't want to be like Steve Falsack."

I agreed with him. Steve was a little bit over the edge. But, you know, things happen that aren't necessarily anyone's fault. I suggested again we try the auto repair.

"No way," said Rick and halfway smiled. "Let's go home."

When we returned to our apartment in Boulder, Rick took up his walking stick and his om and "Inhale the Good Shit…Exhale the Bad Shit" T-shirts but tossed out his white pants in favor of bell-bottom blue jeans. He hiked around Boulder greeting strangers with a big smile. "I've learned my lesson," he told me.

Chapter Twelve

Rick and I attended an antiwar rally in Boulder's Central Park. Allen Ginsberg was on stage in a white robe like a youthful, curly-haired Mr. Natural, reciting "America" in a deadpan voice to a spellbound audience of freaks, grandmas, and such. "America when will you be saintly?" Ginsberg asked his devotees. "When will you strip buck assed naked and check yourself out from the grave." Not the exact words, but close enough.

I sat cross-legged at the foot of the master along with my friends. All of us stoned. Next to me was a lady from Denison I knew only as Rose. She was exotic in a way, dark-skinned, almond eyes, curly black hair. I'd seen her around campus. Never spoke. Maybe nodded a greeting. But right now, she was squeezing my hand tightly as though she needed comfort. I asked her if she was okay.

"I'm fine," she said, teary-eyed more in ardor, as I found out later, for Ginsberg's poetry—and perhaps for me. As we walked home after the rally, I put my arm around her waist. We kissed. She steered me into the woods by the sidewalk. We kissed some more.

"'I saw the freak minds of my generation mangled by madness, hungry hysterical stripped bare,'" she whispered in my ear, playfully misquoting Ginsberg.

"Yeah," I said. "*Howl.*"

This was about the time I turned twenty-six. I was no longer eligible for the draft. My mother told me that she spoke to Dr. Peterson, a friend of the family, who said a doctor in his practice had performed a new type of operation dozens of times with complete success. In the new method, the surgeon cut a three-inch hole in the armpit, stuck some instruments in, and tightened the ligaments. Because of the tightened ligaments, my shoulder would have less of a tendency to pop out. Right now, my ligaments were like rubber bands stretched to the limit. It couldn't hold together a stack of baseball cards, much less my shoulder to the socket. It seemed like a good idea to get an operation, but not until Rose did it become a reality.

When we arrived home to Twenty-Fourth Street with a menagerie of friends, we lit up some more joints and passed them around. It was already dark, and most of us were tired from parading around the park and along the streets of downtown Boulder. We nodded off in corners of the room, Rose and me in a corner by the bathroom. The light was on in the bathroom, the door slightly ajar. Rose wanted to show me her tattoo. She pulled her pants down so I could see the red rose on her thigh. I reached out to touch it gingerly. She giggled at the feathery touch of my hand and rose up in a fit of passion, I imagine, and pounced on me, chest high.

"Make love, not war," she purred as I lifted my arm to encircle her. She pushed up under my armpit in an effort, I suppose, to reach my lips. But she never got there because my shoulder popped out. I screamed. I pushed Rose off me. I jumped up and ran around the apartment in unbearable pain, barely aware that I was stepping on the arms and legs of about twelve or so rally-goers who were crashing on our floor. I ran outside. I draped my bad arm over the porch railing and yelled for Rick.

He came outside, rubbing his eyes. "What? What?"

"Yank my arm."

He looked at me like I was whacked out and then saw it was my shoulder that was out of whack. "Again," he said.

He grabbed my wrist and yanked.

My shoulder popped back in. I sat down on the ground. I held my arm against my side. The last time my shoulder popped out was a month or so before, when Gina had tickled me. And before that, two years, when I was bodysurfing in Rehoboth. And before that, my sophomore year in college when a belligerent drunk took a swing at me. I had backed up, and he had moved forward and fallen on me. It took hours for my shoulder to return to its proper place, and only after a dose of morphine. The fact was, the more my shoulder popped out, the easier it popped out the next time. It was an endless process, like a record stuck in a groove. It was driving me wacko, not to mention the pain and the conditions under which this last one occurred.

When Rick and I wandered in the apartment, Rose was gone. "You scared her to death," said one of the rally-goers. "She thought you were a maniac."

I called Mom up the next day and arranged an appointment and gave Dean Angelo two weeks' notice. He was sympathetic after I explained why I was leaving. He said I could have the job back when I returned.

I jumped in the Mustang along with Hank Hipple, who planned to visit his sister in Virginia. We decided for the heck of it to drive without sleeping. We figured it would take thirty-six hours. We got as far as Topeka, Kansas, when the car started misfiring. Oh, shit, I was afraid we were going to blow a rod. I pulled into a gas station and found out it was the spark plugs. We changed the plugs and were on our way in an hour.

Hank was a wreck. He'd found out that the school friend who was going to hold his girlfriend's hand in Mexico while she got an abortion was her high school sweetheart. He proposed to her on the plane down. She accepted.

"I loved Edie. I wanted the baby," he said as we drove through Kansas City. "I thought she loved me."

As much as I liked Hank, this was a heavy emotional load to deal with on a marathon drive. By the time we reached Columbus, Ohio, he seemed to have calmed down. I was dog tired and let him take over the driving. He drove straight to his sister's house in Arlington. I gave him a hug goodbye and told him I knew everything would work out for the best, though I didn't know that at all. I turned the car north and drove to the house on Twenty-Ninth Place. My mom was visiting my sister for a week and had left the keys in a box behind a bush.

I had two weeks to kill, and I thought maybe one of the things I'd do was invite Robin Gran to a demonstration that was planned for May 10. This one was against the Cambodian incursion in late April and the Kent State massacre that followed. Four students had been gunned down by the National Guard. It was one more step toward anarchy in this country for a senseless war we had no reason to fight. I called Robin's dorm, and she told me to come right over.

I decided to park on Macomb, a block away from where I grew up, because I heard over the radio that American University students were distributing anti-Nixon leaflets to motorists on Ward Circle. They were blocking the flow of traffic that came into the Circle in four directions. The police were on their way. I walked up Macomb. The gridlock started three blocks before I reached Massachusetts Avenue and continued all the way up to the Circle. Horns were honking, and people were jumping out of their cars to get a better look at what was happening. It was rush hour, and Mass. Avenue was one of the main arteries out of DC to the Maryland suburbs. I scurried up the hill, steered right before I reached the Circle, and came in on the other side of the campus.

There was smoke rising in the air, and I knew exactly what it was because my eyes were smarting. Tear gas. The cloud was descending on the motorists. They deserted their cars and fled toward Spring Valley at the bottom of the hill. They were rubbing their eyes, bouncing into each other, falling down. It would have been a riot if the wind hadn't shifted to the west toward campus. I made my way through the crowd and followed a line of hills until I came to the west end of campus to Robin's dorm. She was outside waiting for me.

She looked exactly as I remembered her from the last demonstration: dressed in black from head to toe like a fifties Greenwich

Village beatnik. She grabbed my hand and pulled me back into a secluded corner of the building where our mouths melded in the most delicious peppermint kiss—I think that was her black lipstick—until a finger of gas tickled our nostrils.

"I broke up with Kevin," she said, rubbing her leg against my crotch. She was as aggressive at this as she was at playing *Risk*.

We decided to flee toward the residential area across Nebraska Avenue. When we reached the edge of campus, there were four cops in full riot gear brandishing billy clubs. We veered to the right between parked cars, crossed over into a block of brick homes, and onto New Mexico Avenue past all the swanky doctors' offices where I was supposed to go in a week for an exam before my operation at Sibley Hospital. We made a complete circle around AU in the opposite direction, and when we came out on Mass., traffic was backed up a mile farther to Wisconsin Avenue. We came to the Mustang on Macomb, jumped in, and turned around, heading the opposite direction of the traffic back to Mom's house.

I parked the car, and we went around the house to the garden that was surrounded by a high wooden fence. We sat by a fountain where an alabaster cherub dribbled water from his penis into a pool.

Robin laughed. "Your parents' taste is peculiar."

"That's the previous owners, not my parents. My dad wanted to get rid of it, but then he..."—I didn't want to choke up—"...got sick."

"He died, didn't he?"

"Yeah."

"I'm sorry," she said, leaning closer and patting me on the knee. "My parents are divorced."

"Jeez, wonderful," I said.

We laughed as if it were something funny. It was nerves.

"Let's take the edge off of things," she said. She reached in her purse and pulled out two joints. We smoked them. I think they were laced with a hallucinogenic. The sun's rays poured through the trees like tiny sparks from a live electrical wire. The puffy clouds in the yellowish sky—I think it was near sunset—seemed like red and pink roses. They pulsated and glowed. I turned to Robin. She curled up next to me on the bench where we were sitting.

Later we climbed the steps to the second floor. I wanted to go in my sister's room, but when I told Robin that was where I had slept with Sally, she wanted to go to my room, though it was only a single bed.

I closed the door behind me and reached out to touch Robin, but a bolt of static electricity stung my fingers. I jumped back.

I laughed. She laughed. She pushed me down on the bed and jumped on top of me. We rolled around in bed, the sparks from the sheets flying in a multicolored light show. We giggled. We poked each other. Then we dispensed with our clothes.

She pointed at me. "Your dick looks like a gummy worm."

I looked down. She was right. It was the right color, cherry and blue raspberry, though it wasn't wiggly like a gummy worm. I worried about my shoulder.

She knew I was here for an operation, so she probably treated me gently. I wasn't exactly sure, because I didn't remember the whole process due to my altered condition and faulty memory. But when it was all over and we sat there smoking cigarettes, my body was fully intact, though, I imagine, tingling with all kinds of pleasant physical sensations. Her body was lying inches away from me. She reminded me of a reclining, thick-haired Botticelli beauty.

I asked Robin why she was attracted to me. As soon as I said it, it seemed like something a woman would ask a man. I blushed.

"Oh, I don't know." She assessed me carefully. "Physically, I would say it's the freckles across your nose and your blue eyes. Your eyes are faceted like marbles. All colors. Blue. Gray. Black. White. Green. Very Nordic. Cold like ice. What are you?"

"Part Viking. Part Scottish. Part Welsh. Part German. Part Swiss. Etc. What are you?"

"Russian Jew. My great-grandfather ran with the Cossacks."

"Wow. Way cool. Vikings and Cossacks."

"And Jews. They're tough too."

We wandered downstairs, and I fixed her dinner. My mom had made sure I wasn't going to starve while she was gone. I made one of my dad's old recipes, cowboy steak: T-bone slathered in barbecue sauce and smothered in grilled green peppers and onions.

"You know how to cook," she said. "Man food."

I uncorked a bottle of wine I found in the pantry, and we sat in front of the TV watching *Laugh-In*. Then we went up to bed. I didn't know the world could be so perfect.

The next morning, Robin and I wanted to mellow out on Mary Jane, but there was none to be had. We drove out to Quayle Smith's house on Kirby Road. I think it was his sister who answered the door because she was dark and sharp featured like the mother and son, very pretty with black, soulful eyes. A toddler clung to her leg and looked up at us with the same eyes.

"Quayle's in the basement," she said in a cold voice that made me hesitate. I could tell she didn't like us, especially Robin. She gave her the evil eye as if to say *What are you doing here, fellow female? You should know better.*

We stepped around her, down the hallway, past an ornate grand-father clock that was chiming madly, and down the stairs to the basement room. That was where we saw Quayle sitting on a leather sofa patting Thumper on the head like nothing had changed since the last time we were here.

I asked him if it was his sister who answered the door. He said yes. She was here from Chicago on a visit with her two daughters.

He made a motion for us to wait as if he knew why we were here. He headed into another room and returned a few moments later with a baggie that he dropped on the coffee table. He asked us if we wanted to go to the backyard to test the dope. We said no. We trusted him. We handed over the dough and left as fast as we could. I guess we were paranoid, with the sister being there and all. Maybe she'd call the cops. Like, yeah, she'd turn in her own brother.

We decided to take a weekend camping trip to the Shenandoah Valley with Hank and Bill Barbour, who was home for a visit. Enjoy our dope in a more laid-back milieu. But Robin felt guilty for some reason. She wanted Quayle to join us. She knew him from the old days too. He was a nice guy. Kind of quiet. Maybe lonely, she said. He needed to get away from that creepy sister of his. So did Thumper.

We pitched our tents near Woodstock Tower. The tower overlooked the north fork of the Shenandoah River, which wound through the valley like a silver snake below us. Beyond the river was the town of Woodstock, a series of clapboard houses with tin roofs stretched out along Route 11 with the county courthouse in the middle and a shopping center at each end. To the west was Interstate 81 as straight as an arrow from Pennsylvania to Tennessee and then the Allegheny Mountains and more mountains beyond that. It was a windy day, so the clouds scudded across the horizon in thin, smoky lines.

The tower creaked and rattled. It was open at the top. We climbed up the narrow stairs. Quayle wouldn't follow us. He sat on a rock facing away from the view, staring at the woods, waiting for Thumper, who was off chasing birds.

He was still there sitting on the rock when we came down an hour later, totally blitzed on his superior herb.

It took us a while to realize that he was somewhat distraught, rocking in a slow, tight motion from side to side like the pendulum of a clock. He gestured toward the woods, a heartbreaking gaze in his eyes. "Thumper is gone."

We clomped through the woods for an hour but couldn't find him. We were coming down off the weed. The boys were pissed, but Robin sympathetic.

"He needs that dog," she told us. "Thumper keeps him grounded."

She convinced us to report Thumper missing at the ranger station on the other side of the valley. We packed ourselves in the Mustang and arrived at the station to find the dog running around in circles behind a chain-link fence. Some other person had found him and turned him over to the rangers. Thumper paused in his running and sniffed the air. The ranger opened the gate. Quayle stepped in. Thumper made a running jump into his master's arms, nearly knocking him over.

On May 10, Bill Barbour and Hank joined us for the demonstration against the Cambodian incursion and the Kent State massacre. Hank told me that Edie flew back to Denver after the abortion. Her fiancé rented a car. They picked up her clothes in Boulder and flew to Chicago, where she moved into his apartment.

"He's a stockbroker. Works for Goldman Sachs," said Hank with disdain. We loathed anything that smelled of capitalism. "Can you believe they're getting married in a month?"

I didn't know Edie that well. I met her a couple of times. She seemed nice enough. But why was she giving Hank a running commentary of her life if she didn't want anything to do with him anymore? I was beginning to think, *Jeez, women, they must come from different planets.* I wondered at the same time about my future with Robin. I wondered, why did I care? She was only a stop on the road from one place to another, and I imagined I was the same to her.

Bill Barbour had his camera along with him, and he was taking photos of the march. One of protesters naked to the waist playing in a fountain in front of the Smithsonian; another of the buses in front of the White House, the DC National Guard sitting idly by on the curb, some resting on the ground; another of a bearded, long-haired protester bearing a wooden cross on his shoulder; and a final one of a baby-faced protester in an army uniform festooned with model fighter jets and ribbons and holding a newspaper with the headlines:

WAR DECLARED STUPID!
GENERAL WASTE-MORE-LAND

The one that got me was of a counter-demonstrator dressed like a cowboy. He held up a sign that said:

Beware of
THE NEW WORLD ORDER
The Communist Jewish Party
The Jewish Illuminati
ENEMIES OF FREEDOM

He was trying to make himself heard above our chants: "One, two, three, four, we don't want your fucking war." Someone in the crowd took umbrage and tried to rip down the sign, only to be attacked by the cowboy's allies. They carried nightsticks and started to bust heads. Bill and I blocked Robin's view of the melee to protect her.

"Hey, I want to see," she said, pushing us aside. She chased one of the allies but didn't catch him because the cops came by and restored order.

It wasn't much of a fight, but the offending sign was trampled in the dirt and the creeps run off. They were probably members of the National Socialist White People's Party, formerly the Nazis, that was based in Arlington. Or maybe the Klan. Or who knows what other fringe group existed in those days.

The funny thing was that later, when I wandered around the Mall where they set up tables for one protest group after another, I came upon a table for the American Communist Party. A gray-haired man in a threadbare suit and with a dull expression sat at the table twiddling his thumbs, pamphlets spread out before him. No one paid attention. He was definitely out of step with the times, like the cowboy with the sign. He was, I knew, Gus Hall, boss American Communist. He hardly seemed like an ENEMY OF FREEDOM to me.

The other funny thing was that the dude next to me in a sun hat, the drawstring pulled up to his neck—it was a windy day—seemed to be reading my mind. He was dressed in a white shirt, string tie, and baggy pants. The glare that came off his tortoise-shell glasses nearly blinded me. He was perhaps ten years older than I, but he wasn't at all out of step with the times. He was like one of my professors at Denison.

He asked me how old I was, and after I told him, he asked me how many years during my life had the United States been at peace. I told him in wise-guy fashion that it appeared that most of my life we had been at peace, but in actuality, we had been dispatching troops to one hot spot or another. So, I would say we had been at war most of my life.

"The government has been pulling the wool over our eyes. We live in a national security state," he said, handing me a pamphlet. I looked down and saw that the pamphlet was from the Institute for Policy Studies. Never heard of it. There were so many think tanks, policy study groups, lobbyists, associations, and whatever trying to steer the government in one direction or another that it was hard to keep track.

I looked up to say something to Mr. Sun Hat, but he was gone. Melted into the crowd. I shrugged, stuffed the pamphlet in my back pocket, and rejoined my friends, thinking it took all kinds, the policy-wonky kind like this dude and my kind, who thought the government was there to keep us off each other's backs. I read John Locke, the state of nature, and all that shit. Maybe I was a bit too trusting, because sometimes, like now, it was the government that was on our backs. So, I gave Mr. Wonky Sunhat Dude a little salute for keeping us informed.

The Monday after the march, my mom came home. She took me to Arbaugh's, a ribs restaurant with a blue awning and yellow brick façade that we'd go to often when I was growing up. We sat in the booth of the dimly lit restaurant sipping drinks. Mom wanted to know if I had a girlfriend. She had been cleaning my room and had found a pair of black stockings under the bed.

"Well, yeah, Mom, I do," I said, staring over her head at the orange glow of the Michelob sign on the greasy back wall. This place had seen better times, perhaps around World War II when it originally opened.

"What is your girlfriend's name? Can I meet her?" she asked. Mom always wanted to meet my girlfriends since they were so few and far between. She didn't even care about where she found the stockings. She probably saw that as a good sign.

I told her the name, but she didn't meet Robin until after the operation because, frankly, I didn't meet her either until my last day at Sibley Hospital. Kevin was with her. He was home on his summer break, and I thought—it seemed obvious—that the writing was on the wall. We sat on the front lawn of the hospital. I was in a sling. I guess I appeared glum, because Kevin, in an attempt to lighten the mood, told me one of his jokes, a political one.

"Nixon, Kissinger, Billy Graham, and a hippie are in an airplane," he said, leaning close to me. "The pilot croaks. They need to parachute to safety. There are only three parachutes. Nixon grabs one, saying, 'I am the president of the United States. The people need me.' He jumps out. Kissinger grabs one, saying, 'I'm the world's smartest man and the adviser to the president. The people need me.' He jumps out. Then Billy Graham says to the hippie, 'Go ahead, my son, you can take the last parachute.' And the hippie says, 'Don't worry, Reverend, there's two left. The world's smartest man just grabbed my knapsack.'"

Robin punched Kevin in the shoulder. "That's a stupid joke," she said, though she was laughing. "Don't you see Jeff's not feeling well?"

I don't remember much else of what happened. Kevin had to leave for a job interview, and Robin stayed for another hour. She regaled me mostly about her major and how she hoped to go to graduate school at Johns Hopkins. I told her I flunked psychology in college because my rat went nuts.

I thought of Robin for a couple of days, and when I went home, I called her up. She came over. Mom was shopping with my aunt Janet at Lord & Taylor's. We went upstairs to my bedroom and attempted to make love. It was difficult. My arm was plastered to my chest. Wrapped by gauze.

Robin made a joke about *The Mummy's Curse*: "Funny, you don't look like Boris Karloff."

She lay down on the bed, and I flopped on top of her. But the action was very stilted, to say the least. I was like a beached whale. I could rub my crotch against hers. But I couldn't put the boner in the slot. And when she helped, she jostled my arm. I jumped a mile.

"I'm sorry. I'm sorry," she said. We tried other positions, but it all came down to the same thing. The pain. Either I was going to let my libido control my common sense and end up in the hospital for another operation or quit while I was still in one piece. I rolled off her and sat up on the bed. "This isn't going to work," I groaned.

"That's okay," she said, throwing out a ray of hope. "There'll be other times."

She helped me on with my clothes, and we wandered downstairs to the front hall—and not too soon. Mom barged in the door with her purchases. I introduced Robin. We stood there for an awkward moment until Mom showed Robin what she had purchased, an Ultrasuede jacket with gold buttons, a matching pair of flats.

"I don't wear heels anymore. I don't want to fall and kill myself."

"That's sensible."

I could tell they were both nervous for God knew what reason, but it made me nervous as well. Finally, Mom told us that she had to change. She was going to dinner with Aunt Janet.

I drove Robin home.

"I'll come by to see you before I leave," I said as we pulled in her driveway.

"Yes, please do." She leaned over and kissed me on the cheek. We gazed at each other in a longing way, I guess, because we both knew this was it. I wouldn't come by to see her, nor would there be any other times.

Chapter Thirteen

I FELT LONELY AS THE MILES UNROLLED ON MY WAY WEST ON I-70. Hank had stayed with his sister. She lived on Patrick Henry Drive in Arlington in a three-bedroom brick house with her husband and two children. That left Hank in a cramped basement sleeping on a couch. He said he didn't want to return to Boulder to that apartment. He asked me to pick up his clothes. I wondered if I'd ever see him again.

I pulled into a rest stop west of Terre Haute, climbed in the back seat, and tried to sleep. But that made me think of Pie and when we were in the back seat of the Mustang near Raton Pass and I was groping her. That was a downer. Then I thought I was driving again, though I didn't remember climbing into the front seat behind the wheel. Beside the road a hitchhiker in ragged clothes was sticking out his thumb. I didn't stop for him. Then I saw him again. Someone must've dropped him off ahead of me. This happened again and again until the hitchhiker lifted his hat. It was Hank Hipple glowering at me in an accusatory way. So I didn't pick him up. I couldn't. I was still in the backseat. So I must've been dreaming not driving. I puzzled over this conundrum until a flashlight shined in my eyes.

"Give me your license," said a disembodied voice.

"What? What?"

"Your license."

I reached in my back pocket.

"Keep your hands where I can see them."

"But, Officer, I was reaching for my wallet."

I was ordered out of the car with my hands in front of me, which proved difficult due to my recent operation. But I managed it. The disembodied voice turned out to be an Indiana state trooper all dressed in blue with black boots. He took my license and strode back to his vehicle. I knew what his problem was. I was a long-haired kid with a nice car. Probably stolen.

He returned in a few minutes and asked for my registration. I handed it to him. He checked the registration against the license. Then he ran his flashlight through the interior of the Mustang to see if I had a gun, a Molotov cocktail, or even worse, marijuana. Satisfied, he returned my IDs.

"You're free to go," he said.

I watched as he passed me in his vehicle, the cherry top spinning round and round. I waited ten minutes before speeding off, still sleepy-eyed but anxious to leave Indiana. In downstate Illinois, I was tuned in to a local station that was playing old country tunes when an announcer came on the radio telling us drivers not to pick up any hitchhikers. There had been a recent prison break. I had to laugh. If it wasn't the cops, it was the robbers. What a completely nutty world. Suddenly I didn't feel as lonely as I had before. I was heading on to my next adventure, and I couldn't wait to see what it was.

THAT ADVENTURE WAS J. B. getting busted. J. B. had moved to Boulder. He lived close to the mountains in a sunny apartment with large windows. Once Rick and I visited him during a solar eclipse. We looked out the kitchen window as a black hole seemed to swallow the sun, turning the earth into shadow. First the mountains, then the plains. It was not a total eclipse, so we could see the outlines of the sun through the tinted glass that J. B. had purchased for the occasion. When the sun returned, J. B. regaled us with stories about how the ancients reacted to an eclipse: Vikings thought wolves ate the sun; the Vietnamese thought it was a giant frog; the Chinese a dragon. J. B. was normally not that chatty. He kept to himself, like his father who, I remember, had visited us once in college. He hardly spoke at all but sat in a chair jotting down notes in a small, black leather-bound notebook.

That was J. B. Always calculating. Mr. Businessman trying to make a buck. He went from shooting model rockets in the sky to running drugs in less than three years. But he would only run hash or marijuana—not the heavier stuff. He had his limits, he told me once. Maybe I was paranoid, but I don't think the narcs would care what he was running—illegal was illegal.

What got him started, I think, was somehow through his contacts, he met the drug kingpin in Boulder. This guy—I'll call him Ted because I don't remember his name—lived in a big mission-style bungalow near the University of Colorado. Ted also supplied drugs, it was rumored, to the University of Wisconsin. I don't know where the connection was other than Wisconsin was a hotbed of radicalism and, I imagine, a lucrative market. And while Colorado, at least the university, was far less intense, the town itself and the surrounding mountains were chock-full of hippies to the point where places like Ward, a town thirty miles up Boulder Canyon, had its own hippie sheriff. Ted would fly back and forth from one fiefdom to another. Sometimes he carried small quantities of hash or cocaine. This was before the days of TSA and sniffing dogs. But mostly he would rely on his runners or mules or whatever they were called. He was like a painting contractor. He only showed up to collect the cash.

It was on one of those days that J. B. was on a run to the Mexican border in his blue Volkswagen Bug that we visited Ted at his bungalow for an all-night party. We were almost as stupid as J. B. Ted was a chubby guy with a gray beard and horn-rimmed glasses. His hair was cut short. He wore a plaid vest. He looked like a college professor. He ushered us into the living room where, on a mission-style coffee table next to a leather couch, there was a bowl full of pills.

"Take one," he said.

"What is this, Alice in Wonderland?" asked Rick, taking one of the pills.

"Funny man," said Ted, smiling. He turned to me.

"Take one."

I wasn't as trusting. "What's in those pills?" I pointed at the bowl.

"Speed. You need only one unless you want to stay awake for three days."

I thought about Butch the Speed Freak. I shrugged. What the hell. I'm not mainlining the stuff. I plucked a purple pill out of the bowl and swallowed it.

It took twenty minutes before my tongue loosened up to such an extent that by the time I crashed eight hours later, I had a sore throat. I slid to the floor next to Rick, our backs to the wall, where we stayed for hours before J. B. showed. We touched on the subject of reincarnation.

"If you take the scientific view, reincarnation exists. But not in the Hindu sense," insisted Rick, who preferred the philosophical to the personal. "You're not reborn as a cockroach, for instance. However, when your body disintegrates, the atoms that kept you together scatter, and one may become part of a cockroach's antenna, another part of a drop of water, and another part of the eyelid of the next Einstein."

"I'd rather be in the next Einstein's brain," I said.

"Einstein's brain," said Rick, waving his hands. He was distracted by a few lines from "Wooden Ships" on the record player, the hippie anthem about how we need to leave the straight world before we get blown up or something.

"Dig it," said Rick.

"I do. I do," I said. "I'll take your sister by the hand."

"No, I'll take my sister by the hand. You take yours," said Rick.

"She won't go on any wooden ship," I rejoined. "Maybe an ocean liner. QE2."

We both sniggered.

We sat there for a moment contemplating the guests at the party, only six other than us. Four women, one of whom was sitting on Ted's lap, pulling on his beard and singing along to the music, while two others clad in polka-dotted mini dresses and purple stockings swirled around in circles until one fell on a man in bib overalls sleeping on the leather couch. The last two shared a hookah in a corner of the living room.

We both sighed, kind of bored; then Rick pointed a finger at me. "What do you think it would be like if you lived in the fourth dimension?" he asked.

"It would be like an acid trip."

"All the senses mingled together. Yes. Yes," he said. "Time eliminated. It would be like, I don't know, a swirling circle of intense images where everything blended together: the moment you first saw your mother's eyes and the other eyes admiring you in your crib, saying, oh, what a cute baby, to the moment you were rolling down the hill and got stung by a bee or fell off your bicycle and scraped your knee to the moment of your first kiss from a little French girl named Babette to the moment you dislocated your shoulder when you tripped over your shoelaces and fell face forward in the dirt to the moment you lit up your first weed to the moment you got laid to the moment you tasted your first barbecued ribs, coleslaw, and cornbread to the moment you're at the altar on your knees because you're marrying a Catholic girl and wondering, what the hell am I doing—and all the other moments mixed together like ingredients for a smoothie in a blender. That's what it's like being in the fourth dimension."

"How do you know?" I asked.

"I don't. Just guessing."

So now it was my turn to come up with something, but all I could think of were two lines from a Samuel Taylor Coleridge poem that seemed to relate.

Where Alph, the sacred river, ran
Through caverns measureless to man.

"Yes. Yes," said Rick, "measureless. The universe is measureless. The brain is measureless. That's stupendous."

We decided to write a poem in alliteration that had to do with the stupendous. We were, after all, English majors on speed. I don't remember the lines exactly as we originally spoke them that night, but here are two as I wrote down in my diary in the manner of the poet who wrote his poem down after an opium dream:

While whimpering windless wisteria walk upon
Walls, truth falls like feathers upon fraudulent
Falsehood unmasking phony faces from
Malodorous Milhous.

And:

Detain dribble by delivering lips from
Deviating mouths delivering, dying, detestable
Detritus in deep wells of depthless spite.

There were others I'd rather keep under wraps.

Meanwhile, things happened in front of our eyes that we hardly noticed. The guests were at the windows. The music was off. A red light was going round and round on the ceiling. Ted grabbing the pills off the coffee table and running to the bathroom. He ran back and shook us awake.

"What? What?"

"Your friend," he said, pointing to the window. We stumbled to our feet, nearly falling over stray furniture in the middle of the room. It was then that we noticed that the room—the whole house, for that matter—was dark and that the people at the windows were silent. We looked out. There was J. B. sitting in the back of a police cruiser, his head down, covered by his blond locks. It was hard to tell, but I think he was shaking. Maybe even crying.

The cops—you name it: fed, state, local—were all over his blue VW Bug checking every nook and cranny like the border guards when we crossed over from Mexico. When the cops were finished with the search, a tow truck hauled the Bug away. Ted did not seem as interested in the goings-on as us because he was busy hiding and/or destroying evidence for fear the cops would break down the door and arrest us all. But my guess was that they weren't going to do that. Maybe they didn't have a search warrant. Maybe they were stupid, because if they had waited for J. B. to knock on the door, they could've bagged not only him but one of the biggest drug dealers in the Midwest as well as small fry such as Rick and me.

Later we dragged our bodies back to Twenty-Fourth Street hardly able to keep our eyes open. We didn't notice the message on our screen door from the landlord, but we did the next afternoon when we awoke. We had to vacate the apartment by the end of the month. That was three days away.

We hustled around Boulder, but another apartment was not to be had at a price that fit our budget. We extended the hustle to the mountains and found a motel on a hill outside Nederland, a small town at the end of Boulder Canyon. Norm, the owner, a long-haired guy with a wandering eye, ushered us to a room with two beds, a mini refrigerator, a hot plate, and a tiny bathroom. There were no other guests at the motel, and we were wondering if Norm's last name was Bates, as in *Psycho*. He said that this used to be a lodge for skiers that skied Eldora, but since the slopes were so dinky, nobody came up here except for day skiers. He said he made his real money at the restaurant by the front desk. He named us a price we couldn't refuse.

The next thing we planned was to find jobs in the area, and the only employer, except for a few grocery stores and a bar, was the ski resort. We drove up the mountain to the lodge. We were greeted by Helmud. He was a blond with shifty blue eyes and a thick German accent. He offered us a job that would last until ski season moving boulders off the slope, and then maybe there'd be another job. Maybe not. All this for five bucks an hour.

We decided to keep our old jobs. We had to drive farther, but the pay was better. Just barely. The only thing that worried us was that when the snow flew, we'd be stuck up here. But this was Colorado not Washington, DC, where even a few inches of snow would send the whole town into panic.

One night we visited the Pioneer Inn, the only bar and restaurant in Nederland in the flats near the lake. We sat at a table close to the bar. We ordered hamburgers and beers. We were feeling rich because our rent was half of what it was in Boulder. The Pioneer Inn was a rough-hewn place. Board-and-batten siding painted red on the outside. Worn wood floors inside. A tin ceiling with some insulation sticking out of cracks. Beat-up tables. Beat-up bar stools. And a meager supply of booze and only one draft beer—Coors, of course. We sat there sipping our Coors and checking out the clientele as rough-hewn as the inn. All were long-hairs, except for two older men in cowboy hats. We felt right at home until a woolly-haired freak swaggered in the door. He checked out the clientele as if searching for a victim, but his eyes seemed focused on someplace far away above our heads. He smelled like cat piss. He wore jeans that were patched with leather and pieces of bright cloth. The jeans hung halfway down his hips. He wore a dirty white shirt with an STP logo on it and a denim vest. A skull of a small animal was tied by a string around his neck. He seemed like a modern-day mountain man, a Grizzly Adams type who'd been out in the woods far too long. He came right up to us and stuck out his hand.

"Spare change," he mumbled.

We stared down at his dirty hand. He leaned closer to us.

"Spare change," he yelled, shaking his hand so we could see where to put it.

"Don't have any," said Rick. He told the guy to fuck off. This was not a good way to start our first day in a new town. We didn't know who this miscreant was. But fortunately, a fellow at the bar reached over and dropped four quarters in the dirty hand.

The miscreant looked down at the quarters. He looked up at us and the benefactor. He smiled. One of his teeth was missing, and two that overlapped were as green as moss on the side of a tree. He turned, took one more look around, and swaggered out of the bar, hitching up his jeans. They were almost down to his knees. It wasn't a pretty sight. He was bare assed.

I invited the benefactor to our table and bought him a beer. "I probably just saved your lives," he said, leaning close to us so the others in the bar couldn't hear. "You see that STP shirt he was wearing? It's not what you think. It stands for Serenity, Tranquility, Peace, or maybe just STP, their drug of choice. He belongs to a group of hippies who call themselves the STP family, like the Manson family. You get my meaning. They invaded Nederland a couple years ago in VW buses plastered with paisley designs, so we're thinking, oh, great, flower children. No problem. But no, they're violent. They like guns. They brag about killing bears. Someone once told me that they eat their dead in spiritual ceremonies. That's probably all bullshit. But I'd steer clear of them if I were you."

We wandered back to our new abode thinking maybe we'd made a mistake moving to the mountains.

We changed our minds the next morning when we stood outside our door facing west and watching the sunlight pour down the snow-covered Great Divide like liquid gold. I thought about the Band's Great Divide song. It put me in a good mood.

We drove down Boulder Canyon to see J. B., who had been released from jail two days before. Pie was with him. I think this was the beginning of the committed part of their relationship that eventually led to marriage. I could have been wrong, as I usually was with Rick's sister, but one of Pie's traits was that she was a bundle of intense feelings. Sometimes she could be irrational. You could say it was a woman's thing. But it wasn't. Rick was the same way. Maybe it was tied up with the fact that their father died when they were young. I don't know. I'm not a psychologist.

But what happened was that she dropped everything when she heard about J. B. It didn't seem to matter that she was an A student at the University of Denver or that she had a new circle of friends. What mattered was that J. B. had gotten the crap beaten out of him in jail. The police tried to get him to snitch on his contacts, and I doubt that he did. Ted was still dealing drugs. He was sending people down to the border. Flying back and forth from Madison. There was no big drug bust anywhere in Boulder, as far as we knew. But that didn't stop the cops from telling the other inmates that J. B. had spilled the beans. The inmates laid into him.

When I saw him that day, he didn't look that bad off—a cut under his eye, a swollen jaw, a few bruises here and there like a Nordic hero back from the war. A confident warrior. His ego was still intact, and I could tell by the way Pie looked at him that she was madly in love again.

"I'm through with dealing, forever," he said, leaning forward in his chair and smiling. "You know what I did today? I found a job at an upscale Mexican restaurant on Canyon Boulevard. I mean, they were really impressed that I had a college education. I could see them grooming me for a management position."

"Didn't they ask you about the bruises on your face?" I asked him.

"I told them I got in a car accident," he said, shrugging. "They believed me."

"That's great," Rick and I said, nodding thoughtfully.

"I'm going straight, man," he said finally, clapping his hands together. And it was true. Pie dropped out of college. She moved in with him. He found her a job at the Mexican restaurant where soon he was manager. Plus, J. B.'s lawyer claimed that the shipment of marijuana came under the Marijuana Tax Law of 1937, a law that was repealed a few months later. J. B. paid a hefty fine. No jail time.

Chapter Fourteen

THE NEXT THING THAT CAUGHT MY EYE WAS MOTHER NATURE. Colorado was a beautiful place, full of natural wonders, and since drugs were scarce, we decided to rethink our options. I mean, no more downers or uppers from J. B., nor from Ted. He'd moved his operations to Madison. The authorities were burning the marijuana fields in Kansas. It didn't matter that they were mostly male plants. No THC to get us high. Spooky, one of the Tranquility family members, sold us a lid for ten bucks. We smoked a joint and threw the rest in the trash.

But the final factor that sold us on the straight life was speed. We crashed for fourteen hours after Ted's party, missed our jobs, and nearly got fired.

"I don't want to live like this," I told Rick.

Thus, our interest in nature and, to enhance our interest, yoga. It was Tyrone who helped us with the yoga part. He'd graduated from Denison and was out to visit before he decided what to do with his life. His draft number was low—twenty-seven, I think. He was thinking of hiding out in the mountains with us or going home to face the music. Home for him was Cincinnati, the same as Tyrone Power. So that was what I called him, because he looked exactly like the actor: chiseled face; deep, soulful eyes; dimpled chin; thick, black hair and eyebrows; and flawless body.

He lived in Denver in the back room that J. B. vacated when he moved to Boulder with Pie. Al was still in the front room. He was in love with a nurse at the hospital where he worked. She was there one Saturday when we came to visit on our day off. I mean, we didn't see her. She and Al were in the front room talking, and then later they went out for lunch or something.

Rick and I sat on the front stoop at 1109 scrutinizing the traffic and feeling morose while Ty tried to convince us that yoga was better than getting stoned. He demonstrated a few breathing exercises. We followed suit, but I guess we were doing it wrong because all it did was make us dizzy.

"I'm hungry. Let's go to Taco Bell," said Rick, finally. He slapped Ty on the back. "Our treat."

"Okay," said Ty, though he said he didn't particularly care for fast food. "Too much fat."

We trudged up to Colfax to Taco Bell. Ty consumed more than his share of enchiladas, tacos, and chalupas and on the way home regaled us about how his favorite thing to do was practice his yoga positions in nature like in the mountains with a spectacular view of the plains or next to a mountain brook. We suggested that he come up to visit us, and just as we were about to turn on Corona, we passed three pretty women. I noticed that whenever women were in the vicinity, they'd turn their heads to stare at Ty. They didn't whistle, but sometimes they sighed, ooh and ahh. But one of these pretty women stepped in Ty's path.

"Don't I know you from somewhere?" she asked, losing herself in his eyes.

"You ever been to Cincinnati or Granville or Mackinac Island?"

"No." Her two friends seemed equally enthralled.

"Then you don't know me." He was about to walk on when Rick grabbed him by his arm.

"Maybe these ladies would like to visit us," Rick said.

"Some other time," said Ty, sticking his hands in his pockets and forging ahead.

We followed behind, as did the ladies, down Corona to Thirteenth. I knew what Rick was thinking because I was thinking the same thing. Ty would hang out with one woman and the other two, in a futile attempt to make him jealous, would hang out with us. But it didn't happen like that. All three women followed Ty into his room and filed out a few moments later.

"I told them I was engaged," said Ty, which we found out later was true.

On our next two days off, Ty came up to visit us in Nederland. He brought a book with him called *Yoga, Youth, and Reincarnation*, a copy of which I later purchased at the Buddhist store on the Hill in Boulder. We'd sit on the deck outside our room with a view of the snow-covered Divide playing music on a Philips audio cassette I had purchased in Boulder—the Band's self-titled album, our favorite at the time, with songs like "Up on Cripple Creek" and "When You Awake." I loved every song on that album and the photograph on the cover of the Band members looking like bearded and mustachioed desperadoes out of the Canadian wilderness.

We'd spread out our mats and practice the positions in the book: the headstand, the triangle, the cat, the cobra, the lotus, and so on, but my favorite, and Rick's as well, was at the end where I'd lie on my back and practice diaphragmatic breathing, which meant I breathed from my diaphragm rather than the muscles in my upper chest. Breathing from my muscles made me tired; breathing from my diaphragm made me calm. It made me high, not simply dizzy like the first time in Denver.

The next day off, we traveled to a place we knew about from Joe Johnson, the place with the spectacular view. This was where Bob and Anne lived. Joe and Bob at one time were students at Virginia Tech in Blacksburg, Virginia, though neither of them had graduated. Joe joined the navy, and Bob moved west to avoid the draft, I think. That was where he met Anne. They lived in a tepee in the Arapaho National Forest about three miles off Boulder Canyon on Magnolia Star Route, a dirt road that twisted up the southern canyon wall until it came to the highest point, with a panoramic view of the mountains to the west—some ragged peaks, others tree covered, and a few bare but covered in snow.

We parked the car next to Bob's Ford pickup. We hiked up a short path to a rude cabin made of plywood and beyond that an aspen grove, where I could hear the whoosh of the wind and tinkle of the leaves brushing against each other. Then we came to an open field full of wildflowers and rocks, at the end of which was a twenty-foot wall of jagged rocks. In the middle of the field was the tepee, the poles leaned against each other tied at the top and covered with two layers of polyurethane. Between the layers was insulation, and to one side of the tepee was a wood stove with a hole cut in the plastic for the pipe. The whole contraption sat on a wood frame. The frame was attached to a rope-and-pulley system so Bob could move the tepee if necessary. The rule in the national forest was that you could camp out in a tent for two weeks. Then you had to move. It didn't say how far you had to move, and so far, there hadn't been a forest ranger up here to test the distance.

We hiked up to say hello to Bob and Anne—there was a tension between them that we tried to ignore—then found the path we knew of in the jagged rocks at the eastern end of their valley, climbed up to the other side, and jumped over to a ledge that stuck out ten feet into thin air. Below us a hundred feet were pine trees, a trail that led to the foothills, and Boulder—the sandstone buildings with red roofs at the university, shopping centers, developments, roads, cars, people, like part of a miniature train set—and beyond that the wavy grasslands of the plains. We could even see Denver to the south at the end of a long, black ribbon of highway. We could see the high buildings—not many in those days—the sunlight reflecting against the glass, the brown haze from the stockyards.

We crossed our legs and looked out at the plains and the endless, cloud-studded sky. "Om...Om..." we droned as if we were starving Buddhist hermits in the Himalayas. Then we spread out our mats and practiced the headstand, the cat, the cobra, the lotus, and so on. We lay flat on our backs breathing in and out calmly until we were high, even dizzy. But we didn't stand up suddenly. We didn't want to fall off the ledge into thin air. We waited with our eyes open, drinking in the beauty of our surroundings.

Another day off we visited Grody, Bob and Anne's friend, who lived nearby in an opening between two rocks. I think he was also one of those STP people, but then, I wasn't sure. We followed him down a long path to the left of the aspen grove near the tepee and up a hill to another ledge that overlooked a valley to the southwest in the mountains. There were a few cabins in the valley, but it was mostly meadows, a creek, pines, aspens, and wildlife—deer and elk grazing, an occasional bear lumbering along.

"Sometimes at night when the wind blows," said Grody, leaning close to us, "it makes these funny sounds, like *hoo-hoo-hoo, yoo-o-o-o*. The ghost of a miner, I imagine."

He led us into his abode. There was a small ledge like a table and in the middle an indentation that must have been scooped out by water that dripped from a hole in the rock ceiling. But now there was an exhaust hood with a pipe that poked through the hole. "That's where I do my cooking," he said, "and I keep the fire going so it keeps me warm at night."

In a corner was a polyurethane igloo lined with insulation where he spent the winter nights, but now his sleeping bag was spread out on the dirt floor.

"Where's the bathroom?" asked Rick.

"I'm like an animal. I crap in the woods."

"The running water?"

He pointed down to the creek in the valley.

We sifted through Grody's collection of antlers and small animal bones that he had found in the woods, which included a skull of a bighorn sheep that he found at the bottom of a cliff.

"Can you believe, a clumsy bighorn?" he said. Part of the skull was crushed and a horn was missing.

We spread out our mats in a nearby meadow and practiced the positions in the yoga book: the headstand, the triangle, the cat, the cobra, the lotus, and so on. Grody joined in and seemed to get more excited as we went along.

"This is amazing, very, very amazing," he enthused. I think, like the rest of the STP people, his vocabulary was limited.

When we reached the diaphragmatic breathing, Grody nearly passed out. He rolled through the meadow and would've rolled all the way to the valley if a rock hadn't stopped him. He lay there for a few minutes with his arms splayed out. We ran up to see if he was all right.

Grody's eyes were opened wide and staring at the cloudless, blue sky. A smile creeped on his lips. "Wow, wow, wow."

He stood up, nearly toppled over into the valley, but caught himself on the rock. "I want that book," he said, pointing at the *Yoga, Youth, and Reincarnation* book that lay propped open by a rock on the meadow. "I can't remember these exercises unless I have the book."

Ty was reluctant to give it up, but when I told him he could have mine, and I would buy a new one at the Buddhist store, he acquiesced.

So, we did our yoga in other places, like Russell Gulch overlooking a steep canyon, where six vultures circled in the thermals. One of the vultures lit on a nearby fence post, waiting patiently for one of us to keel over dead. In downtown Denver at a demonstration near the capitol, where we tried to convince two hotheaded teenagers that the way to end war was not to throw rocks at the police who were gathering at the cowboy and Indian statues. In Rocky Mountain National Park, where we were attacked by prairie dogs when we laid our mats down in their village. And in various other inhospitable places until we returned to the peace and quiet of the mountains near the tepee. It was here one day in late October when we were sharing a meal with Bob and Anne that the snow started to fly. Ty seemed antsy.

"I've got something to tell," he said, warming his hands over the cooking fire. "I've decided I'm going to return to Cincinnati. It's no use dodging the draft."

We drove him to the bus station on Twentieth Street in Denver and sat at the luncheonette, chowing down on hamburgers and fries, until his bus left. He told us there was another reason he wanted to go home.

"I'm in love with the most beautiful, sweetest woman in the world. I went to high school with her," he said, showing us her picture. She was all right, but not as pretty as those women who picked him up on Colfax. Though, I had to admit, you couldn't tell how sweet a person was by looking at their picture.

He put the photo back in his pocket and shook his head. "All I want to do after I serve my time," he said, "is marry Cindy and have children."

Rick and I felt cheated somehow. Here was our guru who was leading us toward enlightenment, and all he wanted to do was marry and have children. Samsara. How can that be?

I thought of Grody fifteen years from now, practicing his yoga positions in the meadow near his cave all alone, pooping in the woods like an animal. In a way, like my idea of a Tibetan monk, focused on the hereafter rather than the garden of earthly delights. Was that enlightenment? Maybe yes, maybe no, but whatever it was, it wasn't my bag.

"You know what," I said to Rick after we returned to the motel room in Nederland. I picked up the new *Yoga, Youth, and Reincarnation* that I had purchased at the Buddhist store and threw it in the trash. "I think I'm finished with this shit."

We decided the best thing to make us feel better was to drive down to the Pioneer Inn for a nice hamburger and fries dinner. The fellow who was at the bar the last time we were there, the one who claimed he saved our lives, came over and sat down with us.

"You remember that fellow who came in here and begged spare

change from you?" he asked, leaning closer so he wasn't sharing information with anyone else.

"Yeah, I remember him," said Rick, nodding thoughtfully.

"He's been murdered."

"No shit," I said, pushing up my sleeves. It was getting hot in there.

"No shit," said the fellow. "A couple of months ago, Deputy Dawg—that's the panhandler—was raising a ruckus when in walks the sheriff. The sheriff doesn't like the STP types. They smell bad, act crazy, and such, so he takes the Dawg by the arm and drags him out to his gold Plymouth and drives off. They found him a month ago."

The fellow waved at the bartender, who bought him over a Coors draft. We paid for it. He leaned even closer to us until he was almost in our laps. "It was hunters found a skull near an abandoned gold mine off Oh My God Road, twenty-five miles from Nederland in northeast Clear Creek County. I'm friends with Undersheriff Long, and he told me the skull had only pieces of skin and long strands of hairs attached to it. He surmised that animals had likely carried the rest of the body in pieces deep into the woods. But the reason Long knew who it was was the teeth. One was missing and two others overlapped each other."

"No shit," I said, jumping back like I'd been bitten by the Dawg himself. "You're right. That's the very same guy who panhandled us. I saw his teeth. The ones that overlapped were mossy green."

"I don't know what color they were," said the fellow who saved our lives. "But I can guess who did the murder."

"The sheriff," said Rick.

"I'm not saying yes. I'm not saying no. But I am saying whoever did it did the rest of us a favor," he said, banging his beer mug on the table.

The fellow returned to the bar, nodding to himself and sipping the rest of his beer.

"I think everybody around here is crazy," Rick whispered to me. With all the talk about wild animals carrying body parts in the deep woods and mossy-green teeth, we lost our appetite. We picked at the food and talked about where to go next.

Of course, we didn't do anything except go to work and come home. We were in a funk. It was around Christmas. We clomped out in the deep snow in the woods behind the motel and found a blue spruce that was hanging off a hill, the roots exposed. We chopped it down. We carried it to our tiny motel room and decorated it. I found some cheap lights and ornaments in Boulder.

A couple of nights later—I think it was the day after Christmas, as we were about to pull into the motel lot after work—we noticed a car in the snowfield across the highway. We parked the Mustang and wandered over to the car, following the tracks it left behind. We came up to the driver's side window and peered in at a balding, middle-aged man with a long neck and a pink Adam's apple. He was reminiscent of the vulture at Russell Gulch. His hands were on the steering wheel as if he were still driving and he was shaking his head back and forth, as though fighting off sleep. The headlights were on. The engine was on. It was cloudy inside the car. We knocked on the window. The man jumped about a foot and stared at us wide-eyed. He rolled down the window.

"What? What?"

"Are you okay?" I asked.

"You running beside me?"

"No, we're not," said Rick. "We're standing still."

"What? What?" He looked down at the speedometer. Rubbed his eyes and, when he saw it was zero, switched off the engine. He started coughing.

We dragged him out of the car and put him against the hood. He slid down on his knees and was about to pitch forward when Rick grabbed him. I turned off the headlights and closed the door, though I left the window open so the carbon monoxide could escape.

"Oh, shit. Oh, man," said the guy, holding on to his head. He stopped coughing. "I could've been asphyxiated? Maybe I was asphyxiated? Maybe I'm dead? Maybe you two are angels? How else could you run beside my car?"

Rick turned him around and pointed at the car.

"Oh yeah," he said. "The car's not moving."

We dragged him up to our room at the motel. He was not steady on his feet. At first we thought it was the carbon monoxide, but then we got a whiff of his breath. He smelled like cheap whiskey. When we got in the door, he pushed us away.

"I'm all right," he said as he staggered backward into us, then sideways into a dresser drawer, and forward into the arms of our Christmas tree. They danced around for a moment. The tree lost a few ornaments that broke against the linoleum floor. The man lost his footing and toppled onto my bed. We grabbed the tree and put it back on its stand. We cleaned up as best we could.

"Let sleeping dogs lie," said Rick as he offered me half of his bed. We didn't care if the guy died from lack of oxygen during the night or woke up in the morning with a horrific hangover.

It was a hangover. We gave him three aspirins and dragged him to the motel restaurant where they served breakfast and lunch.

"Oh, hi, Len," said Norm, grinning as he poured us coffee. "See your car in the snowbank across the street. You know we have a parking lot."

The drunk, Leonard Packer, waved Norm off, embarrassed. He ordered a pot of coffee, three fried eggs over easy, two orders of bacon, hash browns, and toast. While he was eating, he called for a wrecker to drag his car out of the snow.

He told us that he was rich. Once owned two Shakey's Pizzas in the Denver area. He had lived in Cherry Creek and been a member of the country club but sold everything and moved up here where it was safe. "The commies are coming."

He pointed a fork at me. "Nixon, you see, is a commie sympathizer. This thing about opening China up to the West. That's just fifth-column talk. What it means is that when we start trading with

China, they infiltrate our system. They beat us at our own game. I know what I'm speaking about."

Leonard Packer rose from the table, nearly knocking over his plate. "I was in the Korean War. We were winning. Then the Chinese entered the war. Then we started losing because they outnumber us a hundred to one. When we open up China, they'll outnumber us a hundred to one. How can you win with those odds?"

"I'm not sure I follow your logic."

He looked at me like I was crazy and went on to another subject, the fluoridation of the water as another communist plot. "There's things happening in this world that you don't know about," he said after I protested.

An hour later, after more talk about communist plots, yellow dye in margarine, United Nations forces flying in black helicopters to take over the US, and such, the wrecker pulled out his car. It was a beat-up Ford Falcon. Before climbing in and zooming off, he clapped us on the backs and thanked us for saving his butt. He handed us his business card that said he was president of the Boulder County John Birch Society.

"That explains everything," said Rick.

Chapter Fifteen

IT WAS NEW YEAR'S EVE. I WAS OFF WORK. RICK WASN'T. HE BORrowed the Mustang, said he'd return at eleven. The clouds rolled in, dropped a few flakes on the ground that didn't stick. Rick said something about celebrating New Year's at the Pioneer Inn.

I decided to take a shower. I turned the handle and waited for the water to turn steaming hot. I took off my clothes. I looked at the water hissing out of the shower head. I looked at the rust-colored water gurgling down the drain. I looked at the bare bulb hanging from the ceiling. I gave it a push so that I could see the shadows rocking back and forth like the shadows of people rocking toward me, their jagged fingers extended as if to strangle me. I jumped in the shower and closed the curtain. I expected the shadow of a man in a wig holding a knife in one hand and pulling back the curtain with the other, but he never materialized. I soaped up. Shampooed. Brushed my teeth. *Maybe at the Pioneer Inn tonight I'll meet a lady. Like, where are the ladies? Do we have to send off for mail order brides?* I waited until the water turned cooler before I stepped out. I climbed into my long johns and socks that I had warmed on the heater.

The first thing I noticed as I stepped out of the bathroom was that the whole room shook and rattled like a freight train was passing by outside the window. I pulled back the curtains. I couldn't see three feet in front of me, it was snowing so heavily. The wind was blowing the snow sideways, so it was smashing against the building. *Chinook,* I thought, the name there for those kinds of gusts. *No Pioneer Inn. Maybe no Rick.*

What to do? I lay down on my bed, opened my sleeping bag, and climbed in. It was nice and toasty, but my head was cold. Not only did the wind rattle like a prisoner banging against a cage but it seeped through cracks around the windows and under the doors. I turned up the heat, put a wool cap over my head, and jumped back into bed.

What the hell am I doing here? I wondered. I remembered telling my mom that my goal in life was to goof off until I got tired of it. What was wrong with that? So Brinton Rowdybush was earning a PhD at Berkeley, Al Stroman was applying to medical school, and Barry Roseman, another Denison friend who moved here for his CO work, was admitted to the University of Chicago's law school. Very smart fellows. Very serious. Very goal oriented, but not in the goofing-off sense. They had bright futures in front of them. Here I was falling into the middle-class myth when I didn't believe in it. But I wasn't falling for the hippie myth either. Living in a commune. Sharing things. Growing vegetables. Crowded in a hut without running water or a pot to piss in. Might as well be a Russian peasant. I was used to the amenities of life. Why suffer when you didn't have to? Which brought me back to Brinton, Al, and Barry.

I slapped Joni Mitchell into the cassette player, and when I came to "The Circle Game," I sang along until I felt dizzy. The world was closing in on me. I mean, here I was in an isolated motel in the middle of a snowstorm. The wind was picking up to such an extent that the walls were breathing, and through the cracks, I heard the sound Grody heard on dark, windy nights: *hoo-hoo-hoo, yoo-o-o-o.* It grew louder.

HOO-HOO-HOO, YOO-O-O-O.
HOO-HOO-HOO, YOO-O-O-O.
HOO-HOO-HOO, YOO-O-O-O.

I couldn't stand it. I ran into the bathroom and stuffed my ears with toilet paper, and finally, after a couple of hours, I fell asleep.

In the morning, the roads were clear. The sun was out. Rick traipsed in with a big smile. I asked him where he'd been.

"I couldn't get through the snow, so I turned around and drove to Denver. I got stoned. I got laid," he said, his big smile wrinkling his nose. "I'm really sorry you were stuck here last night."

"I almost went insane," I said.

"That's too bad," he said, reaching in his pocket and pulling out a Twinkie. "Here."

"Is this supposed to make up for last night?" I grabbed the Twinkie. I was famished.

He shrugged, put his hands in his pockets.

I unwrapped the Hostess treat and stuck it in my mouth. "This isn't left over from our last trip east?" I said in a garbled voice.

"No, Twinkies have a three-day shelf life, though I think they're so full of preservatives they'd probably last until the next ice age."

"Mmm."

Rick reached in his pocket and handed me another Twinkie.

WHEN FEBRUARY ROLLED around, Rick decided that he wanted to spend two weeks camped out in a tent in the aspen grove near Bob and Anne's tepee. He arranged a leave with his boss at the Red Lion Inn. I was pissed off.

"We need the money," I said, "if we plan to do anything this summer. I mean, aren't you getting kind of bored up here?"

"Yeah, there's not enough women," he said, "but, you know, we'll make it somehow. I just want to test myself."

Rick had been a Boy Scout, and survival skills were important to him. He told me once that when he was at a Boy Scout Jamboree in New Mexico, he was paired off with another kid. They were sent out along with five hundred other scouts to see who could last longest in the desert. They were given two days and directions on how to get back if they could no longer stand the ordeal. Rick and his buddy didn't eat much. They couldn't find enough wood to keep a fire going all night, which was necessary, since when the sun went down, the desert turned cold. They shivered in their sleeping bags instead. They ended up lasting the whole time, along with two other pairs of scouts, and were given special badges to commemorate their desert survival skills. I suspected this was why he wanted to test out his skills in the snowy mountains. He wanted me to come along, but I begged off.

"I have to work," I said. I dropped him off at the trailhead on Magnolia Star Route and waved goodbye.

"You're crazy," I yelled after him.

"Thanks," he yelled back. The wind was up. I didn't think he heard me.

Rick asked me to come back in a week to check on him. The weather wasn't that bad, the sun out half the time. On the eastern slope of the Divide, weather was more moderate—sometimes up to seventy degrees, other times down to zero. Mostly somewhere in between. I parked the Mustang next to Bob's Ford pickup at the end of the week. The snow around the trail was well trod, only a few inches deep from new snow. It was easy going. My long johns kept me warm, that and the fact I was lugging a backpack and a sleeping bag. I was going to spend a couple of nights before I headed back to work.

I turned a corner and came up to the crude plywood cabin, and there was Rick chopping wood.

"Hey, man, how you doing?" He put down the ax and hugged me, unusual for Rick because he was the standoffish type. *Probably lonely*, I thought.

"I'm fine. I'm fine," I said, sitting down on a stump and looking up at him. "But what are doing down here?"

"Staying in the cabin," he said. "Bob said it was okay. Belongs to a friend who won't be back until spring."

"How about your survival skills?"

"They're well-honed," he said. "I'm just tired of hearing Bob and Anne arguing all the time. Remember how tense they were when we first came here? I don't know what's up with them. Maybe it's cabin fever."

I helped Rick carry the wood in the cabin. We fed the stove, removed our shoes, and put our feet up until they were warm and toasty.

"Hey, look at this," he said. He shuffled to a corner of the room where on a shelf underneath a window was what looked like a record player. "It's a wind-up."

"Way cool."

"Hey, look at this," he said, pulling a crate full of records from under the shelf.

I shuffled over and perused the collection: *Sgt. Pepper's, Rubber Soul, Highway 61 Revisited, Disraeli Gears, Electric Ladyland, My Generation, Sunshine Superman, Wheels of Fire, Cheap Thrills, The Band*, and on and on.

"We're in heaven," I said as I unpacked the food I had carried up in my backpack. We settled on beans and rice with green peppers and Jimmy Dean sausage mixed in. Rick spun *The Band* on the turntable and motioned me to the window.

"Look out," he said. The glass was dirty. I wiped it with the sleeve of my shirt and stared out at the snow-covered Rockies. When "Whispering Pines" and "Across the Great Divide" crackled out of the box, we got so pumped that we danced around like idiots. There was something about sharing those upbeat vibes that emanated from the music. It was like we comprehended. We were there in the tangible spot. We were following in the footsteps of pioneers.

We settled down to relish our beans, rice, and Jimmy Dean meal at an old, beat-up wood table and thought about a nice, cozy nap on the bunk beds afterward. Then Bob popped into the door.

"Hey, man, I got to go off the mountain to pick up some food, and I won't be back until tomorrow morning," he said. "Would you mind spending the night with Anne? Don't want her to get lonely."

"We'd be happy to," said Rick.

Bob was an elfin man. Very muscular. Dark-blue eyes that always darted around the room as if he were expecting someone to jump out of the shadows. Before he lived here, he lived in a treehouse near the Virginia Tech campus in Blacksburg. I think he was an introvert. For now, he stared at Rick suspiciously. Probably he didn't like the word *happy*, as if it connoted pleasure or something salacious.

"I didn't tell you before, but Anne is pregnant," he said, staring at the floor. "That's the major reason I want you up there. Make sure she's safe."

"Don't worry. She'll be safe with us," I said, looking at Rick. He shrugged. We were a couple of idiots for not figuring out the source of their quarrels.

"Good. Good," he said, nodding before he left. A few minutes later, we heard the rumble of his truck as he drove away.

We grabbed our packs and crunched up the trail through the aspen grove to the tepee. Anne came out to greet us. She wore star-burst sunglasses, a feather boa over her shoulders, a flowery blouse with puffy sleeves, loose-fitting pants, and hiking boots. She was a Janis Joplin lookalike, and I think she knew it. Once I heard her wailing "Piece of My Heart" with the same raw intensity as the original, though, I don't know, something was missing, maybe the emotions. I got the feeling that she wasn't going to let any man take another little piece of her heart, especially if it made him feel good. I was out in the woods wandering by when I heard her that time, but I didn't stop. She made me nervous.

We followed her inside the tent, and we sat down by the wood stove. She kept poking the fire and feeding it with more wood from a huge pile nearby.

"Can we help?" asked Rick.

"No, thanks," she said. "I don't even know why you fellows are here."

We were nervous as cats, having never been around pregnant

women. We knew that any moment she could go into labor. Then what could we do?

"Would you fellows want something to eat?"

"No, thanks. We just had something," I said.

"Hope you don't mind if I do," she said, handing us a half-gallon of Gallo wine. "You fellows drink. I can't."

We found a couple tin cups and poured ourselves a swallow each. We weren't going to get drunk or anything because you could never tell what might happen.

Anne boiled rice on the wood stove. She opened a can of beans and tossed them in with the rice. Then she cooked bacon in a frying pan and fried an egg. She crumbled up the bacon, tossed it in with the rice and beans, and topped it with the egg. She sat down on the floor cross-legged. We couldn't see how she could manage that. She ate slowly, taking occasional sips of water.

"Normally I'm a vegetarian," she said. She brushed the hair out of her face as she leaned down to take another bite. "But I read a birthing book written by a woman's cooperative in San Francisco. It said that protein is the basic building block of the human body and therefore is central to the diet during childbearing."

"How far along are you?" asked Rick.

"Seven months," she said, putting her bowl aside. She spread peanut butter on a piece of bread. "Bob believes in natural childbirth. He wants us to wander off in the woods when I'm in labor and make a comfortable bed for me by a stream. Then when the baby comes, he'll cut the umbilical cord and tie it, wash the baby off, and present her to me. I read the cooperative book. They don't advise that, even though Bob's taken a crash course in midwifery, which means he's read a bunch of books and that's it."

"Is that what you're fighting about all the time?"

"Yes. I don't mind natural childbirth, but I want to move down to Boulder in case there's any complications."

"I don't blame you," I said.

"I love Bob, but sometimes his ego gets the best of him," she said, sweeping her hair behind her head and tying it with a rubber band. She reached for her guitar. "Would you like to hear some music?"

"Love to," said Rick, who sounded doubtful. His sister once belonged to a folk band. They practiced in the basement of their house in Bethesda. They drove him nuts.

Anne leaned over the guitar, running her fingers along the strings. "You know, I wouldn't be the least surprised if Bob doesn't turn up tomorrow. My guess is that he'll stay a couple of days with his friends on Maple Street. Then he'll come back full of contrition, but he still won't take me off the mountain," she said, running her fingers down the strings with more intensity. "But you know, if he doesn't turn up tomorrow, I'm leaving. That is, if you fellows don't mind driving me to Boulder."

"Guess not," we said almost in unison.

"Great," she said, strumming her guitar and smiling inwardly. She looked up at us and winked then lit into Janis Joplin's "Piece of My Heart," the same song I had heard out in the woods, but now with heartbreaking emotion.

Both Rick and I were blown away.

In the middle of the night, I woke up. Anne lay next to me, both of us curled up by the fire. She moaned in her sleep. I wondered if she was having a bad dream. I looked up at the sky through the polyurethane tepee. The moon seemed to race across the sky, but it was the clouds doing the racing, turning the moon on and off like someone fiddling with the light switch. A breeze from the west rocked the pine trees, and a light snow slid down out of the sky, the moonlight turning the flakes silvery like tiny pieces of aluminum foil. Anne moaned loudly. Her eyes popped open.

"Oh, God," she said. She held her stomach. "I think I'm going into labor."

Rick woke up. "What?"

"Labor," she groaned. "Or maybe I'm miscarrying."

I could see the fear in her eyes, and it made me frightened. "Maybe we should take you to a hospital in Boulder?"

"I don't know," she said, breathing more easily, the fear gone from her eyes and replaced by a quizzical look, her eyebrows arched. "The pain's gone away. Maybe it's the food. I'm not used to bacon, too much fat."

She tried to smile, but then the pain returned. She doubled over.

"Contractions," I said. I knew this because once I had kidney stones, and I knew it's much the same as childbirth, except your body is trying to expel a calcium deposit in your urinary tract. I could really have sympathy for what Anne was going through, though I imagined what she was experiencing was ten times worse, and I'm not even getting into the consequences.

"Yes, contractions," she hissed through her teeth. We waited through the ebb and flow of the pain. Three times.

Then we grabbed our coats and scrambled out of the tepee, only Anne was more like bent-over limping. We had to figure a way to get her down the trail fast. Rick suggested the two-person carry that he learned in the Boy Scouts. He grabbed both of my wrists. I grabbed his. We lowered our arms, and Anne sat down. She put her arms around our shoulders. This worked until we came to the aspen grove and the trail narrowed. Then we took turns carrying her on our backs until we came to the cabin, where we resumed the two-arm carry down to the Mustang. We put her in the passenger side and covered her legs with my sleeping bag.

"You fellows are sweet," she said before another round of pain racked her body. We drove down the mountain as fast as we could without falling off the edge. It was slippery with the new, wet snow.

When we reached the emergency room at the Boulder hospital, we ran into some difficulties. They wouldn't admit her because she didn't have insurance. She called her parents in Illinois. It must've been four in the morning there, but parents being parents, they answered and reacted immediately. They asked to speak to the hospital administer, and in a few moments, it was settled. Anne was wheeled into a cubicle in the back of the emergency room. As she went, she asked us to call Bob. We did. He was there within ten minutes of our hanging up.

He thanked us and sat down, stared at his hands. "I really fucked up this time," he said. And that was about all that came out of his mouth except to ask about her symptoms. Our answers didn't seem to relieve his anxieties. He stared at the door she was supposed to come out of, then at the clock, and back at his hands. This went on for two hours until they wheeled her out. She had a big smile on her face, and when she saw Bob, it doubled. He leaned down and hugged her.

"I'm sorry, baby. I should've been up there to help you," he said, rubbing his eyes. He was crying. "I'm really, really sorry."

"It's not your fault," she said, patting him on the shoulder. "You had these fellows come up to watch over me. They took care of everything."

The doctor told us it wasn't labor pains. Maybe it was Braxton Hicks contractions, or more likely, pain caused by the ligaments stretching as her uterus grew.

"The baby's fine. Kicked me in the ear when I leaned down to listen." The doctor advised Anne to stay near a medical facility in case something else came up.

"You never know," he said with a worried expression.

"Maybe he's right," said Bob after the doctor left. "Maybe we can stay in Boulder until the baby is born. Then we'll go back to the mountains."

"That would be nice, but I've decided that I'm going to Peoria to have my baby at my parents' home," Anne said in a resolute tone as if she'd brook no challenges. "And I want you to come with me."

"No way would I stay with your parents. They don't even like me."

"They like you fine. All they want is for you to get a job like everyone else on earth."

"I'm not like everyone else on earth. I like the woods. I want to live with the animals. You can't tame me."

That was how I felt until reality set in. It was like when I was a kid, I wanted to be a cowboy. Then I realized that cowboys were crowded in bunkhouses when they weren't out on the range punching cattle. Sometimes they stayed up all night and didn't make much money to buy toys. That wasn't the life for me, any more than living like a mountain man was the life for Bob.

We didn't stick around for the rest of the fight. We told Bob and Anne that we needed to depart. They both thanked us. Anne put her arms around Rick and me. "If it wasn't for Bob, I'd marry the both of you."

We grinned sheepishly and tripped over ourselves walking out. It was mind-boggling, because for once, we felt a sense of well-being like we'd done something decent.

THE NEXT EVENING after work, I picked up Rick at the Red Lion. I waited in the lobby until he motioned for me to come to the kitchen. I followed him past the hot stoves and dishwashing sinks to a stairway. At the bottom of the steps, he opened a walk-in refrigerator and pointed out a rack of cheesecakes, six in all.

"What kind do you like?" he said, ticking off on his fingers. "We got strawberry, key lime, raspberry chocolate."

"I don't like cheesecake. It makes me sick," I said. I didn't know it at the time, but I was lactose intolerant.

"Then we will take this one," he said, lifting the key lime. He was in the process of lowering it into his rucksack when we heard footsteps on the stairs. Rick didn't have time to put the cake back on the rack, so he handed it to me.

It was the chef who came down the stairs to confront us. He

was a huge guy, the size of a grizzly, it seemed. He sported a long black beard accented by gray thunderbolt streaks. His eyes were as dead as the Dead Sea. He took one look at Rick and then at me. He grabbed the cake out of my hands. He placed it carefully back on the rack.

He turned to Rick.

"You're fired," he said in a soft voice as though trying to contain his rage. "Now you get the motherfuck out of here before I call the police."

Chapter Sixteen

WE DECIDED IT WAS A GOOD TIME TO DEPART FROM NEDERLAND. RICK could've found another job pushing boulders off the slopes at Eldora or something like that. But that wasn't his bag. He'd had enough of the wide-open spaces.

"It was an omen that I was fired," he explained.

"It wouldn't have been an omen if you decided not to steal the cheesecake," I retorted.

"But I did steal the cheesecake. I mean, everybody steals food from restaurants because the pay is shit. Why should I feel guilty about taking back what is mine in the first place?" he asked, pointing his finger in my face. He was upset.

"It's not yours in the first place," I countered. I was beginning to worry about his moral compass, though I was not one to criticize. I felt the same way as Rick that restaurants took too much of a cut out of your salary. But I also didn't think stealing was the answer.

"Okay, maybe I like cheesecake. I mean, what's wrong with indulging once in a while."

We were on our way up Magnolia Star Road to say goodbye to Bob. "I bet if it was caramel cake with caramel icing, you wouldn't be able to resist," he argued.

I couldn't deny that. The thought made my mouth water. Though, hopefully, I'd have had enough money scraped together to buy the cake.

We parked beside the road. Bob's Ford pickup was missing.

"Maybe he's in Boulder," said Rick. We hiked up the trail past the plywood cabin and through the aspen grove. The leaves were coming out. I could hear them tinkling in the wind. In the field beyond the grove, the wildflowers were popping up, mostly a smattering of pale-blue columbine. The tepee was there, though a few feet to the right of where it used to be. We could see the shadow of a woman moving around inside. Maybe Anne, we thought. It was the end of April, after all. It was possible she had had time to give birth and return. We were hoping for a happy ending.

A scraggly-haired man popped out of the tepee and stared at us like we were aliens from outer space, his hand on the hilt of a machete tucked in his belt.

"Hey, Grody," we said.

The woman we'd seen popped up at his side. She wore a torn paisley granny dress and an insolent look in her eyes. He put an arm around her shoulder protectively.

He checked us out for a second, more in a quizzical way, like he was trying to match us to a snapshot in his brain. "Oh yeah, Bob and Anne's friends."

We asked him where Anne was.

"Peoria. She had a baby," he said, shaking his head as if it was a calamity.

"And Bob?"

He laughed. "Where do you think the sucker is?"

"Peoria."

"Yeah."

The next day we left town. We drove by the reservoir. On the left on top of a hill was an idle steam shovel at the entrance of a gold mine. We had seen that shovel all the time we'd lived here and joked about digging for gold. But it wasn't worth it. Gold was at forty-four dollars an ounce. Maybe one day when gold was at twelve hundred, the steam shovel would roll into action.

"We'd come back," Rick joked.

We took one last look at Nederland and turned our eyes to the future. Rick and I mulled over our next move as we drove drown

Boulder Canyon one last time to the plains and east toward DC following I-70. We didn't hit another set of mountains until we reached the Appalachians near Wheeling, West Virginia. A very boring trip except that we nearly collided with a coyote in Kansas and pulled over to the side of the road in Missouri when it rained so heavily I couldn't see one foot in front of me. By the time I dropped Rick off at his mom's in Bethesda, we'd made up our minds about our next move—or rather, Rick had made up his mind, and I decided to go along.

The next day I picked Rick up and drove back to Mom's house. We parked the car. Washington was in the throes of one antiwar demonstration after another, and today was the culmination. It was called May Day. It was put together by the more radical left groups like the SDS, the Weathermen, and a group from New York called Up Against the Wall Motherfucker. The idea was that if the government didn't stop the war, then the protesters would stop the government.

Rick was more interested in scoring an ounce or two of Mary Jane from Quayle Smith. I'd had it with Quayle after the fiasco in the Shenandoah Valley. I mean, I felt sorry for the guy, and maybe I should have been more of my brother's keeper, but it was hard enough keeping myself on an even keel. The guy was a bummer, plain and simple. I convinced Rick that maybe we'd see Quayle later. The demonstration wouldn't wait.

We slogged down Connecticut Avenue toward Dupont Circle and the march. The car traffic was light, and other than a few giggly teenagers and freaks like us, there was little foot traffic as well. About half a dozen troop-carrying helicopters flew low overhead. I heard the chop of their blades, which made me feel like I was in Saigon, not DC. What reinforced that feeling was that a couple of buses sped by full of marines. I could see smoke down by the Circle, and as I was nearing Florida Avenue, I saw an overturned dumpster in the middle of the street spewing trash and a few cars parked askew as if to block traffic. Rick and I hung a right on Florida and approached the Circle via side streets until we came upon the marines, who seemed to be guarding the fountain at Dupont Circle. We scooted across Mass. Avenue to P Street and followed P to Wisconsin in Georgetown. Marching up the middle of Wisconsin was a band of thirty protesters. They held a closed-fist banner and they sang "Subterranean Homesick Blues," the Dylan song the Weathermen co-opted.

We decided to trail along with them until we came to the top of the hill near the Georgetown library. A phalanx of helmeted police blocked our path. We scooted down the street beside the library before the cops pushed forward to accost the protesters, some forcefully with a choke hold, others with an arm to the shoulder, pushing them toward a DC bus parked a block up across from the Boy's Club where I played football when I was a kid. We watched as the bus turned around and headed north.

"Where do you think they're going?" I asked.

"Jail."

We trudged down the side streets past the upscale brick row houses in Georgetown to M Street. Soldiers as far as we could see in both directions. We backed up. Headed east to the other side of the Rock Creek Parkway.

We wandered downtown, and that was where the action started to grow more intense—fewer cops, more protesters. A bunch of protesters linking arms to stop traffic. Another protester lying in front of a car while a group of six dragged a dumpster out in the street and set the trash on fire. Another cop phalanx appeared down the street, but they weren't going anywhere. They were far outnumbered. A woman in a black jacket and jeans ran down the line, stopping on occasion to kiss a cop. The third cop she came to pushed her in the face. The man next to us laughed. He was wearing a top hat that said, "Husband Liberation: No More Doghouses."

We wandered down by the waterfront near the Jefferson Memorial, where a bunch of protesters were gathered holding a black flag. A tear gas canister fell at our feet, and we raced across the street. We sat down near a tree while the cops converged in gas masks to gather up the protesters. They stuffed them into another DC bus.

"I've had enough of this," said Rick, coughing from the tear gas.

"So have I," I said.

We headed home down the sidewalk that fronted the parkway. When it ended at the Lincoln Memorial, we headed into town. We were bushed and felt lucky that we were not busted. It was a demoralizing experience. I felt that the protest movement was taking a wrong turn, and the government was taking full advantage of it. I was a pacifist, I guess. I believed, like the Beatles in *Revolution 1*, that you can count me out for destruction. I admired Martin Luther King, not so much the Black Panthers or the Weathermen. I mean, I could understand the anger. I could understand the desire to tear down things, to lie, cheat, and steal in order to make things better. But it wouldn't make things better, I was convinced. It would make things worse.

Rick and I drove out to Kirby Road a couple days later, after Rick convinced me he would die without more reefer. We knocked on Quayle's door. Mrs. Smith answered. She was thinner than ever, her face so thin and sharp featured that her eyes appeared to have grown larger. She wore a blue pants suit and her usual tired expression. Her hair was no longer in a bouffant. It was down, cut evenly around her ears in a pixie cut that made her appear waiflike. It was weird, such a transformation in a short time.

"Is Quayle in?" Rick asked.

Mrs. Smith seemed to waver like she was making up her mind about something. Her eyes darted over my face, then Rick's. I looked down her long, slender arm to where she was gripping the front doorknob so tightly her hand was turning white. She backed up and motioned for us to follow.

I knew something was up because there were packing boxes piled in the hallway. She led us to the dining room, and we sat down at the dining room table, a highly polished Queen Anne with curvy legs that ended in brass lion-claw feet.

"Would you boys like some coffee? I'm brewing some in the kitchen," she said.

"Sure," said Rick, clearly puzzled. "That would be nice."

When she left, Rick poked me in the side and nodded toward the buffet. Leaning against the wall were two flags folded in triangles. Perfectly folded. We could see both the blue field and the stars and the red and white stripes. I recalled that many moons ago Quayle showed us one of the flags that had been draped over his father's coffin. We both guessed the significance of the other.

Mrs. Smith returned from the kitchen balancing a silver tray. She nearly dropped the tray when she saw us staring at the flags. We hurried to her aid. We sat down. She poured us coffee then offered us cream and sugar and Scottish shortbread cookies.

She ran her hand through her hair and sucked in her breath nervously. I could see the tendons in her long, thin neck stand out. "Well, boys," she said after we'd sipped some coffee and taken a few nibbles of cookie, "you saw the flags."

"Yes," we said, but we couldn't be absolutely sure that what we surmised was true. So, I posed as generic a question as I could think of.

"What happened?"

She seemed as reticent as we were to approach the subject directly, so she said, "I am selling the house and moving to Chicago, where I plan to buy a condominium near where Quayle's sister and her family live. They have two girls. I imagine I will be doing a lot of babysitting. It will be nice to get back to the simple pleasures of life."

Since we were not parents—or grandparents, for that matter—we knew nothing about the simple pleasures she spoke of. We remained flummoxed.

"You want to know what happened to Quayle," she said, heaving a sigh. She leaned closer to us. "About two days after he returned from the camping trip you boys went on, Thumper broke loose. The dog ran down to Greentree, where he was run over by a gravel truck. He died instantly."

She looked straight at me again with those big, dark eyes that seemed so innocent with her new pixie haircut.

"The first thing that happened was that Quayle lost his father," she said in an edgy voice. "Then Thumper. My son went crazy. He wrapped his fingers around my throat and tried to choke me as if it was all my fault. I felt that I didn't have any choice. I consulted a psychiatrist at a hospital, and he agreed that they would take him under observation. Two weeks after they picked him up, he died."

She gazed at us both as if gauging how we were taking this. She was shaking imperceptibly, but I could tell—like an earthquake so low on the Richter scale that it barely rattled the dishes.

We waited for the rest of the story, but it didn't come. We found out later from a friend of Quayle's from high school that he didn't die two weeks after he was admitted but on the very same night when he went to the bathroom by himself. He undid his belt, slid it around his neck, and hung himself from a pipe above the bathroom stall.

Chapter Seventeen

WHAT RICK HAD IN MIND FOR US WAS AN EPIC JOURNEY DOWN A RIVER, like Huckleberry Finn, though it wasn't going to be the Mississippi. We drove across the Potomac on Chain Bridge because we didn't care to have a run-in with the Metro Police, the Capitol Police, the Park Police, the Secret Service, the FBI, the CIA—you name it. We were paranoid. Most of the May Day protesters had been arrested. Kept in holding cells and behind chain-link fences outside RFK Stadium. No use taking chances. We were headed southeast to Alexandria, where they sold the topographical maps we needed in a nondescript government building on Ord Street. We were bummed out thinking of poor, dead Quayle and his sad mother and of Amerika, as we spelled it, barrel-assing down the road to fascism. I turned on WHFS, the local rock station, and what came out was Crosby, Stills, Nash, and Young singing "Ohio." Though it referred to the Kent State Massacre, we thought, hey, this was the same deal in a way. Our spirits were raised, and we started singing along with the music about the tin soldiers and Nixon scurrying after us like we were the troublemakers. We parked in a government lot and slogged inside the topo building. We were confronted with row after row of maps. The river Rick wanted to float down was in Oregon.

"Why Oregon?" I asked.

"Pie's staying in San Francisco this summer. We'll float down the river in a rubber raft then hitch down to meet her."

"How about the Mustang?"

"We don't have enough money for gas. So, we'll hitch."

"We're going to hitch across the country carrying a raft?" I asked, incredulous.

"It'll be deflated," said Rick, and that was as far as we got. Rick found a map for the Prineville, Oregon area, where we planned to start our trip. Then a larger one that showed Prineville all the way up to the Columbia River.

"The idea," said Rick, tracing a line with his finger, "is to float the raft down the Crooked River from Prineville to the Deschutes to the Columbia, past Portland to the Pacific."

I looked at the map. "It's two hundred miles from Prineville to the Columbia, and that's in a straight line. Why do you think they call it the Crooked? The Deschutes is no better. How fast do you think we'll be moving?"

"Oh, let's say an average of four miles an hour."

"Okay," I said, nodding. "Let's say, with all the twists and turns, it's three times two hundred to get to the Columbia and another hundred to reach Portland. Let's say we travel ten hours a day. How long will that take us?"

"Forty days," said Rick, calculating in his head. "If we arrived in Prineville the beginning of July, then we'd have enough time to hitchhike down to San Francisco."

"Yeah," I said, "sounds right. That's if nothing happens like it rains forty days and forty nights." I pointed at a huge lake on the map where the Crooked and the Deschutes came together. "What if there's a dam there?"

"We'll portage. Maybe it'll take an extra day or two. We'll still make it in time to see Pie."

We drove home and thought about what to do next. We needed to purchase two backpacks, a collapsible rubber raft, an inner tube, and some wood to build a frame. The inner tube would float behind the raft. We would top the inner tube with the wood frame where we would stash our gear in plastic bags so it wouldn't get wet. Then we'd tie it all down with rope. We planned to carry everything on our backs: the deflated raft, two oars, an inner tube, the frame, three sets of clothes, poncho, tarp, sweater, freeze-dried food, utensils, Dr. Bronner's soap, and such, plus a fly-fishing rod to catch fish in the river.

But first we needed to make some money so we could pay for all our gear and have enough left over so we wouldn't starve. Mom was moving to an apartment on Connecticut Avenue, and she thought it would be cheaper to have us help her pack everything up. She planned to move some of the stuff to her apartment and some to storage, and the rest would go to my sister, Susan, who was moving her family to Philadelphia.

My step-grandmother arrived from Delray Beach (where she wintered with her country club friends) at the very moment that we were leaving for our epic journey. Mom didn't like the idea of our hitchhiking. She suggested that we ride with her and Nonna as far as Urbana, Ohio, my parents' hometown and where Nonna lived.

When Mom asked her if we could come along, she protested. "I don't want any dirty, filthy hippies in my car." She drove a spotless, black Buick Electra that reminded me of a hearse.

Mom begged long and hard until Nonna relented. "I'm not taking them into town. We'll let them off on the highway." She was not a nice lady. Susan and I used to call her the Wicked Witch of the Midwest and wished that a house would drop on her.

We started on the first leg of the journey. Mom drove while Nonna bantered on and on about how she hated hippies and everything else.

"How often do you take a bath?" she asked Rick.

"Every other day."

"Your hair looks dirty."

"I washed it this morning."

"The way it's bunched up on your head," she said, making a circle gesture like a halo over her head, "makes you look like a Negro. What do they call it?"

"Afro," I said.

"Yes, your hair is so curly you must have some Negro blood."

"If I did, I'd be proud of it," he said, flashing a smile at me.

"Oh, how disgusting," she said, making a face. "When I was little, the Negroes worked in the country club. Now they want to join it."

We were only as far as Frederick, forty miles northwest of Washington.

"The world is a mess," she said as we passed through Hagerstown and looked at all the dilapidated row houses. "It used to be that everybody knew where they belonged. The women knew they belonged at home. The men knew they belonged at work. The Negros knew they belonged in a place like this."

She waved her hands at the row houses. I didn't see one "Negro."

"Now everything is mixed. People can do whatever they want."

"It's says in the Constitution that people have the right to do whatever they want as long as they don't infringe on other people's rights," I said, egging her on.

"Well, they're infringing on my rights. I have the right to peace and quiet. I have the right not to be afraid of every hippie and Negro who comes along. I have the right not to be disgusted by homosexuals who take their shirts off in public parks like I saw in Florida. Hugging each other."

Mom said it was impossible to drive with all the racket in the car. She turned on the radio to a classical station, and we tried to relax.

After a lunch break, the old bag took over the driving chores. She drove at fifty in a seventy-mile-an-hour speed zone. She hugged the far-right lane the whole time, and though I hated feeling cars come up fast behind us and then whip around us, sometimes cutting it close to exit off the highway, at least she wasn't blocking up the passing lanes. She lit into a conversation about Uncle Tom, my dad's brother. "He was low-class. Grew up on the poor side of the town next to the Negros. Always caused trouble. Not like your dad. Your dad was well-behaved."

"I remember one time on Betty's birthday, he came to the back door of the house and gave her a present even though he wasn't invited to the party."

"Why wasn't he invited to the party?"

"Well, you know, he was poor. And some of his relatives were Catholics. The Kerns."

"Yes, I know."

"He'd be uncomfortable at our parties," she said.

Nonna went on in this vein all the way to the Urbana exit. The truth was that she didn't like my dad either until he married Mom. I guess he was acceptable once he married up into the upper strata of Urbana society. Whatever it was, we were happy to leave her foul-mouthed presence, though we thanked her profusely as we clambered out of the car with our gear.

Mom didn't want me to leave. She hugged me goodbye and told me to be careful. There were tears in her eyes that spooked me. Was I going to get run over on my way west?

I waved to her as I went to the other ramp heading west.

We watched them, Nonna still glowering impatiently and Mom still looking sad, drive off and disappear over a hill.

"I feel sorry for your mom," said Rick.

"Yeah, she's been cursed," I agreed as we stuck out our thumbs.

I DON'T REMEMBER many of the rides, but they were usually from fellow freaks in VW vans or such. We had an easier time, I think, because of the gear we were toting. Everyone wanted to know what we were up to, and when we told them, they seemed starry-eyed as if they wished they could join us—except for two long-haired cowboy types in beat-up straw hats in Gillette, Wyoming. We were camped out in a park when it started raining. The two cowboys must've taken pity on us because they pulled up in their pickup and offered to take us to their apartment. They introduced themselves as Glen and Ken, buddies since childhood. They smoked dope with us. They wanted to know what was happening in the world.

Glen said, "We been stuck here all of our lives."

"Why don't you leave?" I asked.

"I'm getting married in September," said Ken.

"For me, it's family," said Glen. "Besides, where would I go?"

The cowboys asked us about our raft. Rick told him we were going to do a float trip down a river in Oregon and that we had carried the raft with us all the way from Washington, DC.

"Don't you have any rivers back east?" asked Ken. They both found this extremely amusing, patted us on the back, and snickered.

"You boys are nuttier than we are," said Glen. We joined in the snickering, though we weren't sure what was so humorous. Maybe it was the dope that activated our funny bones, as it often did.

They took us out to the highway in the wee hours of the morning before they headed off to work. They weren't cowboys. They were coal miners.

In western Idaho a couple of days later, we were picked up by two brothers, teenagers who took us to their parents' ranch home in a suburb outside Boise. Their parents were away, and they were having a party. We were the main attraction, a couple of beat-up hippies on the road like Kerouac and Cassidy, though Rick saw us as more like Lewis and Clark. We seemed to have arrived two hundred years too late.

By the time we made the bridge over the Crooked River late in the afternoon a day later, we were all exhausted. We stored our gear in the nearby woods and slid down the embankment to the water.

"Shit," said Rick, looking down at the brown water. "We fucked up."

The river didn't appear to have much of a current. It was hard to tell whether it flowed north to the Columbia or south to God knew where.

"It'll take us years to get down this river." He shook his head. "Besides, the water's dirty. We might as well float down the Potomac."

"Maybe it will get better once we're outside Prineville."

"Maybe so," said Rick.

The next morning, I trucked into town to buy a steak, four cans of beans, carrots, water, booze, Twinkies, and a ton of beef jerky. I packed all the goods in an empty rucksack and headed back.

It was the Fourth of July, and all the flags were out hanging from the lampposts. The American flag and the state flag. The Oregon flag had a gold beaver on one side and the state seal on the other, but I noticed one that didn't have the state seal but a hammer and sickle. I put down my ruck. I shimmied up the lamppost and grabbed the flag. I tossed the pole in some bushes, folded the flag, and tucked it in the rucksack. It would be the flag for our boat, I thought. I looked around to see if anyone was watching. But they were all down the road at a park at what looked like a Fourth of July carnival.

I wandered over there and sat in the stands. On the other side of a fence, ladies were slinging cast-iron skillets. The judges measured the distance flung and yelled the number to a fellow at a card table who kept the calculations. One small lady, no more than five-two, in rolled-up jeans and a red T-shirt that said, "Wilco Farm Stores," wound up and flung the skillet so far that everyone in the crowd gasped. Someone poked me in the side, and I turned my head.

"You think you could fling a skillet that far?" asked a young lady. She couldn't have been more than twenty.

"I doubt it," I said, checking her out. She was dark-skinned, with thick eyebrows, shiny, dark eyes, and long, silky hair tied in a ponytail.

"She's my cousin," she said, pointing at the skillet thrower who was accepting the blue ribbon from the judges and jumping up and down. "She wins every year."

I wandered into a huge barn and checked out the prize roosters with ribbons hanging from their cages. Brahma, Barbu d'Uccle, Welsummer, Langshan, and Cochin roosters, all different colors—white, black, yellow, green—but all with red coxcombs and beady black eyes waiting for me to stick my finger in their cage to peck it off.

"You like roosters," said a voice from behind me. It was Black Eyes.

I made a clucking noise. "They're okay."

She laughed. Put her hand in mine. We wandered through the barn past the ducks, the bunnies, the sheep, the goats, the miniature horses to a long line of carnival games, food, and crafts on either side of a dirt path. She asked me to win her a prize. I did, a miniature panda at the ring toss. She asked me if I'd like to go for a walk in the woods with her.

"Sure," I said. We followed a path through the parking lot to a trail that went through the woods. At the first bend in the trail, we jumped behind some bushes and sat down where we couldn't be seen. She kissed me, and I kissed her back, a long sloppy, passionate one.

"Yum," she said, wiping her mouth. "That was a good one."

"How old are you?" I asked, overcome by a sudden twinge of guilt and fear that the townspeople might hang me from the nearest lamppost if she was found out.

"Twenty-two," she said. She reached in her purse and handed me her driver's license. "See?"

"Lolita Jackson," I said, handing back her license.

"They call me Lo."

"Like the girl in the book."

"What book?" She tapped her chin and smiled. "You're a college boy, aren't you?"

"Was," I said, grinning sheepishly. "Graduated three years ago."

"I work at the Wilco Farm Store with my cousin," said Lo, "but maybe one day I'll attend the University of Oregon. That's my wish. I don't want to get married yet."

She leaned into me, and we kissed but in a more passionate way to the point that I reached in her blouse and fondled her breasts. I kissed her neck, her shoulder, loosened her bra strap, and nibbled

her breasts. She ran her hands through my hair and made little coo-
ing noises I found encouraging. I reached down between her legs.

"No, not that." She pushed my hand away.

"I'm sorry," I said.

"It's okay. Nobody's perfect."

I didn't touch her between the legs again, but we continued our
passionate groping until she said she had to leave.

"Where you going?" I asked, leaning up on my elbow and looking
in her eyes.

"Church. It's Sunday, you know. But I'll be back tonight for the
fireworks." She reached in her purse, pulled out a notebook, scribbled on a page, and handed the page to me. "That's my number. Call
me. You're a gentleman. Not like most of the creeps around here."

I watched as she disappeared around the bend in the path like
an angel gliding on air. That was my image, but she was not an
angel, and I was not a gentleman. I hate to think what those creeps
were like. I sort of daydreamed for a minute. Then I remembered
what I was up to. I checked my watch. Noon. Rick was going to be
pissed. I slung the rucksack over my shoulder and hustled back to
the carnival.

I came to a food stand that was selling funnel cakes sprinkled
with confectionary sugar and cinnamon. I purchased two. I wrapped
up one and ate the other as I walked down the road to the bridge.

I slid down the embankment, and there was Rick sitting on our
fully inflated raft, scowling. "Where the fuck you been?" he growled.

"I met a woman."

"Bullshit."

I reached in my pocket and handed him the piece of paper that
Lo had written on.

He looked at it, crumpled it up, and threw it on the ground.
"Okay, I believe you. You met a woman."

I could see he was still pissed, so I pulled out the Oregon flag
with the hammer and sickle on it.

"Our raft flag," I said.

"Nice." He crossed his arms and stared up at a car that was passing over the bridge as if he could care less.

So I reached in the rucksack and pulled out the funnel cake.

Rick stared at the cake as if he couldn't make up his mind. "For me?"

"For you," I said.

He grabbed the funnel cake. Scarfed it down. Picked the crumbs off his beard and mustache.

"Nice," he said.

Chapter Eighteen

THE FIRST NIGHT WE CAMPED OUT IN A COW PASTURE. WE HAD TRAVeled six hours. The water was clearer the farther we moved from Prineville. The current picked up, though early on, it was hard paddling. We figured we were about twelve miles into the trip. Rick had a compass, and he found out where we were by comparing the compass reading to the topo map. He told me that in a day we should reach hilly country, probably with more vegetation because it was green on the map. The area we passed through today was white, the high desert. That meant it got more water than, let's say, Death Valley. Mostly what we saw during the day were cows and more cows and one lonely predator slinking along as if waiting to be shot by a cowboy. As to vegetation, there was mesquite and more mesquite and a few scabby trees near the river. We pulled up next to a couple of those scabby trees and made camp. We searched for firewood. It was almost as hard to find here as it was in Mexico. We heard that Indians started fires with buffalo chips. We didn't have any buffalo chips, but we had plenty of cow pies.

At the far end of the pasture was a fence where all the cows congregated, heads down, munching grass. On the other side of the fence was a road. A car drove by about every half hour. We were relatively isolated. It was nearing twilight when we managed to get enough wood together to start a fire. We cooked the steak. This was to be our last good meal before we headed into the wilderness. We checked out the cows, but they seemed unworried that we were cooking one of their own.

We doused our fire and climbed into our sleeping bags. We put a tarp over the bag in case it got wet during the night (fat chance), lay back, and checked the night sky. The stars were out in profusion. We could see the swirl of the Milky Way like an enormous drain sucking in the stars.

I was on the verge of falling asleep when I heard the rumbling of a truck idling on the other side of the fence. I turned my head. The headlights of the truck outlined the cows. They were shifting about. Casting long shadows. Mooing frantically. The driver turned off the engine and doused the lights. I was thinking cattle rustlers, but of course, this wasn't the nineteenth century or a TV cowboy movie. Then I heard some tittering sounds. Teenagers. And I thought cow tipping, but that was an urban legend. You can't tip over a twelve-hundred-pound cow even if it was asleep. Then I saw the flare of a match followed by the *boom-boom-boom* of a long string of firecrackers they tossed over the fence amid the restless cows. The cows hesitated for a moment as if not quite sure what to think. Then the foremost cow took off down the fence line. The others followed, then the teenagers. They lit another string of firecrackers. The cows took off. The teenagers followed. Back and forth six times before they grew bored and screeched off in the truck to their next prank.

I imagined this wasn't the first time that they had bothered the cows and that the cows were grateful. They needed entertainment as well. I was a city boy and couldn't imagine the ennui I would suffer from in a rural area like this where there were not so many rock concerts, museums, movie theaters, and restaurants. No professional sports. Not as much thinking out of the box. My dad once told me that he was glad to leave his small town of Urbana because no matter how successful he turned out to be, he'd still be the poor boy who grew up on the wrong side of the tracks. Maybe that was why one of the cowboys from Gillette had said, "We been *stuck* here all of our lives."

We settled back down in our sleeping bags. We checked out the swirl of the Milky Way again, and Rick started to lecture me about black holes. Giant stars that explode and suck in all the energy so that even light cannot escape, he said.

I pretended like I didn't know this.

"Do you know that there may be a black hole at the center of our galaxy? About the size of a large ball."

"Is that why the Milky Way is in a swirl? We're being sucked into the black hole?"

"No, no, no," said Rick, scratching his head. "A black hole is a huge mass of energy with a huge gravitational pull. Like, the one in our galaxy has the pull of four million suns. Yet our galaxy is so much huger that only the closest stars can be sucked into a black hole. Not the Earth. Too far away."

"Well, couldn't our sun explode one day and turn into a black hole?"

"No, it will probably explode one day, but it won't turn into a black hole. Only supernovas do that."

"That's reassuring," I said.

We lay there quiet for a moment, watching a shooting star leave a trail of smoke behind it before it disappeared on the horizon. Rick sighed. "Beautiful."

The next morning, we packed up and ate on the run. Beef jerky. Hostess Twinkies. We waved goodbye to the cows who wandered over to our camp as soon as we left. The current picked up. We saw ripples on the water caused by a light breeze coming in from the west. Rick pulled out his fly rod and cast it a few times. Not even a bite. We looked into the water, which reflected the glare of the sun, though in spots I could see the bottom. I don't imagine it was deeper than five feet. Fortunately, we brought along sunglasses and wide-brimmed hats because the sun was beginning to beat down on us. It was hot, maybe in the nineties, and the breeze didn't help much.

We were paddling along lazily, and Rick kept asking me about that woman I had picked up in Prineville. What did she look like? Was she nice? Did you screw her? I told him it was she who picked me up at the skillet toss. I told him what she looked like.

"Sounds like she was Mexican," he said, smiling, "a beautiful señorita. Oh, I'd love to sleep with a beautiful señorita."

"I don't know if she was a señorita. Her last name was Jackson, and she didn't have an accent or anything."

"Her mother could've been Mexican."

"Her mother could've been Nez Perce as far as I know."

We went on like this for a while, and then he got into the sex thing. I refused to enlighten him in any way.

Along the banks of the river, we saw what looked like a bull. A big, beefy, brown guy with a tuft of hair on his forehead and a short tail that he was swishing like a cat swishes its tail when it's angry. He gave us the evil eye, and I thought there was a chance he might charge, but he couldn't get too far in the deeper water. We hugged the right bank, away from him.

When we got past the bull, Rick resumed talking about women, only it was Rose with the almond eyes and curly black hair in the crowded apartment on Twenty-Fourth Street in Boulder. The one who dislocated my shoulder and ran away.

"Remember I told you that I got laid on New Year's Eve," he said, grinning as he paddled the raft and checked back at me. "It was Rose, the one who was making the moves on you in our apartment."

"You're kidding!" I exclaimed in an incredulous tone. "Why do you think I want to know that?"

"I don't know. I thought it was funny, a coincidence that she was in Denver, I guess."

I could tell by the smirk that wasn't it at all.

I flattened my paddle and slapped it against the water. The water sprayed in his face, wiping off the smirk.

"What's the idea?" he sputtered.

"What the fuck you think the idea is?" I sprayed him with water again.

He flattened his paddle and sprayed back. We splashed back and forth several times as we drifted around a bend in the river toward shore. That was when we came face-to-face with the cowboy, only he didn't see us at first. He was sitting at the bottom of a small hill in a lawn chair in a plaid bathing suit, cowboy hat, and sunglasses, a bottle of bourbon and one of suntan oil by his side. He was reading the Sunday comics, I thought, because he was laughing to himself.

"That Beetle Bailey," he said as he put down the paper. He stared at us for a few minutes as if he was seeing a mirage. Then he slowly pushed himself up from his chair, wandered over to us casually as if we were an everyday occurrence, and bent down. He grabbed a blade of grass and stuck it in his mouth.

"Who the Sam Hill are you?" He was an older man with a face the texture of leather and mud-gray eyes.

We told him our names and that we were floating down the Crooked to the Columbia River. We asked him how long it would take.

"Six weeks, maybe longer," he said, grinning. "You'll be doing more walking than floating."

He invited us to come ashore and take a snort of his bourbon. We did. It tasted good and burned the throat. He said this was his ranch, and it ended right there. He pointed at a barbed wire fence over the river.

"You lift the fence carefully lest you blow a hole in that tiny yellow raft of yours."

"We'll be careful," said Rick.

"I got two boys about your age. They'd probably be doing the same thing as you if I hadn't sent them to cow college in Corvallis."

We didn't know if this was a form of criticism, because he just smiled kindly.

He offered another nip, which we took gratefully. We thanked him and headed back to the raft.

He returned to his lawn chair. "You boys be careful." He waved at us. "Watch out for the sharks."

"What sharks?" asked Rick as we slid the raft under the barbed wire.

"The sharks that come up the Columbia River to feed on the salmon. They could feed on you."

"Thanks for telling us," Rick waved, turning to me. "That guy's full of shit."

We went around another bend in the river, and we were alone again.

In the distance, we glimpsed the hills that Rick had pointed out on the topo, only they seemed much steeper than I imagined. Like half-hill, half-rocky cliffs climbing up about one hundred feet at a forty-five-degree angle. It reminded me of the mesas in the southwest because they were flat on top. The current picked up a few notches. The river widened. We could see an opening between the hills where the river seemed to be flowing. We thought about pulling over to scout things out before we went into what we thought might be a canyon.

"I mean, maybe it's a canyon. Maybe it isn't," said Rick. He was looking at the topo map while I steered the raft. The mule that was supposed to follow directly behind us was coming up even, bumping the side of the raft. The current seemed to move backward and sideways, slowing our progress. No way I'd jump in that river. May have an undertow. I felt a knot in my stomach, unwarranted fear, as it turned out, because as soon as we made the gap between the hills, we lost the crosscurrent. The current sped up, but it wasn't the four miles an hour that we needed to keep on schedule. To our left was a rocky shore with knee-high grass and, on one of the rocks at the water's edge, a long, skinny creature, the wet fur reflecting the light from the sun.

"What's that?" I pointed out to Rick. The creature dived into the water and swam along in our direction as if it were curious to see who we were.

"It's a river otter," exclaimed Rick as it swam no more than five feet away before it turned and went back to shore.

"You're right," I said, looking at its pointy head. I had seen them swimming in a glass enclosure at the National Zoo in DC maybe a hundred times when I was a kid.

"Damn," said Rick, grinning happily. This was his kind of place, I could tell. Mine too.

We were coming around a bend in the river when we heard a roaring sound. We looked to the right at a waterfall cascading maybe a hundred feet off a cliff and, above the spray of the falls, a tiny rainbow. And above that, a huge bird of some sort spread its wings. It dipped down to check us out. I could see a white chest with gray spots, gray wings, and a pointed flat head like a snake.

"That's not an eagle," I said.

"Probably a falcon," said Rick as a flock of about twenty geese or ducks flew over us in perfect formation. The falcon swerved away.

"Do falcons eat ducks?" I asked.

"How do you know those are ducks? They could be carrier pigeons," said Rick.

They were gray.

"Carrier pigeons are extinct."

"Bullshit."

I knew it was true because I'd read it somewhere. They had died out for the most part after World War I, when they were used to carry messages. In the days before the west was settled, there were so many carrier pigeons they darkened the skies when they flew over.

"Look there," said Rick, pointing to the opposite shore at what looked like a weeping willow tree high up on a hill overlooking the river. Below the tree was a rock, and on the rock a large, yellow-colored animal stared down at us.

"A cougar," insisted Rick.

"Bullshit." It could've been a bear. It could've been a cow, though

I'd never seen a cow lounging on a rock, or a large dog, maybe a coyote, but a cougar? They were nearly as extinct as the carrier pigeon.

"I wish I had my binoculars," said Rick.

I squinted, and sure enough, the creature was licking its paws and swishing its tail like a kitty would. I think I even saw whiskers and sharp teeth as it snarled. Did it snarl?

Rick and I were so preoccupied that we didn't notice that, as the roar of the waterfall receded, another ominous roar downriver took its place. The current picked up considerably. We rounded a bend.

In front of us, we saw two huge pipes coming out of pumping stations to the flat plateau above us. They were sucking the water out of the river for irrigation, and what they left behind was a large number of rocks of all shapes and sizes and not as much water. We had to think fast. We were heading to the right of an immense rock that stuck four feet above water. The water around the rock was a frothing maelstrom that we wanted to avoid. We also wanted to avoid going straight because what we saw was more frothing water and, beyond that, thin air like there was a drop-off, maybe a waterfall. No telling how far it dropped and what was at the bottom. More rocks? We tried to change course, making for a chute four feet wide that dropped a couple feet into what seemed like a protected pool of water, an eddy that swirled gently around and around. Beyond the eddy was a sand beach. We moved sideways, parallel to the big rock, jamming our paddles in the water as deep as we could and trying to push forward toward the chute. But we seemed to be standing still. Then Rick's paddle broke, and the raft turned toward the rock. Rick was on his knees, and the second before we smashed against the rock, he sprang onto it. Fortunately, there were some handholds. He managed to pull himself up.

The raft folded beneath me and slid over to the left, carried by the mule. But I didn't see that because I was underwater. I was caught in a hydraulic, I found out later, water that spins around and around against a rock like in the spinning cycle of a washing machine, only it was not on a timer. I could drown and spin around like that forever.

I hit the bottom of the rock and kicked off upstream. As soon as I came to the surface, I kicked sideways and tried to swim toward the chute, but the hydraulic had me in its grip. Before I went down the second time, I saw Rick reaching out his hand with a terrified grimace. He touched one of my fingers, but then I was underwater. I didn't have the momentum I had before. I wasn't able to push off. Instead, I crashed against the rock, feeling myself heading toward unconsciousness as much from the blow as from lack of air. On my way up the second time, I grabbed at a fistful of empty air, then I slammed against the rock again and reached up as high as I could. I missed Rick's hand and grabbed his belt. As I slid down to the water, his pants slid down to his ankles. He grabbed me by the wrist and somehow directed my hand to the same notch he had used to pull himself up. I was losing strength and breathing hard the wonderful air that I had been denied. I felt so dizzy that Rick had to lift me all the way up, and when I reached the top of the rock, I clung to it like shit to a shovel.

Chapter Nineteen

"Thanks, Rick, for saving my life," I said as we crawled off the rock into the calm part of the river where the mule was turned upside-down with all our possessions underwater.

"I don't think I exactly saved your life," said Rick the Modest as we pulled the wet stuff out of the trash bag and dried it on the beach. "I mean, I had to grab your hand, or you'd drag me into the river with you."

We walked down to the end of the beach to scout the river, and all we saw was white water, sharp rocks, and sheer cliffs on both sides.

"I don't think we're going down that," I said. Rick agreed, and furthermore, he thought we should forget the whole thing. The cowboy was right: we'd probably do more walking than floating to the Columbia.

"It was a harebrained scheme in the first place," he said, "but how was I to know there was a pumping station sucking out all the water? It didn't show on the topo map."

We packed up our gear after it dried. It wasn't that wet, thanks to the plastic bags. We deflated the inner tube and raft. I suggested we leave them there, but Rick was a Boy Scout. We'd pack everything out. We dragged our stuff up the steep, rocky slope, and by the time we reached the top, we were exhausted. We sat down to catch our breath and sip some water from our canteen. We were next to a dirt road.

"I think we should head north," I said, pointing down the road where it curved into the woods. One of the things that we lost when the raft tipped over was the topo map, so there was no telling if I was right, though Rick agreed.

"My guess, if we go south, we'll end up at a farmer's place. I mean, that's why they pump the water up, for his crops," he said, nodding thoughtfully. "And north is where the main road would be, or there wouldn't be a dirt road here heading north."

"Yeah, I get what you mean," I said.

A big yellow dog wandered out of the woods and nudged me in the shoulder. I jumped about a mile thinking it might be the cougar Rick had pointed out on the rock. I turned. The dog had a green tennis ball in its mouth. The dog dropped it in front of its paws. I picked it up and threw it. The dog raced after the ball. Retrieved it and dropped it at my feet. Our ball game went on for about ten minutes, and then Rick wanted to leave. We lifted our packs and headed north. I looked back one more time at the big yellow dog. It sat on its haunches in the middle of the road, the ball in his mouth, whining.

"Some cougar," I said.

We trudged a mile to a two-lane road that led up to the mountains. In the distance, snow-capped Mount Hood glistened in the sun. We waited an hour. Only two cars and three lumber trucks passed us by, the third one scaring us to death with its diesel whistle blaring as it blew past. Then a cream-colored convertible with red interior pulled up in front of us. We tossed our gear in back and jumped in front with a platinum blond. Her hair was dyed, the dark roots creeping up like kudzu.

"Where you going?" she asked in a husky voice. She was wearing rolled-up jeans and a plaid shirt opened in the front so I could see her cleavage. She was hot.

"To the coast. Route One-oh-one."

"I'll take you as far as Eugene."

Rick and I looked at each other like we were both in love and wondering who would get the upper hand. Neither of us, as it turned out. Her name was Dolly. She was a student at the University of Oregon and a maniacal driver. She raced up and down the mountains at breakneck speed, taking corners too fast, nearly running into Douglas firs that would've smashed her convertible and our bodies as well. But the worst thing she did was pass the lumber trucks. She'd creep up to them slowly until I could see the logs swaying from side to side and threatening to topple on our car. Then she'd pull out and gun the engine. It didn't matter if it was a solid or a broken line. I remember speeding around a corner as we were passing a truck while another was coming in the opposite direction, blaring its horn. She pulled in with an inch to spare.

"Sorry, guys. I'm late for an exam."

We were so spooked by this woman that we looked at each other and wondered who was going to tell her to pull over. We'd find another ride. Neither of us, as it turned out.

For one thing, we couldn't get a word in edgewise. This was familiar in our hitchhiking experience. The drivers were lonely or tired and wanted to stay awake. So they ran at the mouth.

Dolly's commentary had to do with how she loved to spearfish for salmon. That was why she was late for the exam. She had been fishing with her dad.

"Used to be," she said as we were coming out of the mountains into a valley, "that you could walk across the Columbia River on the backs of salmon. But that was before the white man came."

"What are you, an Indian?" asked Rick.

"No, but I'm not a white man."

She pulled in front of a bungalow on a tree-lined street in Eugene and raced inside. We took our gear out of the back seat and were about to head off when Dolly stopped us.

"Hey, you can spend the night at my place. My roommates won't mind." She jumped into the car and waved. "The door's open."

We slogged inside and cleared a place in the corner of the living room. The truth was we were dog tired. We spread out our sleeping bags and lay down on top, not even bothering to take off our shoes. We fell asleep almost instantly, even though it was four in the afternoon.

The next morning, Dolly's roommates invited us for breakfast, Mickey Mouse waffles made in a special waffle maker they had in their kitchen. In exchange, we gave them the Oregon flag with a gold beaver on one side and the hammer and sickle on the other, which they loved, and our much-damaged river raft, which they didn't. We asked them what happened to the maniacal driver.

"Oh, she drove back home after the exam. Don't expect we'll see her until the fall."

Within an hour, we were out on the highway with our thumbs stuck out. I don't remember any of the rides, but the last one let us off south of Coos Bay near a dirt road that led down a hill to a cove by the ocean. A huge rock about ten feet high curved around protecting the cove from the cold wind that blew off the water. Clinging to the rock were crustaceans of some sort. I pointed them out to Rick.

He stared at them for a second and snapped his fingers. "I got an idea."

He rummaged through his backpack and came out with a small hunting knife and a plastic baggy. He handed me the baggy.

"Follow me," he said.

We went to the end of the beach and climbed the rock. The waves crashed below us, sending up a fine mist that coated the rock. It was slippery. I got down on my hands and knees to follow Rick, who was still standing. He slipped and almost fell before he got down on his hands and knees to dig at the crustaceans.

"Mussels," he called them as he put them one by one into the baggy until we got about ten.

"So, what's your idea?" I asked as we jumped off the rock.

"You'll see." We headed over to his pack. He pulled out his fishing rod.

"You're going to fish in the ocean with a freshwater fly rod?"

"No harm trying." He cut open the shell, removed the mussel inside, and baited the hook.

He cast about four times near the rock. Lost the bait. Opened another shell. And on the fifth caught a red snapper.

"You're shitting me," I said.

He baited the hook again. Took him three more casts to catch another snapper. The next cast, another one.

"We hit the motherlode," I said as I searched for firewood. That wasn't difficult with all the driftwood tangled in the brush on the hill. I built a fire and cut two green sticks I didn't think would burn for skewers. Rick gutted the snapper and tossed the waste in the ocean. We sat on our haunches to watch them cook. That was when the cop came down the hill.

He was an older guy with a white mustache and thick glasses, sergeant's stripes and a patch that said, "Coos County Sheriff's Department," on his sleeve. He stood beside us with his hands behind his back at parade rest.

"You can't fish here," he said, pointing up the hill. "There's a sign up there—I know it's hidden behind some bushes, but it says, 'NO FISHING.'"

"Sorry, Sergeant," I said, looking up at him, but his eyes had wandered over to the five fish lined up in a row then over to Rick's fishing rod.

"You mean you caught all those fish with a freshwater fly rod?"

"That's the only one we had, sir," said Rick. He told the cop about rafting down the Crooked River.

"I suspect you were below the dam. I wouldn't fish below the dam," he said, then turned serious again. "You have a fishing license?"

"No, sir."

"I could haul you in, you know," he said, rubbing his chin, "but you know, when I was a kid, I used to fish here, and I didn't have a license."

We both looked up at him in amazement, a policeman who almost seemed human. Maybe he was trying to trick us. Looking for dope or something.

"You fellows wait here," he said, clambering up the hill. We finished cooking the first two snappers, set them aside, and started on the next two before he stumbled back down the hill with a couple of lemons and Chesapeake Bay seasoning.

"Never can tell when you need this," he said as he bent over to season the cooked fish. We divided the fish in three equal portions.

"That's really tasty," said the sergeant, cleaning his fingers with a handkerchief and stuffing it back in his side pocket. "Now, you young fellows finish cooking your fish. You may not eat it all, but you'll dip into it on down the road."

We asked him if he wanted another snapper.

"No, thanks. But I don't want you fishing anymore. When you finish the cooking, put out the fire." He went up the hill.

And we went back to our cooking, and when we finished, we put out the fire. He had left the seasoning and lemons behind.

"I don't get it," said Rick, "a friendly cop. He didn't want to bust us or anything."

"Maybe it's because he's near retirement."

A couple days later, we camped out by the freeway behind the bushes in somebody's backyard. In the morning after some moist, tasty snapper and a Twinkie each, we walked to the ramp that led down to the freeway and stuck out our thumbs. Within about five minutes, a motorcycle cop pulled up. He wanted to see our driver's licenses.

"Hey, Greene," he yelled after looking at mine.

"My name isn't Greene. It's Richards."

"Says here Greene," he said pointing at the license. He was doing a slow burn, so I didn't enlighten him that my last name came first then a comma then my first and middle names. Maybe it was different in California, but I had a DC license.

He gave it back to me and ordered us up the ramp. He pointed at a sign that said no hitchhikers on the freeway.

"You're supposed to stay behind this sign if you want to hitchhike."

I didn't point out to him that it didn't say we had to stay behind the sign, but I could tell Rick was about to.

"Yes, sir, we'll stay behind the sign," I yelled before Rick had a chance to chime in.

The cop nodded, strutted back to his motorcycle, and roared off.

"Jerk," said Rick.

"Yeah," I agreed. "But he didn't arrest us."

When we reached San Francisco, we called Pie. But she wasn't at the number she had given us, so we called Boulder, and there she was. "I got delayed," she said. "I'll be there in a week." So we decided to keep hitchhiking down the coast to see how far we could get before we had to turn back.

We followed Route 1 out of San Francisco. We were picked up by a green Ford Econoline. On the side of the van were a couple of paisley flowers and painted in red the words "Mystery Machine." Bolted onto the roof was a black wooden container where the driver insisted we store our gear. I climbed in next to the driver, a fat, ginger-haired, mustached freak who reminded me of Fat Freddy. He even had a cat with orange rings around its tail. Fat Freddy's cat. Rick sat in the back with three other hitchhikers.

The driver was on his way to Santa Cruz, where he lived. "It's a real hip town," he said. "The university there is far left. It's like the polar opposite of San Clemente, you know, where Nixon lives, the summer White House."

"I'm from Washington, DC," I said.

"That's a cool place too. They have a lot of demonstrations there. I was thinking of going there sometime. But I'm lucky if I can make it to San Francisco. Ha-ha."

He stroked his kitty, who was rubbing his butt up against my leg.

"The only problem with Santa Cruz," said a guy behind us in

tie-dyed T-shirt and floppy leather hat, "is that there's a murderer on the loose."

"What murderer do you mean?" asked Freddy.

"I mean I heard last year the cops found five people floating in a pool at a fancy house in the Santa Monica Mountains. They were shot in the back of the head, gangster style."

"They caught the murderer," Freddy said. "He was tried and convicted, and now he's in jail forever."

"Yeah, I heard he showed up at the trial with one side of his head shaved. The other side of his head was long hair. He called himself the yin-yang hippie."

"He was crazy. He heard voices that told him to kill these people," said Freddy, who was definitely steamed.

"I heard he had an accomplice," said the guy with the floppy hat, who leaned forward so I could only see one of his gray, wolfish eyes. "Did you hear there was a fellow going around campgrounds in the mountains lopping off hippies' fingers? He made them into a necklace, like a bear claw necklace."

"That's disgusting," said Freddy.

We stopped for gas, and Floppy Hat found another ride. He was headed southeast to Yosemite. When Freddy finished pumping gas, he asked for help, and we gave him a few bucks.

We drove down the road. We were silent until Freddy spoke up.

"I'm sorry about that jerk. If I had known that he was such a creep, I'd a left him by the road."

"He could've been the accomplice," said the lady in the back seat wearing bell-bottoms with heart patches on the knee.

"Nah, he was a loudmouth," said Rick. I knew he was interested in her, but I guessed the guy sleeping in the back was her boyfriend.

We tuned in the Beach Boys on the car radio to lighten the mood and sang along with "Wouldn't It Be Nice" while Rick was whispering to the lady. The guy in the back stirred. He was a behemoth surfer dude who could twist my buddy into a pretzel.

Rick whispered something that must've set the lady off, because the next thing that happened was that she embraced him. "Oh my God. Oh my God," she gasped.

I turned around. "What's the commotion?"

"We just figured out that Shelby and I sat next to each other from kindergarten to third grade at Bradley Elementary in Bethesda," said Rick in disbelief. "Shelby...what's your last name?"

"Sage."

"Yeah, that's why I was next to you! Alphabetical order," he said, shaking his bushy hair so that it moved down over his forehead. It needed cutting. "I hitchhike all the way across country only to find the girl I sat next to in elementary school."

They hugged each other and bounced up and down in their seats like they were still the same age they had been when they last saw each other. "Hey, I think you were at Walter Johnson."

"Yes, I was there for one year, and then I moved with my family to California."

"Yeah, you went out with Quayle Smith."

"You're kidding. You knew Quayle. How is he?"

"Oh, shit," said Rick, hesitating before he told Shelby that Quayle had died. He didn't say that Quayle hanged himself, but dying was enough. Shelby started to blubber.

The behemoth surfer leaned his head against the seat, rubbing his eyes. "What the hell you making my girl cry for?" he asked, raising his fist at Rick.

Shelby explained to her boyfriend, and he said, "Man that's a bummer. I once knew a surfer friend of mine who overdosed on horse."

"I knew a college friend who swerved off the road on some loose gravel on his Harley. His bike slipped out from under him, and he rolled off into the road. He was run over by a school bus," said Fat Freddy from the front seat.

I told them the story of the drunken frat boy who hung his head out the window, and then the car he was in grazed a telephone pole, and his head smashed like a pumpkin. Freddie was about to launch into another story when Shelby covered her ears.

"I don't want to hear any more," she screamed.

We sat there for a long moment in the depths of despair over all the casualties until Freddy told us that he and his girlfriend, Jewel, planned to see *Woodstock* at the local drive-in that night, and would we like to come along? We all, of course, jumped at the chance. We picked up Jewel and drove to the drive-in in Santa Cruz, then we stuffed all the gear in the Econoline, climbed a ladder up the back, stuffed pillows in the black storage container, and relaxed. We had a perfect view of the screen. It was almost like being at the festival without the downside of the rain, the mud, the lack of food, and such. Rick and Shelby climbed down the ladder. They danced to "Summertime Blues" and "At the Hop." We were all transfixed by Jimi's rendition of "The Star-Spangled Banner" and then "Purple Haze," the most natural guitar player in the universe, a lefty who played a righty guitar upside down, or so I'd heard. The behemoth didn't seem bothered that Rick was taking up his girlfriend's time.

When it was over, we all hugged and jumped up and down with excitement. We thanked Jewel and Freddy, though we paid their way in. Rick tried to kiss Shelby on the mouth, but she turned her head. He ended up kissing her hair. The behemoth hugged both of us and wished us a good life.

Then Rick and I hiked onto the two-thousand-acre campus of UC Santa Cruz, much of it in forest. We found an isolated spot at the bottom of a hill near a creek, laid out our sleeping bags, and crashed. We were bushed.

In the morning, we cleaned ourselves off in the creek using Dr. Bronner's soap so we wouldn't pollute the water, changed into our alternate outfits, and stashed our belongings in the woods under some brush and leaves so they wouldn't be found. We were hungry. We headed for the college cafeteria. Rick knew the ropes, so when we walked in the entrance where the checker stood behind a desk,

Rick maneuvered himself behind him where he could see the list of names. I distracted the checker by saying that I'd left my student card back in the dorm and that I could go back and get it.

"Don't worry," he said with a bored expression. He was a long-hair like us. "Give me your name."

Rick wandered by and whispered the name in my ear.

"Joe Shmoo," I said. He checked me off his list. I wandered in coolly. Grabbed a tray and piled it with food. Coffee, eight pieces of bacon, sausage, waffles, three eggs, toast, butter, and jelly. I sat off in a corner. Rick came over, his tray as full as mine.

"Oh, by the way," he said grinning, "the name I whispered in your ear was Snow, not Shmoo."

"Oh." We both laughed nervously and wolfed down our food. I was afraid the real Joe Snow might show up and we'd be found out. Rick wasn't afraid.

"This thing happens all the time." He went back for seconds.

We finished. Hustled down the hill into the woods. Picked up our belongings. Hiked out to the highway. By nightfall, we were in Big Sur.

Chapter Twenty

WE ARRIVED AT BIG SUR AT TWILIGHT. WE HIKED DOWN A STEEP trail, tripping over rocks. Rick fell once. We halted at a cliff because we were afraid we weren't going to get any farther before the sun set, and there was a place behind a couple of trees where we could camp out. We sat down at the edge of the cliff, a few-hundred-foot drop to the ocean. The waves crashed against the rocks. A bird behind us in the trees trilled *tweet, tweet, pa-chew, pa-chew*. A familiar song. A long white line of clouds hung on the horizon, and the sun set behind it, squashed together like an accordion. The clouds turned colors from dark red on the edges to pink in the middle, surrounded by the slate gray of the ocean and the yellowish-orange aura of the sky until the darkness descended like a rock.

We crawled up the hill to our hideout place. Rick turned on his flashlight so we could see well enough to rummage through our backpacks for food. We polished off the rest of the red snapper, which was beginning to turn rancid. We hoped we didn't contract ptomaine. We polished off the rest of the Twinkies, two each.

"I feel like shit," said Rick.

"So do I," I said.

Rick crawled up the hill a bit farther and vomited. I was not the type to vomit. I drank water, and though it was lukewarm, I felt better. We climbed in our sleeping bags, lay back, and looked through the trees at the swirling pattern of the Milky Way.

"Oh, shit," said Rick.

"What's wrong now?" I groaned.

"What happens if we are so restless in our sleep that we roll down the hill and off the cliff into the ocean? We'll be killed."

"That won't happen. The trees will catch us."

"Maybe we'll slide between the trees."

We tied one end of the rope left over from our boat trip around our waists and the other around the tree trunk, making sure the rope was short, so we wouldn't slide far. Then we jumped back in our sleeping bags and fell asleep feeling kind of flaky, but we were in California.

We awoke in the morning to the *tweet, tweet, pa-chew, pa-chew, pa-chew, pa-chew* trill of a gray bird a few branches above us in the tree. I could easily identify it as a mockingbird, a familiar sight when I was growing up. We untied the rope from around our waists, packed up the gear, hid it in the bushes, and headed down the steep trail to a campfire. We were hungry and thought we'd beg some food off these folks. But these folks turned out to be four nasty-looking badasses: three hairy Hells Angels in dirty jeans, chains, and tattoos, and a fourth—the guy in the floppy hat and tie-dyed shirt. He sneered at us.

"I know these jerks. They caught a ride with me and a bunch of other jerks in a Ford Econoline on the way to Santa Cruz," he told his buddies. "I think the whole bunch were afraid of me." They all laughed.

"I thought you were hitching a ride to Yosemite," I said.

"I was, and now I'm here," he said, sneering at his Hells Angels buddies. We, of course, were shaking in our boots because what he did next was brandish a huge knife that reminded me of the knife Jim Bowie carried in the Walt Disney show I used to watch on TV as a kid.

But this Jim Bowie, while he might be a bold and adventuring man, wasn't, I thought, battling for right. He swished his knife around in a threatening way like one of the evil pirates that Bowie met along the river. Then he played mumblety-peg with his foot.

He missed the side of his boot by inches, leaned down, grabbed the knife, and grinned at us before he tossed it again. What I pictured in my brain was that while we were distracted by his antics, the three Hells Angels would grab us from behind. Floppy Hat would turn to us with that same malevolent sneer and chop off a couple of our fingers for his gruesome bear-claw-like necklace. We'd either bleed to death on the spot or go through life with an interesting tale to tell.

But that was not the way it happened. Instead, he played mumblety-peg with my foot. I jumped back. I nearly fell on my ass in the fire. He and his buddies broke into laughter. Punched each other in the shoulder.

Floppy Hat pulled the knife out of the dirt, wiped it on his jeans, and sheathed it. "Scared you, didn't I?"

"Yeah, you did," I said, grinning out the side of my mouth like I thoroughly enjoyed being humiliated.

He slapped me on the shoulder. "You freaks look hungry," he said. He reached down to his saddlebag and pulled out six small packs of beef jerky. "Here you go."

To the left of the campfire was a creek that came trickling out of the forest above us and cascaded down a gently sloping field of rocks to the ocean. I nibbled on my beef jerky and looked hungrily up the hill at smoke from another fire drifting above the trees.

We thanked our benefactors and headed upstream following a small but well-trod trail. It couldn't have been more than a hundred yards when we came upon a clearing. In the middle of the clearing was a large army surplus tent that fit four and above it a plastic rain tarp and four chairs, two occupied by long-haired freaks in fringed shirts and beaded moccasins. One wore jeans, the other a loincloth and jockey briefs. They were munching on carrots and nodded at us as we came up. Two women busied themselves around the fire. They were cooking beans and rice in a pot. They offered us some, and we gladly took them up on it. We sat in a circle around the fire with tin cups in our hands and sticks fashioned as spoons. We offered some of our beef jerky to spice up the meal, but they turned us down.

"We don't eat anything with a face."

"That's nice to know," said Rick, chewing on the undercooked beans and rice. "Then you won't eat us."

The freak in the loincloth gave us a deadpan stare. "We're not cannibals."

"Only joking," he said, but they didn't seem to find it funny. So Rick decided to add some fuel to the fire by delivering a lecture that we had heard from a biology teacher at Denison about how herbivores were no better than carnivores because both had to kill to eat.

"It is egotistical to think that, let's say, a mushroom has less feelings or capacity for pain than a cow. I mean, that's why you don't want to eat animals, because they are more like you than a mushroom."

"What is he trying to say?" asked one of the women in a long, rainbow-colored granny gown.

"I'm saying that mushrooms have feelings too. But since they're further down in the food chain, they're harder for us to relate to, unlike cows, who are more like us."

"Hmm, that makes sense," said the rainbow granny. "What do you think, Job?"

Job was the guy in the jeans. He was rubbing his chin thoughtfully. "I think that this is a very wise thing to say. But there is nothing we can do about it. In order to live, we must eat. In order to eat, we must kill, whether it is high up in the food chain or low down. It is what it is."

They all nodded in agreement.

I stood up, having finished my meal, and brushed the dirt off my jeans. "Well, I think we should head on out."

"Yeah," said Rick. We shook hands with our benefactors. Job in particular was enthusiastic, hugging me gently and squeezing the life out of Rick.

"You are a very wise man," he said. "We fed your body, and in exchange, you fed our minds."

The others nodded in agreement.

Rick stood there transfixed, so overwhelmed by his wisdom, I suppose, that he thought he was the Second Coming of Christ. I had to grab him by the arm and drag him uphill to the next encampment, a religious one, I assumed, or maybe it was a Jewish wedding because they were dancing in a circle singing though I don't think it was "Hava Nagila," more like some Gregorian chant.

We bypassed this group and stopped at the next because it was more familiar to us—a gathering of freaks dressed like us passing around several gallon jugs of Gallo wine. I sat on a stump next to a lady in bib overalls, her hair covered with a blue bandana. A cute blond with a button nose that looked like she belonged in a beach party movie with Frankie Avalon.

"What's up?" I asked her.

"Oh, nothing much. We're dinking around doing our own thing," she said, smiling and passing the jug of Gallo.

I took a whiff followed by a deep swallow. I nearly choked. It tasted funky.

"You didn't cut this with anything?" I asked. "I mean, this isn't a Kool-Aid acid test, is it?"

"No. Wine, that's it," she said. She leaned against me. A bit tipsy, I surmised. "Do you know Li Po?"

"If you're talking about the Chinese poet, I've heard of him," I said, recalling the Asian lit course with our guru professor, Stoneburner.

"Have you ever heard his poem 'Alone and Drinking Under the Moon?'" she asked, squeezing my shoulder as if we were old comrades.

"Not sure," I said.

"Well, here it is," she intoned, stumbling on a log. I caught her before she fell. "Here it is."

Amongst the flowers I
am alone with my pot of wine
drinking by myself; then lifting
my cup I asked the moon
to drink with me, its reflection
and mine in the wine cup, just
the three of us; then I sigh
for the moon cannot drink...

"Do you want me to go on?" she asked, smiling sweetly.

"No, you don't have to. But that was a very good job." I clapped my hands. She bowed and nearly toppled on the ground.

"You know what happened to Li Po?" she asked. Her lips, I noticed, were wet, a gloss of some sort that shimmered in the sun's reflection. Very enticing.

"Li Po was drunk from too much wine when he saw a reflection of the moon on the surface of a lake. He jumped into the reflection and drowned."

I leaned over to kiss those enticing lips, and she leaned over as well but caught herself on the stump where I was sitting.

"Oh," she groaned, holding her stomach.

"Are you okay?" I asked.

"I don't know. Too much wine too early in the day." She looked like she was about to puke, so I backed off. A skinny-armed guy with a long beard who reminded me of a biblical prophet hustled over and leaned down.

"Are you okay, Tess?" he asked. We lifted her to her feet, took her to a tent, and laid her on top of a sleeping bag. She closed her eyes. I took one last look at Sleeping Beauty and followed the prophet back to the stump. His name was Will. Will and Tess came from Antioch. I asked him if he knew my high school buddy, Brinton Rowdybush.

"I knew him. He was always in the library studying."

"Yeah, that's him."

"He graduated. Getting his PhD at Berkeley."

"Yeah, I heard."

Then I asked him what he was doing out here. He said that he and Tess were studying crustaceans. I told him about the crustaceans we used for bait to catch red snapper up in Coos Bay. "Mussels, my friend called them."

"Mussels! Why, you should've forgotten the fish and eaten the mussels. They're tasty," he said, licking his lips. "A month ago Tess and I were in Fells Point, where they served up a mess of mussels at a seafood restaurant. I almost died. Mussels and crabs."

"You mean Fells Point in Baltimore? You from there?"

"Not me, Tess. I'm going to marry her one day."

"That's nice."

He stood there sizing me up for a long moment like I was his rival. "Traveling around, huh?" he asked finally.

"Yeah."

"Where you headed?"

"San Francisco."

"Well, hitch a couple of hours north of there to Mendocino. We just left there. It's a happening place."

We trudged farther up the trail. Our aim was to get to the top, a huge round hill with the most beautiful view in all of California, or so Will told us. We passed other groups of people camping by the stream, a group of mellow freaks strumming on their guitars, a group of bums in tattered clothing cooking things out of a can, but finally we came to a flat area where the trail bent away from the creek and into a thick forest. A few yards in, we came upon a clearing, in the middle of which a man in army fatigues and a red beret leaned back on a blue leather sofa, staring at a squirrel chattering in a tree above him. He looked down at us in a casual but interested way as we came up.

"Are you Charlie?" he asked, stretching out his legs and crossing them. Beside him he had a nasty-looking Lugar. He was inching his hands toward it.

"No, I'm Rick," said Rick, his voice cracking.

"I don't think he means Charlie the person. I think he means Charlie as in Viet Cong."

"Victor Charlie," said the soldier. He had his hand completely around the gun, but his finger wasn't on the trigger.

"We're not Charlie," I said. "We're Americans like you."

Rick stared at the Lugar.

"Don't worry—it isn't loaded," he said, reaching in his breast pocket and pulling out a magazine. "Come on in."

I moved in slowly, Rick behind me.

"Welcome to Camp Bravo," he said gesturing with his hand at the sofa, a metal table, and a mattress on the ground. "If it rains, all I need is to cover the mattress and sofa with a plastic tarp. Doesn't matter about the table."

I wandered over to the table. On the top were a couple of mess kits neatly packed up and silverware scattered about. I noticed the insignia of a swastika on the handle of one of the spoons and looked up at the soldier.

"I got that at an army surplus store," he said proudly.

"And the gun?"

"I stole that off a dead gook." He introduced himself by pointing at a white nameplate above his breast pocket that said, "Don."

"Hi, Don," I said. "I'm Jeff." We shook hands.

Then above us, the squirrel started to chatter again. It was messing with a plastic bag hanging from a branch, probably food.

"Damn squirrel," said Don. He jammed the magazine into the Lugar's handle and pulled the trigger twice. We jumped back, expecting a loud *KA-BOOM* instead of two innocuous *click-clicks*. Must've been no bullets in the magazine. But this didn't bother Don. He smiled as the squirrel jumped from branch to branch, down the trunk, and across the clearing to another tree.

"Good shot, huh?" he said as he holstered his gun.

"Yeah," we said. Rick and I looked at each other knowingly. The soldier, we suspected, was as squirrely as the squirrel.

He wanted us to secure the perimeter, so we went out on patrol, Rick taking the point, because, as Don whispered to me, he was the most expendable of us three. We wandered around in the woods for a while until he came to a halt suddenly, waving his hands.

"Oh my God, I can't look. I can't look." He sat down on the trail and closed his eyes.

"What is it?" I asked, looking around. All I could see were trees, bushes, the blue sky, and the birds flitting from one branch to another.

"Over there. Over there. Over there," he said, pointing in one direction after another.

"What?"

"Body parts. An arm. A leg. Hanging from a tree. And on the ground like a ripe apple, a bloody head."

"I don't see anything," I said. I leaned down and put my hand on his shoulder. "Are you sure you're okay? Are you sure you're not going mental on us?"

He opened his eyes slowly and looked at me. Then he looked around the forest as if trying to catch his bearings. "I'm fine. I'm fine. I was hallucinating that I was at Firebase Zero. Charlie was lobbing in mortar fire. We jumped in our hooches and fired back, *rat-a-tat-tat*, *rat-a-tat-tat*, and *BOOM-BOOM* from the big guns. Then there was a lull. No more incoming. So we went out to count the bodies as we were instructed to do after every firefight. Ha-ha-ha. No wonder the body counts are so high. One leg here. One arm there. One head. That makes three dead. Ha-ha-ha." He paused and pointed at Rick, who was clomping up the trail toward us. "Who's that?"

"That's our point man."

"What did you see out there?" he yelled to Rick.

"Nothing."

"Then the perimeter's clear. We can redeploy at Camp Bravo." We helped Don to his feet and lugged him back to his couch, where he lay down with a sigh.

"Are you all right?" asked Rick.

"I'm tired," said Don, waving the Luger in our faces. "Now leave me alone."

"Sure, sure." We crept off.

We followed the trail until we came to a dirt road, where the forest ended. Beyond it was a steep hill covered in lemon-colored grass. We climbed five hundred feet or so to the shade of a few windswept, gnarly evergreens, sat down, and checked out the view that Will had told us about. It was well past noon. The sun slipped behind a cloud. We were in shadow for a moment. The grass turned brown, the forest black, and beyond it the water's surface no longer slate gray but the darkest blue that suggested to me the depth and coldness of the ocean. It made me shiver to think what was underneath. Giant squids. Huge jellyfish. Manta rays. Whales. Orcas. Killer sharks.

We were so high up in the hills the earth seemed to curve on the horizon. The sun slipped from behind the cloud. We turned around, glimpsed one lemon-covered hill after another. No human life, no human habitat, nothing but nature. We felt like we were at the edge of the world where civilization ended.

"What do you think of that cast of characters that we passed on the way uphill?" asked Rick, finally. "Do you think we'd fit in? Do you think we ought to stay here?"

"I think if we stayed here long enough, we would fit in," I said. "But I don't think I want to fit in."

"Why not?"

"I don't want to be a vegetarian and live in a tent in my underwear or pass out drinking rotgut wine, though I wouldn't mind spending some time with Tess. Nor would I care to dance in a circle chanting whatever. Nor would I care to be part of a group of mellow freaks sitting around a campfire strumming on my guitar. I have a tin ear. Nor would I care to be a bum in tattered clothing cooking things out of a can. I have an aversion to poverty. Nor a pretend Vietnam veteran sleeping on a couch in the middle of the woods."

"How do you know he's pretend?"

"I don't," I said, "but either way he needs help so he won't harm himself or anyone else."

"So you're going straight on me."

"No, I'm not. I'm just saying that you need your head examined if you want to live in the woods like this. Not that I think civilization's that great, but it's less precarious. I mean, twenty years from now, these freaks will either be dead or holding down a job."

We both laughed at this, like reality was a joke, and checked out the majestic view one last moment until a green tractor drove by on the dirt road hauling a load of hay.

Chapter Twenty-One

WE HITCHED TO BERKELEY AND CAUGHT UP WITH PIE. SHE WAS STAY-
ing with a friend. I forget who it was, but I remember for sure that
she didn't want any part of Rick and me. I think her friend might've
had a fling with my friend—there was a lot in his life, especially his
relationships with women, that he kept private. Besides, I figured
out that I didn't stand a chance with Pie, an idea I had held in the
back of my mind, thinking that she was out here because she was
breaking up with J. B. But I was wrong. She needed to get away for
a short time. But they were in love.

"This place is a bummer," insisted Rick after a few days of doing
basically nothing. "Let's take Will's advice."

We hitched up the coast to Mendocino. Our last ride let us off
at the south end of town. We strolled down a dirt road that hugged
the cliffs. To our right was the town, a collection of saltbox and
Victorian houses and shops like a New England village and to our
left, Mendocino Bay. A small beach at the end of the bay was littered
with log-sized driftwood. A flock of freaks built shelters out of the
driftwood on the beach while another flock built a raft. One of their
numbers scurried from one flock to the other, gesturing wildly. He
towered over the others. Long, curly red mane. Long, curly red beard.

A stairway led down to the beach, but we decided to forge ahead
to where we saw another flock of weirdos jumping into a hole. As
we moved closer, we saw the walls of the hole were lined with sharp
volcanic rock, and at the bottom there was water. The water poured
in from the ocean and poured out to the bay. All frothing white
water. It seemed like a dangerous proposition to jump in this water.

It was a fifty-foot drop, and no telling what was underneath the froth. But these weirdos jumped like a herd of lemmings, rode the wave to the bay, and ran back for more. We stared down the hole, our mouths agape, until a woman in jeans cutoffs and a wet T-shirt suggested we jump off as well.

"Oh, I don't have a bathing suit," said Rick.

"You don't need one," she said as she stripped down to the buff. "You can go naked."

She jumped in the hole, and Rick and I followed her all the way to the water—though only with our eyes.

We trudged back to the stairway that led to the beach and made our way down the steps carefully. They creaked under our feet and seemed to sway slightly, as if they were not securely tied to the cliff. When we reached the bottom, we were welcomed by the red-headed giant, who called himself Erik the Red.

"We're building a raft that we plan to sail up that river," he said, pointing toward the land where waves broke against a sandy beach, though I could see a gap in the beach. I guessed that was the river.

"The Big River," he said. His eyes were as blue as the water, and they seemed wild. He reminded me of Butch the Speed Freak in Denver, though of more substantial build. A Viking.

We put down our gear and wandered over to a log where a bunch of long-hairs were munching peanut butter and cheese sandwiches.

"I mean, help yourself," said one, a curly-haired blond lady with the bluest eyes. It was no wonder her name was Iris. "I mean, thanks to Ronald Reagan, socialist governor of California."

On top of one of the logs was a gallon can of peanut butter, a block of cheese, a knife, three loaves of bread, and a couple of gallons of Gallo wine.

"Does Reagan buy the Gallo?" I asked as I spread the peanut butter on the bread, sliced the cheese, and slapped it on top.

"Nah," said a guy in a straw cowboy hat. I'll call him Jerry. "We go to Fort Bragg once a week to the warehouse where they hand out food. It depends on what they want to get rid of. Sometimes potatoes, sometimes grapes, sometimes sandwich meat, but always plenty of peanut butter and cheese."

"But we all divvy up for the Gallo," Iris informed us.

I saw a can full of sliced dill pickles, plucked out three, and made a peanut butter and pickle sandwich.

"Disgusting," said Jerry, but Iris said she ate peanut butter and pickle all the time when she was growing up, but with mayonnaise. "It's Southern food, like fried green tomatoes."

"Are you a Southerner?" I asked.

"No, I'm from Philadelphia. My mom's from North Carolina."

"Oh, we're neighbors," I said, looking at her carefully. "I'm from Washington."

Jerry didn't seem pleased with the eye contact. He moved closer to Iris, who seemed nervous somehow and went back to how Ronald Reagan was a socialist. She remembered a campaign speech she saw on TV where he promised to "put those welfare bums back to work and clean up the mess in Berkeley."

"Now, I was a student at Berkeley when he was elected, and I didn't see him cleaning up any messes. I mean, People's Park, the Summer of Love, what hey, messier than ever. And what is there about a food giveaway that encourages welfare bums to work?"

"Maybe he's a communist in disguise," said Jerry. He was another Antioch student, but he was here studying seals. "In the Soviet Union, they brainwash the kids, I heard, by putting them in front of cabinets. One says 'Capitalist Pigs,' the other, 'Communist Comrades.' You open the capitalist cabinet, it's empty. You open the communist cabinet, it's full of milk and cookies."

"What's that got to do with Reagan?" asked Iris.

"Well, that's what Reagan's trying to do. He's trying to brainwash us by giving away food. That way we'll be on his side."

"That's logical," said Iris, giving Jerry a push. He fell off the log laughing.

I turned to Rick, who was on another log making time with a tall, dark-haired lady with big, round eyes. I felt lonely all of a sudden. Left out like I had felt in Taos when Pie paired off with the guru.

I didn't feel better until later that afternoon when I was wandering out by the rocks trying to make sense of a sucking sound I heard from below the water's surface. I sighted a seal as it disappeared into the sucking hole. It was an underwater cave, I figured, and I wanted a look at it. I crawled carefully on the slippery rocks. I kept a sharp eye out for how high the waves broke and stopped a foot above that point. I leaned forward as several waves slammed against the rock, sending spray into the air and soaking me. But I couldn't see anything. After the fourth wave receded, I bent lower. I not only saw the sharp, volcanic walls of the cave glistening in the sun but the big, round eyes and the shiny skin of the seal. I should've known better, the way the water slid out so far like in a tsunami. In a tsunami, you can walk on the ocean floor and watch the fish flop around while the ocean gathers force to roar back at you in the form of a tidal wave thirty feet high. That was what was happening to me, though on a much smaller scale. I leaned forward, totally entranced by the seal in his cave, when I heard a voice yell from the top of the cliff. I turned around. It was Iris. I waved. She pointed frantically in my direction, a fearful gaze in her eyes. I turned back and gasped at the wave that was coming at me. It had to be fourteen feet high, maybe eight feet above my head. I plastered myself against the rocks as the wave washed over me, dragging me down into the water. I felt that the end was near. I'd be sucked into the cave and dashed into bloody unconsciousness against the jagged rocks and drowned. But as luck would have it, another jagged rock caught me between the legs. It wasn't as painful as it might sound, and what did it matter? I was saved. I scurried to the top of the cliff and collapsed at Iris's feet.

"Thanks," I said.

The next morning, we visited the nude beach on the Navarro River. Rick was with the tall lady, a telephone operator from San

Diego. I will call her Landis because I don't remember her name. She cozied up to him. I cozied up to Iris. Jerry was in Fort Bragg picking up more food. He had wanted Iris to come along, but she refused.

"I want to relax in the sun," she said.

I asked her if there was something going on between her and Jerry.

"No," she said, laughing. "He was a friend, but not anymore."

We parked in a sandy lot next to some trees. Erik the Red carried a duffel bag where we were supposed to stash our clothes once we got down to the beach. Or we could keep our clothes on and gawk. It didn't matter.

"Whatever turns you on," he said.

We sauntered down a winding path to the beach, a long strip of white sand full of nude people. The first thing I saw was a naked one-armed man tossing a Frisbee to his dog. Then an old naked couple under an umbrella and two kids playing in the sparkling, clear water of the river. They were chasing a fish—a trout, I think. I could see the speckles on its back. We disrobed. I tried not to look at Iris because I didn't want to well, you know, get a hard-on. She was beautiful, no doubt.

I sensed that I better act soon. *Carpe diem.* My day had come. I was more appealing to her than Jerry. She put her hand in mine. We wandered over to a corner of the beach where most of the nudists were gathered. They were watching a couple screwing.

The man was standing with his legs bent slightly. The woman straddled him. He had his arms around her waist trying to keep her steady as she bounced up and down on his dick. She made a couple of flourishes with her arms like a ballet dancer. He made a couple of flourishes as well and wiggled his eyebrows at the crowd like Groucho Marx. Then they went at it hot and heavy. They ignored the applause from the crowd. I thought it was kind of weird, but, you know, I'd never been on a nude beach before.

Iris squeezed my hand. We wandered to the other side of the beach away from most of the others and lay down facing each other. We went at it very slowly. We looked at each other intently. We fiddled with each other's organs. I played hers like a violin. She played mine like a slide whistle. I rose to the occasion and was about to head on to the next step when the dog jumped over us, chasing the Frisbee and spraying sand in our faces. We sought more privacy in the woods.

We found a nice, soft, secluded bed beneath an evergreen tree. A fallen tree blocked the view of the path. Though we could hear people wandering by, they couldn't see us. We kept quiet and resumed our organ fiddling. That led to kissing, fondling, and other stocks of the trade, until Iris rolled on her back, and I rolled on top of her. I entered her. I moved up and down in a slow rhythm that would've been fine if she hadn't been moving down and grabbing my ass as I was moving up. I was afraid I was going to spill the beans prematurely, but then we heard a noise and looked up. A funny-looking man in thick glasses stepped over the fallen tree and sat down beside us. He wore cordovans, green pants, a plaid shirt, and a pen holder full of pens in his breast pocket. He put his hand on his chin and stared at us.

"I'm lost," he whined. "I was on my way to Mendocino because I heard it was a happening place, and I had a week to kill until I had to show up in San Jose for a job, but somehow I made a wrong turn and saw all these parked cars and thought maybe someone could help me. Sorry to bother you," he whined as if suddenly aware of what we were up to, though he didn't seem embarrassed. He stared at us more intently.

"No problem," said Iris as she pushed down as I pushed up, though she didn't grab my ass, thank God. "You follow the river west toward the ocean until you come to a dead end. Take a right. Follow Route 1 for ten miles until you cross a bridge. You'll see Mendocino on your left."

"Thanks." He repeated her directions. "Is that right?"

"That's right," I said in a not-too-friendly tone.

He stood up and saluted us then crunched through the brush toward the beach, not his car. As he disappeared, I fired off my cannon. Iris groaned but not in delight. She turned on her side and pointed at the white, creamy liquid sliding down her rear end to the ground.

"You missed," she said. I looked down at the pine needles stuck to my limp weiner.

"I guess I did."

I followed her down to the Navarro River to clean off.

I didn't see Iris for a few days. She said she was visiting a friend who lived a few miles down the road, but I figured she had dumped me.

But Landis didn't dump Rick. She clung to my buddy like moss to stone, and I was afraid I'd never see him again. But maybe I was wrong, because he hung around with us as much as he did with Landis. By us, I meant Jerry and me. We spent some of the time helping Erik the Red build the raft. While we helped him attach the logs with duct tape and rope, he regaled us about the explorers Sir Francis Drake, Vasco de Gama, Coronado, and his namesake.

"I think we'll find something when we explore the Big River," he said, his hands flying. "I'm not sure what. Maybe arrowheads. Maybe something Lewis and Clark left behind when they passed through here. Who knows? At the very least we could have fun."

Every morning we'd trudge up the long stairs to the cliff and across a field to the edge of town to the Lumpty Dump, a muffin-and-coffee shop in a wood shack with a big window that overlooked the ocean. We'd chow down on blueberry muffins, sip coffee, and check out the ocean. No one seemed to mind us, as unkempt as we were.

One time I stubbed my toe so badly that it got infected, so I went to the medical clinic in town where the doctor cleaned and bandaged the toe. He gave me penicillin. All for free. I left a couple of bucks in the donation jar.

One morning Rick and I climbed the stairs and came upon a structure that hadn't been there the day before. A two-floor saltbox that looked like the other houses in town. It was a drug store, according to the sign that was offering ice cream cones for five cents a scoop. We galloped up the wooden stairs. Rick opened the door and fell five feet to the ground. I nearly toppled on top of him.

"Shit," he said, standing up and brushing himself off. "I could've broken my leg."

"Must be part of a movie set," I said, checking out the one-sided house propped up by wooden beams. "The inside must be on a sound stage in Hollywood. No cheap ice cream for us."

We wandered around Mendocino checking out all the commotion. Hollywood had taken over the town. We heard that the movie was *The Summer of '42* and they were looking for extras. The only stipulation was that we cut our hair.

"No, thanks," said Rick, turning to me. "It's like stealing my identity. I'm a freak. Like David Crosby said, 'I feel like letting my freak flag fly.'"

I was not as enthusiastic as Rick about the length of my hair, though I understood it was a sign of our rebellion against the establishment. I thought it was a righteous rebellion, antiwar, equal rights, freedom, and all that shit. But I thought there were a fair amount of creeps hanging around muddying the waters. Creeps like Charlie Manson, the Hells Angels at Altamont, the Weather Underground and their kind who promoted murder and mayhem to get their way. I was pointing this out to Rick, that violence was counterproductive, but his mind was elsewhere.

He returned to the beach and I to Lumpty Dump. I spent an hour or so there, conversing with Jerry about my freak concerns, but his interest was in Iris. He was wondering if I was finished with her. I told him I wasn't finished, though I said I wasn't sure what that meant.

"It means you horned in on my territory, and I was wondering if I could have her back," he said, adjusting his straw hat. He was about my height and skinny as a starving horse—and as ugly. A small wind could blow him over.

"I don't own Iris," I said in a relaxed tone that I hope projected my true lack of concern.

I got up from the table finally, bid Jerry goodbye, and returned to the beach. I got halfway down the stairs when I noticed Rick in his sleeping bag, his hands behind his head, a blissful smile on his lips. About waist high in the bag a big lump was moving up and down, up and down at a dilatory pace. Oh, jeez, Rick was getting a blow job.

I sat down on the steps, my hand on my chin, thinking, *Rick's got all the luck.* Not that a blow job was that desirable—you could get one in any bathroom in a seedy part of town—but it certainly trumped nothing.

As it turned out, Iris resurfaced the next morning. We piled in the back of Erik the Red's truck, drove up to the hills behind the town, and parked on the side of a dirt road near a wood pile where a half dozen other cars were parked. Trucks, VW buses, and such. We carried as many pieces of wood as we could handle down a path to a sauna in the middle of the woods. We stuffed some of the wood in a furnace and tossed the rest on the ground.

Erik explained that the rich freaks who owned the sauna and the land around us believed in sharing, but there were two rules. We fulfilled the first by hauling down the wood. The other was to take off our clothes. We did. We entered the sauna and sat down on the wooden benches. The benches were arranged in levels. The higher up you were, the cooler you were. So we went up to the top and worked our way down. One of the nice things about the sixties was that you came across many naked people, like at the hot springs in New Mexico, only those people were in the steamy water for the most part. Here I could see everything. Breasts. Pubic hair. Thighs. Pretty faces and not so pretty, all shiny and dripping sweat. I didn't look at the men except once to see if they were reacting to all this female flesh in the same way I was. Some were. I turned to look at Iris, but she was looking down at me. When she noticed my eyes, she looked up and smiled.

"Let's move down to the next level," she said, taking my hand. When we finally reached the bottom level, she sniffed my skin. "You smell like peanut butter."

I took a whiff of her. "I hate to say what you smell like…"

"What?"

"Garlic."

She laughed. "I was visiting my cousin who lives in Albion, a small town south of here. Last night we had spaghetti and meatballs. I'll bet there was garlic in the sauce."

When we couldn't stand the steamy heat anymore, we soaked our bodies under an indoor shower. We squirted each other with Dr. Bronner's soap. Soaked again and ran outside. Our skin tingled in the cool air. We put on our shoes and picked up our clothes, but we didn't dress. We followed the path deeper into the woods until we came to a clearing. On the far edge of the field, there was a half-finished geodesic dome. We went inside. We found a secluded place where we couldn't be seen from the outside. I grabbed a packing blanket from over a crate. I put it down on the ground. Iris wanted me to sit down first. I sat down. I leaned against a wall. She sat down on top of me, straddling my hips like the couple at the Navarro River. She rubbed her crotch against mine. I felt her prickly soft pubic hair and reacted to it in a positive way. She lifted up slightly and guided my dick into her. She was wet, but not enough. I fiddled around down there until I hit a spot. She jumped.

"Ohh, that feels good," she purred.

I hit the spot again, and this time when she came down, I was fully inside her. She yelped. Bounced up and down, up and down, but once she bounced too high. My dick came out and waggled from side to side like a metronome. She grabbed it and pushed it back in.

Bounced up and down. Grabbed my hands and put them on her breasts. I tweaked her nipples. She bounced harder. The dick came out. She pushed it back in. I gritted my teeth. Narrowed my eyes.

"What's wrong?" she asked, looking at me with concern. Her eyes were wide and seemed feverish with desire.

"I'm trying not to cum."

"How sweet of you." She caressed my cheek. I looked into her bluer-than-blue orbs. I fell instantly in love, but I shouldn't have, because that opened the floodgates. As soon as she commenced to bounce up and down on me again, I came. Fortunately, not like the first time. Not on her butt. But inside of her.

She purred, "Ohh." I think I purred as well. She leaned forward and buried my face in kisses.

"Nice," she said.

"Let's do it again," I said.

"Maybe later," she said.

We stood up. We cleaned ourselves off with the packing blanket. We were freaks, after all. We dressed and walked slowly back to the sauna, hand in hand.

THERE WAS NO later. A fog bank rolled in during the night. When we woke, it was thirty feet high and white as snow, like a bank of tundra inching toward us. It covered us like a wet blanket, and everyone was packing to leave.

This was the day we were going to launch the raft. Erik the Red was intensely agitated. He ran from one group to another, begging for us to stay. "I mean, what a perfect day," he cried, cutting his hands through the fog. "Like, like, like the old days in the fjords."

He managed to convince six volunteers—one was Iris, another Jerry. I wanted to go, but Rick didn't. Too wet. Too cold. No fun, he said. Besides, Landis had left for her job in San Diego yesterday. Rick wanted to hitch back to San Francisco. It was decision time for me. I watched the volunteers splash through the water to help Erik shove off. He scrambled to the mast while the others grabbed canoe paddles and jumped aboard. Iris waved at me. I looked at Rick. He shrugged. The last I saw before the raft faded in the fog was Jerry with his arms around Iris and the distressed look on her face like *Come on out here, Jeff. Rescue me.*

We hitched back to Berkeley, where we found out that Nat Koenig had dropped by on his way back east. He was in the army stationed at Fort Dix in New Jersey, but he had devised a plan to get out before his unit was shipped off to God knew where—Vietnam, Germany. He heard a rumor that Margie Walker had been married in Atlanta in a *Gone with the Wind*-themed wedding. He didn't know if her wedding dress was red like Scarlett O'Hara's, but one thing he did know was that she didn't marry Earl Harris. Earl was in Central America. He was not a missionary as he had hoped but a marine guard at the embassy in Managua. He had been drafted. That pleased Nat to no end. He wrote down his parents' address and telephone number in Boston and suggested we come by in a few months. He'd be there if things worked out as he planned.

Chapter Twenty-Two

THE NUMBER ONE RULE OF THE ROAD WAS THAT THE LONGER YOU waited for a ride, the longer the distance it would take you. We were on the last pass in the Sierra Nevada mountains, that is, Rick, Pie, and me. She had decided to come along with us. I guessed she had had enough of Berkeley and was anxious to see J. B. We had eaten the last of the gorp. We had shared the last Granny Smith, and now we shared the final contents of my canteen, cherry Kool-Aid mixed with vodka. The air was thin. It was hard to breathe. The cars rumbled by slowly, but none of them stopped. We had been waiting two hours.

Our last ride was in a semi-trailer truck that picked us up outside Sacramento. We piled in, Rick and Pie in the back behind a curtain where they sat on a bed, me in the front with the driver. He pulled out, grinding his gears.

"Is that your girlfriend?" he asked me, gesturing toward the rear.

"No," I said.

"Do you mind if I sleep with her?"

"That's not up to me," I said.

He grinned out the side of his mouth. He wore a Boston Red Sox baseball cap and spoke with a South Boston brogue. I knew what he was thinking: *Hippie chick. They'll fuck anything.*

About twenty miles down the road, he pulled over at a truck stop and asked Rick and me to buy some coffee and donuts. As soon as we jumped out of the truck, I grabbed Rick by the arm and told him what the truck driver was up to. Rick decided to wait near the truck where he couldn't be seen while I purchased the goods. I guessed he was thinking that if things got out of hand, he would be there to rescue his sister, even though the driver was twice his size. But things didn't get out of hand. We scrambled into the truck and distributed the coffee. The truck driver ground the gears and pulled out on the highway with a donut in his mouth and a scowl on his face. On Pie's face was a look of determination. The trucker promised to drive us all the way to Denver but instead let us out in this godforsaken place on top of a mountain.

Pie said she was sorry. "Maybe I should've slept with the guy."

"No, you shouldn't have," said Rick. "You don't sleep with anyone for a ride to Denver. Not my sister."

"Thanks for caring, brother." She pecked Rick on the cheek.

"Hey, I care too," I said.

She pecked me on the cheek, but I could tell she felt guilty. She was looking around for a way to get a ride, and that was when she eyed the hole behind us—four feet deep, dirt, rocks, and an empty Pepsi can at the bottom. We knew that it was totally against the rules, but we were desperate. Rick and I ducked down in the hole so we couldn't be seen from the road. Pie giggled. She stuck out her thumb. The cars rumbled by, but within a minute, we heard the screech of brakes. We peered over the hole. Pie was at the window of a beat-up International Harvester pickup. Depression-era vintage. We saw two blond, curly-haired heads bobbing behind the glass. Pie waved in our direction. We emerged from our hole. One of the heads leaned out the window. "A couple of jokers," he yelled. He motioned us to the back. We opened a door to a corrugated metal cabin that sat on top of the truck bed.

A wood bench lined each side of the interior. We saw four pairs of eyes and heard one disembodied voice intone, "Hey, man."

We climbed in. Pie was in the front between the two men. One of them put his arm around her shoulder. She took it away. He put it back.

"Hey, how far you going?" Rick asked the driver.

We pulled over the rough gravel to the road.

"Denver."

"That's how far we're going." Rick poked me in the side.

"But we're stopping off in Reno. We don't have money for gas," said one of the heads, "but we have twenty promotional cards worth five dollars each at the casinos." He waved the cards in front of our faces.

"Take your arm from around my shoulder," said Pie.

"Yeah, letch," said the driver. His name was Kelvin. The letch was Kurt. They were brothers and looked exactly alike.

"But we're not twins," said Kurt. "My dick's a foot longer than his."

We chugged down the mountain, across the border, and into Reno. The first casino we saw, we pulled in the parking lot. We piled through the glass doors of the casino and headed off in all directions. Rick and I played the slots. We lost the three quarters we had between us in a matter of seconds. Two casino guards tapped us on the shoulder. They were dressed in blue suits and cowboy hats. They escorted us to the door.

"Don't ever come back," they said.

Kelvin and Kurt leaned against the International Harvester a few feet away. "They threw you jokers out too?"

Then Tiny, who was squeezed next to us in the back of the pickup—he must've weighed 250 pounds—shuffled out the door, followed by more cowboys who delivered the same message to him as they had to Rick and me.

Then came the Three Stooges, as they called themselves. Three friends from Winnetka, Illinois. One of them asked, "Isn't our money as good as anyone else's?"

"What money?" answered Kurt.

We sat around the parking lot glumly, the cowboys eyeing us through the glass doors.

"Where's Pie?" I asked Kurt.

"Oh, she's inside. I gave her all the promotional tickets. She's trying to win some money," said Kurt, scratching his head thoughtfully. "You don't think she'll run away?"

"She's my sister," said Rick.

An hour later, Pie emerged from the casino waving a wad of bills: two fives, the rest ones, forty in all. She handed them over to the brothers.

Kelvin climbed behind the wheel of the truck and commanded us to push. "You got to jump-start this heap," he said.

The truck hiccuped down the road a hundred yards before the engine caught. We jumped in.

Pie sat across from me in the back of the truck, glad to be away from Kurt. Our knees touched as we bounced down the highway. I gazed at her in a longing way. She gazed back at me with her big, sympathetic, doe-like eyes.

"What's up?" she asked.

"Oh, you know, you and J. B. getting married. Seems like the end of an era."

"What are you going to do?"

"Move back east, I guess. I don't know. I haven't really thought about it. Maybe I'll go to graduate school."

"Why would you want to do that?"

"Gives me a chance to think about what I want to do next." I shrugged.

"When you go to graduate school, you already know what you're going to do next. That's why you go in the first place," said Rick. He was sitting beside me.

"Okay, I'll follow in my father's footsteps. I'll go to the Ohio State University School of Journalism. I could probably get a scholarship, considering that Dad was the editor of *The Ohio State Lantern*," I said without much conviction.

"I hate school," said Tiny, who was listening in to our conversation, though it was hard to hear with the wind whistling through the cracks in the metal shell we were sitting in. "I'm a bartender, though I'm not working right now. Heading for my next job."

"That's great," I said, turning back to Rick. "How about you?"

"I want to get married, have children, and live out in the country. But not in a commune. This commune thing was another one of our harebrained ideas, like floating down the Crooked River."

We both laughed.

"You know what I want is a house with a lot of acreage," said Rick, furrowing his brow reflectively. "I'll find a job somewhere but spend most of my time with the wife and kiddies cultivating a huge garden, in the middle of which I'll grow marijuana. I'll plant a statue of Buddha at the entrance of the garden to protect us from negative vibrations."

"That sounds great," said Pie. "You want to know what I have in mind?"

"Sure."

"Well, J. B. and I decided we're going to work at the Mexican restaurant another year, move to Tempe, and work in a food co-op that a friend of his owns until we learn the ropes. Then we'll start our own food co-op, probably in a small town in Arizona where the closest grocery store is twenty miles away," she said as if it was a plan set in concrete. "We'll corner the market."

"When will you get married?" I asked, feeling a bit downtrodden by the thought.

"Oh, we've planned that as well. Next spring, we'll have a sunrise ceremony at Flagstaff overlooking Boulder and the plains. It'll be beautiful. Then we'll have a breakfast buffet and sip champagne by ten in the morning at our restaurant, of course. You're invited," she said.

"Thanks." Jeez, I thought, Rick and me left in the lurch treading water without any mates, careers, and so forth while she had her whole life spread out before her like a road map.

We stopped for gas. The brothers grabbed some food for themselves. We purchased some as well and a pint of vodka that I mixed with lime Kool-Aid. We scrambled back in the truck, Pie next to me. We shared the booze and a huge bag of potato chips with our fellow passengers.

Pie put her hand on my knee, gave me her doe-eyed sympathetic look. "You're not depressed, are you?"

"Me? No. Too many endorphins. That is, of course, unless I knew that I was going to die," I said, nodding. "That would definitely depress me."

That put me in mind of Flakey Foont, the skinny, long-nosed, slump-shouldered R. Crumb comic strip character grossing one time that one day he would die. No more consciousness. No more pleasure. No more me. It's inconceivable. And Mr. Natural in his thought balloon replies, "Get used to it."

I would like to have thought of myself as more like Mr. Natural. Relaxed. Laid-back. Ready to accept anything that came my way. But that was more Rick's style. I wasn't uptight like Flakey either. I was somewhere between, though, in this case, I decided to take Mr. Natural's advice.

I leaned over and kissed Pie. It wasn't a peck on the cheek but a wide-open French kiss, though I was the only one with the open mouth until I knocked on her lips with my tongue and she opened the door and our tongues touched long enough to taste lime Kool-Aid and vodka.

Tiny, who was sitting across from us, slapped his hands together and exclaimed. "Way to go, man."

The Stooges guffawed mindlessly, and Kurt stuck his head through the sliding window. "I saw that," he chortled, while Rick shook his head in disapproval.

"Hey, man, just getting a jump on the wedding," I said lamely.

"Kissing the bride," said Rick.

"Yes."

We pulled in at a truck stop in Winnemucca, Nevada. The brothers moseyed inside and sat at a booth in front of a plate glass window. The sunlight reflected off the window, so we could barely see the two bobbing-head jerks chowing down on hamburgers and fries between sips of ice-cold Coca-Cola. We sat outside at a picnic table shaded by a cottonwood tree. It was as hot and dry as the inside of an oven. From far off, I could hear the shriek of a train whistle. I stared at the desert that fanned out to a low line of hills. Somewhere out there was the actual town. Trees. A river. A high school. But here it was pure desolation. Flat. White. Like Venus on a cold day.

We shared what was left of the potato chips and filled our canteens with water, mumbling the whole time about the greedy brothers spending the money Pie had handed over to them at the casino.

Tiny wanted to strangle the two, take what was left in their pockets, and race off in their International Harvester. But it was so damn hot, it wasn't worth the effort, nor were they.

"Don't worry, I'll get us something," said Pie. She hustled to the mini-mart next to the restaurant.

An old, stubble-chinned fart stumbled up to us with his hand out. "You got any spare change?" he asked, taking off his beat-up, dusty homburg and bowing slightly.

We all laughed. "We should be asking you the same question," said one of the Stooges. We gave him some water from our canteen and let him dig into the dregs at the bottom the potato chip bag.

"You wouldn't know it by looking at me," he said, shaking his head sadly, "but I am a graduate of Harvard University with a PhD in musicology. I taught at the University of Chicago, and about the time I come up for tenure, they fired me because they found out I was affiliated with the Communist Party. That was the 1930s, you know."

I took a close glance at him, and sure enough, he reminded me of a seedy college professor down on his luck, threadbare tweed jacket with leather patches at the elbows, dirty tan chinos, dirty plaid shirt, and bow tie tied loosely around his scrawny neck.

He leaned in close to us. "I took to the rails after they fired me. Went from town to town just like all the hobos in those days. You know who I met one time I was on the rails?"

"No, who?" I asked mildly interested.

"I met Woody Guthrie. You know who he is?"

"Yeah, Arlo's father," said Rick, whose ears seemed to perk up.

"Why, you're a smart fellow," said the codger, slapping Rick on the arm. "Sure you don't have any change?"

We shook our heads.

He sighed. "Now, where was I? Yeah," he said, rubbing his chin thoughtfully. "Once Woody and I were riding a boxcar with the sliding door open. We watched the countryside speeding by and heard the rails singing, *clickity-click*. It was an exhilarating feeling. I turned to Woody, and I asked, 'Isn't this land the prettiest land you ever seen.' He said, 'It sure is.' 'We're lucky,' I said, 'even as poor as we are, we can still wander this land as free as a bird. It's our land,' I said, poking Woody. It was like I saw a light bulb pop on in his head. He strummed his guitar and mumbled to himself in an unsure way until I pitched in. Before long we came up with the first stanza to a song. You know which one it is?"

"Yeah, I do," said Rick, singing:

This land is your land, this land is my land
From California to the New York Island...

"That's it. That's it," the old fart exclaimed, doffing his homburg. "Sure you fellows can't spare a dime?"

I reached in my pocket and handed him a lint-covered Ben Franklin fifty-cent piece. He grabbed it and hustled off as fast as he could to the mini-mart. We could see him talking to Pie though the glass window. She came out of the swinging doors a few minutes later with a smirk on her face and a small bag of goodies in her arms.

We rummaged through the goodies—Clark Bars, Butterfingers, Dots, M&Ms, bags of peanuts and raisins, and such.

"Where'd you get the money to buy that?" asked her brother.

She reached in the pocket of her jeans and pulled out a twenty and some change. "You think I was going to give those two blond creeps all the dough?"

"Hey, you're a real smart lady," said Tiny as he reached in to grab a Clark Bar. Pie slapped his hand.

"Hey, what's the idea?"

"I'm going to mix these all together in little plastic bags and hand them out individually like gorp. Energy food," she said. I noticed at the bottom of the bag was a box of plastic bags.

The two bobbing-head creeps ambled out of the restaurant and jumped in the cab of the Harvester. "Time to jump-start this heap," yelled Kelvin.

We gave it a heave. The truck hiccuped down the road a hundred yards before the engine caught. We jumped in.

While Pie blended all the candy and such and put them in plastic, Rick told her about the college professor from Harvard and how he knew Woody Guthrie. The smirk we had seen on her face when she came out of the mini-mart grew wider.

"What did he say to you?" asked Rick.

"He said that he had the biggest dick in the world. It was so big that he had to strap it to his leg. And wouldn't I like to come in the bathroom so he could show it to me."

After our gorp repast, I fell asleep. I had a dream. I was six years old at a horse show in the country in a big crowd, and I was scared. I was all alone. I scanned the crowd but didn't recognize anyone. A bunch of horsey people—men, women in jodhpurs and felt hats. Nasty looks on their faces. Then I heard a familiar cough in the distance. Mom. She was a smoker. She was moving closer. The crowd parted. She walked up, leaned down to where I was sitting on the ground, and lifted me in her arms. I woke up spooked out of hell remembering the last time I dreamed this I was about to leave for Colorado to start my new life. Was this the old subconscious bubbling up? Was I about to disregard my mother's warning? Was this the end of my hippie dreams of freedom?

I didn't have time to answer these questions because Kelvin pulled over to the side of the road. He came around back and pulled out a ten-gallon gas can.

"I'm getting gas," he said. "You jokers wait here."

He sauntered off casually, smoking a cigarette. He slid down a gully and reappeared on the other side, climbing a hill. He threw the gas can over a barbed wire fence, parted the wires and slipped through gingerly. At the top of the hill was a house with a porch light on and, about a hundred yards off, a huge tank. Kelvin emerged from the shadows near the tank. He put down the gas can, stamped out his cigarette, and dived to the ground.

A police car pulled up behind us. A cop slid out the driver's side and marched up to us, hitching his pants.

He shined a flashlight in our faces and then on the patch at his shoulder. It said, "Ute Reservation Police."

"I been working for two weeks," he said proudly. He was a kid. A patch of black hair, shiny black eyes, and a big smile that exposed his pearly white teeth.

Two more police cars pulled up behind the first. Four cops piled out. They were dressed in blue uniforms and cowboy hats like the casino guards.

"They're from the state police," said the kid. He was dressed in tan. "In case I need backup."

"Backup for what?" asked Kurt. "We're no trouble."

"That depends," said one of the cowboys, the one with stripes on his shoulder, as he walked up, "whether you been stealing gas or not like the lady in the house told us." He pointed up the hill. The lady was under the porch light shading her eyes, staring down at us.

Two of the cops climbed up the hill to talk to her. They searched around the house. They searched around the tank. They blended into the shadows of the hill and a few minutes later came out on this side of the gully, holding a gas can.

"There's nobody up there," said one of the cowboys. "But we found this. It's empty."

They wandered off to their cars to consult, leaving the Ute kid behind to guard us. He smiled gingerly at us and tucked his thumb in his belt near the gun holster. The cowboys wandered back.

"An empty gas can isn't evidence," said the policeman with the stripes, "so I guess we got to let you go, as much as I don't want to. There's too many of you. We don't want to start a revolution." He snickered at his buddies.

"We're going to have to jump-start the truck," said Kurt.

"Okay," said the cop. We leaned our shoulders into the back of the truck and pushed. The truck hiccuped down the road. The engine caught. We jumped in.

The cop wandered over to the driver's side window and leaned in. "I want you to get out of here as fast as you can. Off the Ute Reservation. Out of the state of Utah. And I don't want you to ever come back again."

We trundled down the road in fits and starts. "We got no more than ten miles of gas," Kurt whined. "What are we going to do?"

We rolled into a sleepy Indian reservation town. A few adobe huts, dilapidated wood shacks, and a brand-new gas station and grocery store, open twenty-four hours.

"I still have twenty bucks left over from the casino," said Pie.

"Why didn't you tell us that before?"

"You never asked."

Kurt laughed and shook his head. "Poor Kelvin," he said.

We purchased fifteen gallons of gas and a bag of groceries. We pulled the truck out to the road. It hiccuped for a few yards. The engine caught. We jumped in.

Pie was in the front seat between Kurt and one of the Stooges. I could see her ponytail bob from side to side as we shimmied down the road. Kurt leaned over and whispered to her, words I couldn't hear above the roar of the engine and the whir of the road.

When we passed a sign that said we were leaving the Ute Indian reservation, we pulled over at a rest stop. It was a bunch of picnic tables on a grass plot surrounded by cottonwood trees that blocked the view from the highway. The wind swayed the trees and blew against our faces, a welcome relief after the heat of the day. I could hear the burbling of a nearby brook.

Kurt said we were going to wait here. "I know Kelvin," he said. "He's circling around to the highway. He'll hitchhike to where we are."

"That is, if the cops don't catch him," said one of the Stooges. "He's only one revolutionary."

We took the groceries out of the car and munched idly on the contents while Rick gave us a lesson on the constellations in the night sky. Kurt had trapped Pie over in the shadows of the truck. I think he was talking dirty to her, because all of a sudden she let loose with a couple of foul-mouthed oaths. He grabbed her breasts. She slapped him. He jumped back out of the shadows, pursued by Pie. She landed a left hook on the tip of his chin. He fell in the bushes, less from the force of the blow than from being knocked off-balance.

He was like a cat. He leaped to his feet and turned toward Pie. He was a thin and wiry guy like his brother. He looked quick. I'm sure he could've beat the crap out of her. But he hesitated when we came over.

"Can you believe this girl?" he said, swiping his chin. "I don't think I want her in my truck."

He marched over to the truck and scrounged around the back until he came up with a backpack. He dropped it on the ground.

"That's my bag," I said.

He reached down to pick it up.

"Don't bother," I said. He watched with a disgusted sneer as Rick and I pulled Pie's and the rest of our gear out of the back. Then he sneered at Tiny and the Stooges, who were standing in a clump by the picnic table.

"How about you guys? You coming?"

They gave us a baleful look and shrugged.

"Then get your fucking butts over here and give this piece of shit a shove." He climbed behind the wheel and waited. Tiny and the Stooges shuffled over dejectedly. They gave the Harvester a half-hearted shove. It started immediately. They jumped in, and before Tiny closed the back door, he whispered in a voice loud enough for us to hear, "Sorry."

We dragged our sleeping bags down by the brook near a stand of cottonwood, but not too close. We wanted a view of the night sky. I had never seen so many stars in my life. It reminded me of a silvery cobweb attached to the edges of the earth.

"I guess we're not going to make it all the way to Denver in one ride," said Pie as we climbed in our bags.

"I'm not surprised," I said. "We cheated. We climbed in that hole."

We lay back for a while and checked out the sky. I saw a shooting star on the horizon. Rick pointed at a tiny light that appeared and disappeared.

"That's a rocket," he said. "It's turning end on end so that when it turns toward us, the light appears, and when it turns away, it disappears. It could be one of the rockets from the moon shot."

"Hey, Pie," I mumbled, trying to work up some humble pie. "This has been a rotten day for you, hasn't it?"

"Are you kidding? I thoroughly enjoyed myself, especially when I slugged Kurt. If anyone deserved getting slugged, it was him."

"Well, I regret kissing you like that."

"Well, I don't," said Pie, turning on her side toward me and smiling. "I enjoyed your kiss even more than I enjoyed slugging Kurt."

"You did?"

"Yes, I did. I love you." She hesitated. "I mean like a brother."

"A kissing cousin," corrected Rick.

We heard rustling sounds over by the cottonwood on the other side of the creek. Two fawns slid down to the water's edge, dipped their heads to drink. Behind the two came the mother deer. She peered in every direction until her eyes came to rest on us. We remained stock-still. We could see the father standing on the hill next to the tree scanning the horizon, shaking his antlers as if preparing to charge us. There was another rustling sound, and the deer family bolted, jumped the creek, and raced past us within a few feet of our bags.

"Wow, amazing," said Rick. We couldn't figure out what that other rustling noise was, probably a squirrel, because we heard chittering noise coming from the tree and from far off, the howl of a wolf. Or maybe it was a dog.

We lay back quietly and looked at the endless stars in the night sky. We could see the swirl of the Milky Way, the star at the end of the Big Dipper that Rick claimed was a double star so close together that it was used by people in ancient times as a way to test eyesight. I felt like one of those people, a nomad stopping off on an oasis on a desert plain for the night to rest between one destination and another.

Acknowledgments

ACKNOWLEDGMENT IS MADE TO BARRY MUEHE WHO COMMENTED, after reading one of my efforts, that he thought it was good. But where was the rest of the story? Well, here's the rest of the story, Barry. Hope you enjoy it. Kudos also to all those characters inside the story and out who made this memoir possible. There are too many of you to name, but I am grateful. And to Rick Sager, a great buddy. I'll see you downstream.

Share Your Thoughts

Did you enjoy *Nothing Left to Lose*? Then please consider leaving a review on Goodreads, your personal blog, or wherever readers can be found. At Circuit Breaker Books, we value your opinion and appreciate when you share our books with others.

Visit circuitbreakerbooks.com.

JEFF RICHARDS is a native Washingtonian who moved to Denver with his wife, Connie, and their shichon, Billy Bones, to be near his two children. He has two novels and one short story collection under his belt. Richards' short stories, essays, and cowboy poetry have appeared in over thirty publications and four anthologies. He has worked as a teacher, dishwasher, door-to-door salesmen, farm worker, wilderness counselor, newspaper carrier, radio reporter, and busboy. He has hitchhiked across the country five times, but that was a while back. He is a graduate of the Hollins Writing Program and an avid blues music and rock and roll fan.